AMERICAN SOCIETY FOR YAD VASHEM

1981 2011

30th Anniversary

TO OUR PIONEERS, VISIONARIES
AND SUPPORTERS

IN FRIENDSHIP

ELI ZBOROWSKI
Chairman and Founder

A Life of Leadership
ELI ZBOROWSKI

From the Underground
to Industry
to Holocaust Remembrance

A Life of Leadership
ELI ZBOROWSKI

From the Underground
to Industry
to Holocaust Remembrance

George and Rochel Berman

KTAV Publishing House, Inc.
Jersey City, New Jersey

in association with

Yad Vashem Publications
Jerusalem, Israel

Library of Congress Cataloging-in-Publication Data

Berman, George Richard, 1935-
  A life of leadership : Eli Zborowski, from the underground to industry, to
Holocaust remembrance / George Berman, Rochel Berman.
    p. cm.
  Includes index.
  ISBN 978-1-60280-190-5
  1. Zborowski, Eli. 2. Jews--Poland--Zarki--Biography. 3. Jewish
children in the Holocaust--Poland--Biography. 4. Holocaust, Jewish
(1939-1945)--Poland--Personal narratives. 5. Holocaust survivors--United
States--Biography. 6. American Society for Yad Vashem. 7. Zarki (Poland)-
-Biography. I. Berman, Rochel U. II. Title.
  DS134.72.Z36A3 2011
  940.53'18092--dc23
  [B]
                              2011035149

Dedicated to
Eli's parents
Zisel and Moshe Zborowski *z"l*
Whose loving memory continues to inform all that he does

Contents

Acknowledgements

Presenting a portrait of a man whose life has spanned more than eight decades, who has lived and worked on several continents and has been in the forefront of both the Jewish communal world and the international corporate stage is a daunting task. We are deeply indebted to Eli Zborowski for entrusting us with the many threads of the intricate tapestry from which his life has been woven. The story told in these pages is based on Eli's own absorbing narrative, expanded through the personal experiences and observations of family members, friends, and colleagues. It is a record of both the inner and the outer man.

Our interviews with Eli took place during the winter of 2009 in the Florida offices of the American Society for Yad Vashem. For each of the many sessions, we would arrive mid-morning to a conference table spread with coffee, cake, and fruit thoughtfully provided by his wife, Elizabeth. Armed with a series of questions that we provided, Eli began to recount in astonishing detail the events of his life, starting with his childhood memories of Żarki. Interviews often ran for five or six hours. There was a distinct rhythm to these sessions that assured us from the outset that we were witnesses to an incredible drama. Just as each session began with gracious hospitality, it ended in the late afternoon with our being escorted to the elevator by Eli in his signature courtly manner.

Our greatest debt of gratitude goes to Elizabeth Mundlak Zborowski, Cultural Director of the American Society for Yad Vashem. Elizabeth is responsible for much of the archival research. She spent countless hours examining documents and photographs that are part of the Society's files as well as Eli's personal records. Her support and enthusiasm for this project were unbounded.

Each member of Eli's family to whom we spoke welcomed the opportunity to share thoughts about his influence in their lives. We are grateful to his children, Dr. Lilly Zborowski Naveh and Murry

Zborowski, his brother Marvin Zborowski, his sister Tzila Listenberg, and his niece Yaffa Zilbershatz for allowing us into their lives and for the candor of their narratives.

Our understanding of Eli's leadership in the perpetuation of Holocaust remembrance and education and his involvement in a wide array of Jewish communal activities was enhanced by Dr. Yitzhak Arad, Barbara Arfa, Elinor Belfer, Julius Berman, Adina Burian, Dr. Herbert Dobrinsky, Ira Drukier, Eugen Gluck, Dr. Yosef Govrin, Saul Kagan, Ruth Kastner, Manya Knobloch, Rabbi Norman Lamm, Rabbi Marvin Luban, Rabbi Israel Meir Lau, Sam Halpern, Caroline Massel, Samuel Norich, Avner Shalev, Dr. Alvin Schiff, Selma Schiffer, Stella Skura, Keren Toledano, Prof. Feliks Tych, and Joseph Wilf.

We acknowledge with thanks individuals and organizations that helped us gather information: Shulamith Z. Berger, Curator of Special Collections at the Mendel Gottesman Library of Yeshiva University; Dr. Jeffrey Gurock, Libby M. Klapperman, Professor of Jewish History, Yeshiva University; Dr. Joshua Zimmerman, Associate Professor of History, Eli and Diana Zborowski Chair in Interdisciplinary Holocaust Studies, Yeshiva University; Judith Cohen, Director of Photo Archives, United States Holocaust Memorial Museum; Gella Fishman; Oren Rudafsky; Dr. Robert Shapiro; Rabbi Yeshaya Metal, YIVO; Yefim Krasnyanskiy, Editor, *Martyrdom & Resistance*; Ruth Lemberger; and Rabbi Zvi and Hassia Yehuda. Dr. Bella Gutterman, Director, International Institute for Holocaust Research at Yad Vashem, reviewed the manuscript, offering several incisive comments.

Sir Martin Gilbert graciously agreed to write the foreword. We are profoundly grateful to him for his thoughtfulness and his insights. Professor Feliks Tych's contribution of the final chapter, "The Aftermath of the Holocaust," highlights the research he spearheaded on this topic in Poland and the proceedings of the inaugural conference of The Diana Zborowski Center for the Study of the Aftermath of the Shoah,[1] which took place at Yad Vashem in October 2010. Diana Zborowski's death in 2004 prompted Eli and his children to establish this Center at Yad Vashem in her memory. Professor Tych's pioneering work in the post-Holocaust era provides a model for what Eli hopes will become the stimulus to pursue similar research in countries throughout the world where survivors settled.

Assistance in interviewing people who live in Israel was kindly provided by our son, Rabbi Dr. Joshua Berman. Finally, we wish to thank our longtime colleague and friend Zoya Pisarenko, Finance Director of the American and International Societies for Yad Vashem, for her aid and support, and for her dedication to the mission of the organization and to its chairman, Eli Zborowski.

Rochel and George Berman

---

1. Shoah is the Hebrew word designating the Holocaust.

Foreword
Sir Martin Gilbert

Eli Zborowski has had a remarkable life that has been a source of inspiration to those who know him—a life that Rochel and George Berman have brought together in these pages. His achievements, as they emerge through this highly readable book, are many: among many other achievements, it was he who opened the door to diplomatic relations between Israel and Poland, he created the first Yom Hashoah commemoration of the Holocaust in the United States, he endowed the first chair in Holocaust studies in the United States. Under his leadership, the American Society for Yad Vashem remitted more than $100 million to Yad Vashem, the Holocaust museum, memorial, research and education authority in Jerusalem, and he was one of six survivors who welcomed Pope John Paul II to Yad Vashem—in Polish.

I first came across Eli Zborowski thirty years ago, when I was working in Yad Vashem on my *Atlas of the Holocaust*, and saw at first hand how highly regarded he was by the whole institution. His story mirrored so many of those who would come to Yad Vashem to give testimony, and whose hometowns and places of incarceration I was mapping. At the age of fifteen, he was a courier for the Jewish underground in Poland. When he was seventeen, his father was murdered by Poles. At the end of the war he escorted a hundred Jewish war orphans from Poland to the displaced-persons camps in southern Germany.

Eli Zborowski was born in 1925 in Żarki, a small town in prewar Poland, two-thirds of whose inhabitants were Jews. The pages about his childhood are heartwarming. His Hebrew high school was in Częstochowa—my own family's town—where he learned both Jewish and general studies. Then came the war: its opening days are vividly described through the eyes of a fourteen-year-old boy.

The two and a half years in the Żarki ghetto are harrowingly described. Eli was one of the youngsters who distributed the clandestine
Jewish newspaper. He then worked as a courier for the Jewish underground organization. At one point his mission was to escort a hundred children out of the doomed ghetto of Radomsko—my paternal
grandfather's hometown. He was, however, unable to complete this
task because the day following his arrival, the final liquidation of the
ghetto took place. In the Żarki ghetto, he met—and was inspired by—
that great leader of Jewish resistance, Mordechai Anielewicz, who
was then on his way from Warsaw to Zaglembia-Bendzin, Sosnowiec
Region, to participate in the resistance there: "He instilled hope in me
and in my small group of friends."

For the last two years of the war, Eli, his mother, and his two siblings were hidden by two courageous Polish families, poor peasants,
who risked their lives to take in the wanderers. I was proud to be able
to tell that story in my book *The Righteous*.

Half of this book tells the story of Eli Zborowski's life after the
war: his struggles, his initiatives, and his successes, culminating in the
extraordinary efforts that he made to sustain Holocaust remembrance,
and to ensure that the words "never again" would not be a mere catch-
phrase. Returning to Żarki in 1983, he provided the funds to restore
as much as possible of the destroyed Jewish cemetery where he had
walked with his father in prewar years.

In this book there is not a single dull page, not a single story that
does not resonate today with the capacity to inspire new generations.
Eli Zborowski went through hell and emerged to take his place as an
active, productive, thoughtful, and ethical member of society.

*Sir Martin Gilbert is the biographer of Winston Churchill, and a
historian of the Holocaust. He is also a pioneer of historical atlases,
including his Atlas of the Holocaust. In 2008, he accompanied the
British Prime Minister, Gordon Brown, to Auschwitz. From 2009
to 2011 he served as a member of the British Government's Iraq
Inquiry commission.*

Introduction

The immigration officer was persistent in his advice that one would never make it in the United States with a last name like Zborowski. Although young and still inexperienced in the ways of this new country, Eli explained that the name Zborowski was one that generated deference and pride and had been the family name for generations. Eli's refusal to accept the suggestion expressed not only his respect for the past, but also his determination and confidence about the future.

Having survived the Holocaust, Eli Zborowski began his life in America with no money, no contacts, and very limited knowledge of English. Only ten years later, he became president of Sheaffer Latin America, subsequently making a credible bid to purchase the entire Sheaffer Pen Company. He opened the door to the resumption of diplomatic relations between Israel and Poland, created the first synagogue-based Yom HaShoah commemoration of the Holocaust in the United States, spearheaded fund drives that changed the landscape of Yad Vashem, the Holocaust memorial in Jerusalem, welcomed Pope John Paul II to Yad Vashem in Polish, and endowed the first chair in Holocaust Studies in the United States, at Yeshiva University.

After the initial question one is likely to ask—How did Eli Zborowski get from there to here?—a flood of other questions arise. What kind of person has such a wide range of successes? Why would people follow him into risky ventures, both commercial and philanthropic? From what wellsprings of knowledge, philosophy, and experience does he draw? What motivates him, and, in turn, stirs those who join in his endeavors?

This biography of Eli Zborowski not only tells the story of his life so far but seeks to provide the answers to these questions. More accurately, we have presented the evidence, and hope that each reader will find answers in the text. Your questions may be different than ours.

In Judaism, the phrase *tikun olam* means "repairing the world": reducing chaos, bringing order. Doing so is seen as the mission of man on earth: the perfection of the social order. From his earliest days, fixing a broken world has been Eli's principal motivation. When he was seventeen, his father was murdered by Poles. Eli stepped in as *pater familias*, the de facto head not just of his immediate family, but also of his extended family of aunts, uncles, and cousins. After the liberation, when he encountered a carload of a hundred war orphans with no leader, Eli stepped in again, putting his personal plans on hold, and shepherded his flock from Poland to the Feldafing displaced-persons camp, picking up similarly detached orphans along the way.

In Feldafing, Eli created a kibbutz for his orphans where he continued to look after their needs. During the next several months, younger children, many separated from their parents, arrived at Feldafing. They wandered through the camp with little or no supervision or educational opportunities, in surroundings that were unsuitable for them. Stepping in once again, Eli organized a residential youth center for these children that became a model for the American forces administering similar camps throughout West Germany.

This has also been his pattern in business: find a need for which he is uniquely qualified by experience or by chance, and fill it. That, of course, is why we reward entrepreneurs. They fill a need. But to Eli, fixing the problem was key. As he taught his family, any material success is by the grace of God. One's primary motivation should never be just to make money, but, having it, to use it for *tikun olam*.

Leadership is the expression of courage that compels people to do the right thing[1]

Ernest Hemingway said that guts meant "grace under pressure." Hemingway would have liked Eli Zborowski. Most of us are risk averse. To Eli, risk is a familiar companion. At the age of fifteen, he was a daring courier for the Jewish underground. He dismisses this, saying that in a time when a Jew could be shot just walking down the street, risk loses its meaning. Nevertheless, the experiences he had, the constant weighing of risks against objectives, further sharpened Eli's skills in speculative ventures.

True commitment inspires and attracts people[2]

With a tenacity that has been noted by many of his colleagues, Eli made things happen that could easily have failed to materialize. At a time when most Holocaust survivors wanted to leave such memories behind, Eli took up the cause of Holocaust remembrance. Against all odds, he organized support for Holocaust education, creating the American Federation of Jewish Fighters, Camp Inmates and Nazi Victims. He went on to organize the American and International Societies for Yad Vashem, which have remitted over $100 million to perpetuate the memory of the Holocaust and to better understand it.

By far the most powerful influence in Eli's life, his primary source of inspiration, has been his father, Moshe Zborowski. Throughout this book, we find Eli asking himself, "How would my father have dealt with this?" When Moshe Zborowski built a house, he sat with the workers and shared their vodka; when Eli acquired a factory in Mexico, he built a subsidized cafeteria for his employees.

It was only through Moshe's careful planning that the Zborowski family survived the Holocaust. Julius Berman, Eli's confidant and attorney, says of him, "He is able to think three steps ahead. That's the key in business."

Good leaders never embrace a victim mentality[3]

One of Eli's strengths is his refusal to embrace victimhood. In his teens, he learned from experience that resistance was possible. He was never helpless, and, indeed, was able to help many others. This has given him a basis for the self-confidence that is essential to leadership.

One last question: Is the capacity for leadership learned, or is it inherent? It is difficult to imagine that the requisite qualities are to be found in one's genes. More likely, some leadership elements are absorbed, early on, from such influences as Moshe Zborowski, though their source may be less apparent than in Eli's case.

. . . the one quality that all successful people have is the ability to take on responsibility[4]

In the final analysis, there is one factor that is neither inherent nor learned. Regardless of his fundamental qualifications, the leader must choose that role, with all its risks, responsibilities, and limitations. In seeking a source for this personal decision, we may just have to accept that source of individuality we commonly call the soul. Brigadier General Avner Shalev, Chairman of the Yad Vashem Directorate, says of Eli's determined support through the American Society for Yad Vashem: "Eli shouldered the mighty responsibility, bringing along his talents, his unrelenting devotion, his *neshomeh* (soul) and the determination that we admire so much."

---

1. John C. Maxwell, *The 21 Indispensable Qualities of a Leader: Becoming the Person Others Will Want to Follow* (Nashville: Thomas Nelson, 1999), p. 41
2. Ibid., p. 18
3. Ibid., p. 114
4. Ibid., p. 111, citing Michael Korda, editor-in-chief of Simon & Schuster.

❧ Chapter 1 ❧
THE ROOTS RUN DEEP

Three Generations
Top: Moshe Dauman
Right: Shmuel Dauman
Left: Moshe Zborowski

The Roots Run Deep

Żarki is a town in the southwestern corner of Poland, a short distance from the prewar German border. It nestles in a bowl of broad green farmland and forest surrounded by steep hills, where Jews from surrounding industrialized communities came in the heat of summer to refresh themselves among the cool breezes. The Jewish community of Żarki dated back six centuries. Legend has it that the town was named for a Jewish woman called Sarah. Jews no longer live in Żarki; in fact there are less than 7,000 in the entire country. Today, it is a favorite spot for hang-gliding.

In 1936, there were some 3.5 million Jews in Poland—and the majority of the 6,000 residents of Żarki were Jewish. It was, therefore, not remarkable to see Moshe Zborowski, a giant of a man dressed, despite the midsummer warmth, in the long black coat and black cap often worn by Jews, walking through Żarki with his son, Eli, at his side. Moshe had dark hair, and was easily identifiable as a Jew. The boy, however, might have attracted the notice of a visitor. In contrast to his father, he was lightly dressed, and wore a navy blue beret. His slim, athletic build, his blond hair and blue eyes gave him the appearance of an "Aryan" Pole. He chatted comfortably with his father in Yiddish. Eli, named at birth Yitzhak Eliezer after his grandfather, unlike most Jews spoke perfect Polish.

These two contrasting figures walked slowly to the outskirts of Żarki, and stopped before the looming gates of the Jewish cemetery. It was the fast-day of Tisha b'Av, the ninth day of the Hebrew month of Av. The fast commemorates the destruction of the First and Second Temples in Jerusalem, which occurred on this same date, 656 years apart. Many subsequent disasters have befallen the Jewish people on this date, making it a time of communal mourning. It is traditional to visit a cemetery on Tisha b'Av, after the morning prayers in synagogue, to remind us of the frailty of our existence.

The high proportion of Jewish residents in Żarki was a direct result of Poland's historical relationship with the Jews. Most Poles lived in rural, agrarian settings. Jews, however, were barred by long-standing laws from owning land. Engaged in commerce and the professions, they concentrated in the cities and towns. Throughout Poland, most retail businesses were Jewish-owned. More than half the physicians, one-third of the attorneys, and nearly half of all teachers were Jewish.[1] As a result, their proportions in urbanized areas were far higher than in the country as a whole, where they amounted to merely ten percent. Even the capital city, Warsaw, was one-third Jewish. Only New York City had more Jewish residents than Warsaw.

For over eight centuries, Poland had been a haven for Jews fleeing persecution elsewhere on the European continent. The first permanent Jewish community on record was well established by 1085. Jews seeking refuge from the ravages of the First Crusade began arriving in 1098. King Bolesław III, who ascended to the throne in 1102, recognized the value of the Jews in developing Poland's commerce and trade. They managed the lands of the Polish nobility, increased trade with other countries, and stimulated domestic trade. In short order, Jews became essential to the economy. Indeed, several medieval Polish coins even carried Hebrew inscriptions.

In 1334, King Kazimierz the Great made tolerance of Jews the law of the land. Kazimierz was said to have a Jewish lover named Esterka; whatever the reason, he was especially friendly to the Jews. He proclaimed severe punishments for such activities as the desecration of Jewish cemeteries and forced baptism of Jewish children. However, the need for these legal protections gives us some insight into how Jews were regarded by many Poles.

Despite the objections of the Catholic Church, Jews found protection in Poland for nearly a millennium. With the expulsion of the Jews from Italy in 1282, and subsequently from England, France, Switzerland, Hungary, Germany, Austria, Spain, Lithuania, Portugal,

Bohemia, and the Netherlands, Poland became the cultural center of European Jewry.

During the succeeding centuries, the environment of tolerance waxed and waned in response to several forces. Jews were blamed for the bubonic plague that decimated Europe in the middle of the fourteenth century. The Black Death was one of the deadliest pandemics in human history. Unaware of the bacterial origin of the plague, people blamed it on the Jews. Apparently, the impact was noticeably less in Jewish communities, perhaps because of different hygienic customs, perhaps simply because of their cultural and thus physical isolation from the larger community. Altogether, at the peak of the epidemic, 60 major and 150 smaller Jewish communities throughout Europe were destroyed.

Late in the sixteenth century, the Jewish *kehilah*, or community, of Poland was granted administrative autonomy. It took responsibility for collecting taxes from Jews and for all civil functions, including providing for education. While this further isolated the Jews from the social and political life of Poland, it also provided a sheltered environment within which Jewish learning flourished. Throughout the next century, the academies of Poland, including Lithuania, grew in stature to a level of preeminence never equaled since.

In 1648, the tide turned once again, when the Cossacks revolted against the Polish government, and slaughtered thousands of Jews. The protective power of the ruling class waned, and the underlying anti-Semitism of the populace took over. The state's forces ignored attacks on Jews.

In 1772, exhausted by civil war and threats from neighboring countries, Poland agreed to a treaty with Russia, Prussia, and Austria that cost the country half its population, and a third of its territory. Consistent with the Church's insistence on isolation of the Jews, in 1791 Catherine II of Russia ordered the Jews within her domain confined to the Pale of Settlement, a region of Eastern Europe that included western Poland. Once again, although this ghettoization was intended to constrain the Jews, they flourished in their isolation from the Poles.

In 1793, Poland ceded more land to Prussia and Russia. Finally, in 1795, what was left of Poland disappeared, divided amongst these two states and Austria. It would not emerge again, reconstituted as an independent nation, until the end of World War I, in 1918.

By the late nineteenth century, the number of Jews living in what is now Poland had reached over four million. Restriction to the Pale offered no security for the Jews, however. A series of terrible pogroms, attacks unimpeded by the state, plagued the community under Russian rule, and led to large-scale emigration, principally to the United States. As Żarki was one of the westernmost sites of Jewish presence, the impact of the pogroms was less, and there was little or no emigration. The roots of the community extended back many generations, and its members saw no reason to live anywhere else.

The Jewish cemetery of Żarki

As Moshe and Eli Zborowski entered the cemetery, the tall stone arches loomed over them ominously. Moshe and his son became somber. Moshe guided the boy to the part of the cemetery where their family was buried. Moshe turned to Eli, addressing him by the Yiddish form of his name: "Our family has lived in Żarki for more than five generations. See here, Lazer, the grave of my father, Yitzhak Eliezer Zborowski, for whom you were named. And here are Menachem Mendel and Surka Zborowski, your great-grandparents. And over here, the family of your great-great-grandfather, Shmuel ben Shmuel Zborowski." As it is contrary to Ashkenazi Jewish custom to name a child for a living person, Eli understood that this meant that Shmuel's father had died before he was born.

Other Zborowski graves, their stones now almost illegible, stretched out before them. Not far off, Eli could see the huge gravestone of his maternal great-grandfather, the "Groiser Moshe" (Big Moshe), looming over the surrounding plots. The boy wandered among the graves, thinking about how very long his family had been part of the life of Żarki. He felt that his existence revolved about these lichen-covered stones. He counted seven generations among the markers, noting that there was still room for several more graves. Staring at this gap, where still more Zborowskis would lie beneath the earth, he suddenly paled, turned, and ran back to his father, nestling close in his protective embrace.

During the years of the Holocaust, many Jewish cemeteries were destroyed, and Żarki's cemetery was no exception—all but the huge stone over Groiser Moshe's grave were broken, overturned, or removed entirely. In 1983, Eli returned and, at his own expense, partly restored the cemetery to its former grandeur. It was his principal connection to the past, to the long train of souls whose succession had led to him, and whose lives had been so intimately intertwined with the town of Żarki that he loved.

Moshe and Eli began the walk back home. As they passed through the outskirts of Żarki, the homes became more substantial. Rude cottages, some with dirt floors, gave way to solid frame houses; whitewash to white paint. A solitary figure approached them, with a yoke over his shoulders, and two large metal cans hanging from the yoke. Yomely the *wassertreger*, the water carrier, had completed his rounds and was on his way to refill his supply. Żarki had the benefit of electric power since 1925, the year Eli was born, but still had no public water supply or sewers. Moshe Zborowski, successful businessman that he was, nevertheless greeted Yomely respectfully by name, and received in turn a tug of the burdened man's cap.

Zborowski made his living as a wholesale leather dealer. Twice a month he set out through the countryside buying leather, selling it to shoemakers in Żarki, and to retailers and other trades in the cities and towns he visited. Over the years he had built a solid business on his reputation for strict honesty, service, and trust. He had a gift for matching each exchange with terms that were reasonable and considerate but not foolhardy. He would transmit this gift to Eli, although he could not have known how critical it would be to his success in America. Even at the age of thirteen, Eli often accompanied him on his trips to Częstochowa to sell leather.

In addition to his careful relationship with suppliers and customers, Moshe Zborowski had great respect for workingmen. He did not think twice about greeting the water carrier as a fellow traveler through life in Żarki. By the same token, when he built his home he came by each day to observe the progress and paid the workmen their wages on the spot. Then he shared a bottle of vodka with them. At the same time, he developed a warm relationship with Placzek, the Polish contractor. The lesson was not lost on young Eli. Many years later, when he acquired his first factory, in Mexico, he would install a cafeteria for the employees where whatever they ate cost them only one peso.

Żarki had a vibrant Jewish community, governed by the *kehilla*, an elected body of townspeople, with representatives of every faction—religious, socialist, Zionist. Although its members disputed the town's issues passionately from their own viewpoints, the *kehilla* was nevertheless an effective, cohesive force in Żarki, binding together a broad array of Jews.

Even among the religious Jews there were divisions. Some *davened*, prayed, in *shtieblach*, small congregations whose members were followers of one particular *rebbe*, or leader, believed to have been especially saintly or knowledgeable. Others attended services in the main synagogue on Moniuszki Street, built in 1870. Moshe Zborowski was a loyal member of the Trisker *shtiebel* near his home. Nevertheless, out of respect for his father, on the anniversary of his death every year he recited *Kaddish* in the Aleksander *shtiebel*, his father's congregation. This diversity of worship would become particularly important during the German occupation, when only very small, inconspicuous groups could gather safely for morning, afternoon, and evening prayers.

The *kehilla* assessed taxes from all but the poorest Jews, in proportion to their wealth. These revenues were used for Jewish education and for many other institutions essential to life as an observant Jew. They paid the salary of the rabbi . If a male child was born, he was circumcised by a *mohel* who was paid by the *kehilla*. When a woman bought a chicken for the Sabbath meal, it was ritually slaughtered for free by a *shochet* also paid by the *kehilla*. The ritual bathhouse, the *mikvah*, where men bathed before Sabbath services, and women rinsed away the *tumah*, or ritual impurity, of their menstruation, was also subsidized by the *kehilla*. As a result, no one in Żarki had to weigh their spiritual needs against their financial needs, however pressing. The community also maintained a free loan society, where one could borrow money for an approved purpose without interest.

Żarki had a Jewish library, containing over 6,000 volumes, donated by Abraham Josef Sztibel, who had emigrated, in 1912, to America, where he became a renowned publisher of Hebrew and Yiddish books. A street in Tel Aviv is named for him. Nevertheless, here in Żarki stood a library named for his wife, Zisel, who had died in childbirth. It was said that from Warsaw to Kraków one could not find such a fine, large library. Use of the library was free of charge, and Eli had become virtually addicted to the books he found there. He brought them home and read all night in the kitchen while the rest of his family slept.

Father and son continued walking, the intense July heat relieved by a cool breeze from the surrounding hills. At last, they arrived at the Zborowski home, a fine one-story brick building that had risen under Moshe's daily supervision. In front of the entrance was a massive doorstep of stone that would play a significant role in the family's survival. Eli ran ahead to tell his mother about his day and his thoughts at the cemetery.

Chapter 1 Notes

1. Iwo Cyprian Pogonowski, *Jews in Poland: A Documentary History* (New York: Hippocrene Books, 1993), pp. 27–28.

❧ Chapter 2 ❧
AT HOME IN ŻARKI

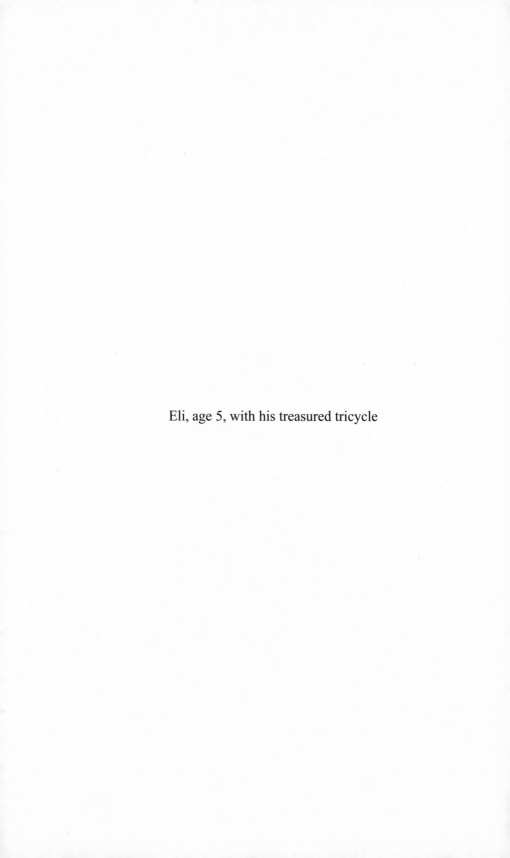

Eli, age 5, with his treasured tricycle

CHAPTER 2

ॐ

At Home In Żarki

Eli's third year of life was marked by several significant events. Perhaps the most dramatic was his *opshern*—his first haircut. In this religious practice, a boy's hair remains unshorn until he is three years old. It is a custom based on the dictum of Rabbi Isaac Luria, a sixteenth-century mystic in Ottoman Palestine, that children are like trees in the field which, according to sacred law, may not be harvested during their first years of blooming. Eli sat dejectedly staring down at the floor as the family members and friends who had gathered to witness this milestone sat staring at him. Eli fought back tears as one golden lock after another fell to the floor. He would miss his long blond tresses. so frequently and affectionately caressed by his doting grandmother and aunts.

In 1928, the Zborowski family moved into the new, one-story brick home whose construction had been meticulously overseen by Moshe Zborowski. Shortly after they moved, they welcomed their second child, Mendel, later known as Marvin, whose *brit milah* (circumcision) took place in the new house.

At the age of five, Eli received the gift of a tricycle. This wondrous possession, the only one in the neighborhood, was a source of instant fame and popularity for its owner. Several disasters rendered the joy short-lived, however. Once, when Eli was riding the tricycle with a friend, Moniek Fiszer, on the back, they fell. His friend broke his nose. On another occasion, Eli rode the tricycle in the house and fell off, hitting his head on the heating stove. Blood cascaded from the open cut on his forehead. Upon seeing the profusion of blood, his father fainted. He was so upset that he took the tricycle, broke it in pieces, and threw it out.

Lessons Learned at Home

The Zborowski home stood out among the other houses in the neighborhood because it was considerably more substantial. It had a wide center hallway with a smaller dining area and kitchen on one side. This area was sufficiently large to accommodate a bed for the maid. On the other side of the hallway was a formal dining room where guests were entertained and where the family ate on the Sabbath and holidays. In addition, there were two bedrooms—one for the children and one for the parents. In every room there was a free-standing stove that kept the room warm. Like all the homes of that period in Żarki, the house had electricity but did not have indoor plumbing.

Eli felt that the family's home was "one of the nicest houses among my friends." It was the only one constructed with a built-in *sukkah*.[1] Part of the hallway had a removable roof that could be covered with *schach* (fresh-cut branches) during the Sukkot holiday so that it could serve as the temporary booth Jews construct at this time. All the other families had to erect free-standing *sukkot* in their backyards.

Weekdays, Moshe Zborowski, went to the Trisker shtiebel twice each day to *daven*—to pray. The Zborowskis were committed to the Jewish commandment of *hachnoses orchim,* sheltering the wayfarer. Their hospitality extended to the poor and lonely amongst them as well as to the boys from neighboring towns who were studying at the local yeshiva.[2] Eli's brother, Mendel, recalls becoming very fond of one yeshiva *bocher* (boy) named Yosef who came for lunch once a week. Sitting next to each other, they talked and laughed, ignoring everyone else at the table. Later that day, Mendel felt sad, hoping to see this boy again. He sheepishly inquired of his mother, Zisel,

"It's a mitzvah (good deed) to have a yeshiva *bocher* for a meal, isn't it?

"Yes that's right," Zisel replied. "It's the best meal they get in a day."

"Wouldn't it be the same mitzvah if we had Yosef every day, instead of a different boy?"

A family photo in 1935

Back row left to right: Zisel Zborowski, nee Dauman;Tzivia Jonisz, nee Dauman; Shlomo Jonisz; a Dauman cousin; Bella Monat, nee Dauman;

Seated in the center, left to right: Sheindl Dauman; Rochel Dauman
Children left to right: Eli, Tzila, Marvin Zborowski; Hela Monat; Moshe Dauman (the youngest of the Dauman children)

Marvin, Uncle Wolf Dauman, Zisel   Eli, Marvin, cousin
Zborowski (1939)   Chaim Shlomo Dauman(1939)

Zisel hesitated a moment, and then replied, "No, not quite. We are fortunate enough to have meat every day. Most of the homes that host students don't serve meat except on the Sabbath, so we are obligated to share our good fortune with as many students as possible."

Loving Grandparents

Blessed with good looks, charm, and a fine mind, Eli was treated like a golden prince by his maternal grandparents, who lived close-by in Żarki. Eli says, "On my own, I often ran to my grandmother's house, especially when my mother was busy or annoyed with me. My '*Babche*' had all the time in the world for me, and I enjoyed it when she patted me on the head and placed me on the table during the Passover *seder* to recite the *Ma Nishtana* (Four Questions)."[3] His fond and vivid memories of a proud grandfather continue to this day:

My grandfather, Shmuel Dauman, was the town's jeweler. He was a very busy man and could not spend much time with me, but as I was the first grandchild, he was very proud of me and enjoyed taking me with him on special occasions. When my grandfather arrived with me at a wedding or some other simcha (celebration) guests always jumped up to offer him their seats.

Many people in our town davened (prayed) in shtiblach (small houses of study and prayer) that were established for followers of a specific rabbi. In addition there were two synagogues, one next to the other. My grandfather, on the other hand, prayed in the large synagogue that was built by his father, my great-grandfather, Moshe Dauman.

My grandfather was highly respected and served as the gabbai rishon—which was analogous to the president of the synagogue. When he entered the synagogue he always made his way to the front of the sanctuary, where the most prominent seat, inherited from his father, was reserved for him. In all of my adult life, I have followed his example. Whenever I walk into a synagogue in a strange country, be it Argentina, Costa Rica, or Mexico, I immediately gravitate toward the front of the sanctuary, just as my grandfather did.

Esther and Shmuel Dauman, Eli's maternal grandparents

Eli's grandparents' commitment to family did not preclude communal responsibility and *gemilat chesed*—acts of loving-kindness. While they saved every penny for their four unmarried daughters' dowries, they still invited people to their home for *Kiddush*—wine and a collation of sweet treats—on holidays and festivals

During his formative years, Eli's life was significantly affected by positive and reinforcing role models.. As his journey unfolds, we will see how they have repeatedly provided him with the confidence and courage to make decisions in trying situations that he could not possibly have imagined during his carefree and happy childhood.

Parents as Role Models

Zisel Zborowski managed the household and helped the children with their homework. She spoke to the children in Polish because she felt that one had to be able to get along with people outside of one's immediate sphere. This attitude was more common in the big cities, where Jews sought to be progressive and even emancipated, but in Żarki it was unusual. As a result, Eli spoke Polish without an accent, a skill that enabled him to survive during the war because he could pass as a Pole.

By example, Zisel encouraged the children to share what they had with those who came from households where food was not as abundant. Eli recalls: "There was a pale thin girl in my class who lived in our neighborhood and whose mother was sick. The girl would often come to our house for a glass of *wishniak*—a cherry concentrate. For her family this cherry drink was a luxury, while for us it was simply a staple of life."

When Eli left for school, Zisel handed him a snack to eat mid-morning consisting of a roll with butter and sometimes cheese. Since he had already eaten a full breakfast and would have an ample lunch waiting for him when he came home, Eli would regularly give his snack to a friend whose stomach had rumbled from hunger on more than one occasion. The snack was so welcome that it was devoured before the first class of the day even began.

Zisel and Moshe Zborowski, Eli's parents (1923)

On Sunday mornings, as a special treat for the children, Zisel would sometimes prepare French toast, known in Yiddish as *gefrishte broit*—refreshed bread—which she made from left-over challah. Eli remembers with great pleasure the sound of the sizzling butter in the pan and the gentle plop of the eggs, each dropped separately into the waiting bowl. Zisel next poured in milk, fork-whisking with a sure, quick hand until the mixture had an even, creamy consistency. Eli's mouth watered as he watched his mother coat each slice of challah and place it carefully into the frying pan. The final presentation was a work of art—each piece had a soft yellow center encased in a golden-brown frame.

It is not surprising that Eli continues to view French toast as the ultimate comfort food, ordering it over other menu items almost every time he goes out for lunch.

* * *

Moshe Zborowski's early years were marked by poverty and struggle. His formal education was abruptly terminated when World War I broke out in 1914. He was orphaned at the age of sixteen. As World War I ended, he became involved in the leather business. At that time leather was a precious commodity. The most desirable hides, used to make boot soles, were imported. As leather was a rarity, most of the hides came from Argentina. In the early years Moshe would travel to Kraków, which was the closest business center, and buy as much leather as he could carry back by himself. As the business grew, he always saved some portion of his profits.

Once, upon returning from Kraków, Moshe found that he had been undercharged. The next time he went there, he paid the difference. This established his reputation as an honest businessman. The dealers began to trust him and offer him credit. His wholesale business expanded, and within a short time he was able to provide leather dealers in several nearby cities with goods by extending credit. The fact that he saved money enabled him to pay tanneries in advance for the six-month period it took to properly tan the hides so that they could be used for soles. He would then sell the tanned hides all over the region, and what remained he sent back to Żarki to be sold to local shoemakers. When he returned home from a business trip, he eagerly shared stories about his transactions with his wife in the presence of his children. Eli reflects on the impact of these tales and how his father taught by the simple eloquence of example:

Unquestionably, I learned about business and the moral underpinnings of business from my father. Every step I've taken in business is rooted in stories my father told us about his business dealings—how he dealt with the people from whom he was buying, how he dealt with the people to whom he was selling. For example, a tanning factory where he was paying in advance was destroyed by fire. The owner did not have either the leather or the money to pay my father back. The owner took off an expensive ring he was wearing and offered it to my father, at least as part payment, for the money he had paid down. However, my father refused to accept the ring.

My father believed that *a soicher muz hoben breite plaitzes*—"a businessman must have broad shoulders." There is always a rainy day, and one has to be prepared for that. One must be prepared for the downside of business, and this must be calculated into your business plan. He dealt kindly with clients who went bankrupt, unlike other creditors who stripped them of their homes. He never belittled people who were in need. And he was angry with the people who did not behave with compassion. So what did I learn? I learned how one has to apportion one's business income and how to be compassionate to those who did not manage their businesses as well and came on hard times. I learned from him to make a living and save a dollar. And saving the dollar was just as important as making the living. He would often tell me about visiting tanneries after the season and buying up goods with saved money at a reduced price. In sharing stories about his business life. the importance of saving money was a consistent and recurring theme.

Moshe Zborowski was well-to-do, but very modest and unpretentious. He owned a fur-lined coat, but rarely wore it. Similarly, his wife owned a fur coat that she rarely wore. Moshe was careful to behave in a way that would not cause envy in the eyes of others or set him apart from his community.

The Zborowski family was close-knit, but like most families, amidst the love, there were feelings of favoritism and sibling rivalry. Eli recalls:

My mother was very devoted to my younger brother, Mendel, and doted on him. I thought he was very indulged. And when my sister was born, she became my father's little princess. When I felt left out, I would run to my grandparents, who always had time for me.

I never had bad feelings toward Mendel because he got more attention. I felt it was my mother's fault. I ultimately accepted the fact that Mendel needed more attention and ended up having a good relationship with him as we grew up together.

Our father was an attentive, unifying force in our family. Every night he tucked each of us into our beds and placed a piece of chocolate in each of our mouths before we fell asleep.

Starting School

Long before Eli was of an age to attend school, he could read and was quite knowledgeable in math. He was very eager to go to school. but the starting age was seven. When he was only six, the principal of the public school, Mr. Fantazyjski, a neighbor and friend of his grandfather, was persuaded to accept Eli into the first grade. So that he could be formally registered, his parents stated that he was seven years old. Eli remembers the long, exhausting days: "Public school began at 8:00 a.m. and ended at 1:00 p.m. I then came home for lunch, which was the main meal of the day. I recall that the whole family ate together. We did not start our meal until my father came home and sat at the table with us. After lunch I went to *cheder* (religious school) until about 8 pm. Then I came home and did my homework. It was a very long day that left me no time for anything else.

Many children, Jews and non-Jews alike, dropped out of school at age eleven or twelve because their help was needed at home. Moshe Zborowski, whose education had been truncated in his teens, was determined that his children should have as fine an education as possible. Following the seventh grade, Eli applied for admission to a Hebrew high school in Częstochowa, twenty miles from Żarki. It required travel by horse and wagon to the station in Myszkow and from there by train to Częstochowa and then by foot to the school. Eli was the only Jewish child of his age in Żarki who went out of town to attend high school.

The school emphasized the Hebrew language and embraced a very Zionistic philosophy. Eli passed all the entrance exams except the one in Hebrew, a subject that was not emphasized in the *cheder* he attended in Żarki. The other children who went to the high school had previously gone to the Hebrew elementary school connected with the high school, so their facility with the language exceeded Eli's. With the help of a Hebrew workbook provided by the school, Eli studied on his own to prepare for the test. He wanted desperately to attend the school, so he applied himself diligently, completing all of the thirty-six lessons in the workbook required for the second test. He felt triumphant when he heard that he had successfully passed the test that ensured his acceptance into the school.

Eli's parents were certain that this success was but one of the many that he would achieve in life. He says: "When I was growing up my parents hoped that I would be a lawyer. I can't recall having any special thoughts about aspiring to any profession when I was a child. However, it made me feel very good about myself that my father thought I would be a good lawyer. He would often say that I would be another Pawelek, a prominent lawyer in our region. Had it not been for the war, I probably would have entered the legal profession."

The Holy Sabbath

The Sabbath was the highlight of the week. The warmth of the experience continues to radiate in Eli's mind and heart to this very day: "I treasure the memories of ushering in *Shabbes* with prayers in the shtiebel on Friday night, *Kiddush* chanted by my father, a festive meal, singing *zmirot*—songs, and relaxed storytelling between meals."

Preparations began on Wednesdays, when Zisel would go to the weekly market in the center of town to shop for poultry, fruit, vegetables, butter, and eggs. There were some permanent vendors in the marketplace, but most of the space was devoted to small rented kiosks where farmers displayed the wares they had transported from neighboring villages by horse and wagon. Live poultry bought in the market would be taken by one of the children to the *shochet* (ritual slaughterer). Thursdays were devoted to washing and cleaning the house, a day when children generally tried to be out the way.

Of all the days of preparation leading up to the Sabbath, Eli remembers most fondly going to the public bathhouse with his father on Fridays, while his mother cooked. The bathhouse was another service supported by the community, but it could not make ends meet. Those who could afford it paid some small amount. Those who were not able to pay were allowed to use the facility, but usually at the end of the day, just before the Sabbath. Eli describes the pleasurable experience of male bonding with his father.

I started to accompany my father to the bathhouse when I was about three years old. We generally went in the morning when the bathhouse was reserved for those that paid and was therefore less crowded. Because there was no secure place to put your belongings, we dressed in old clothes reserved only to wear to the bathhouse. If an item of clothing disappeared, the loss would not be so great.

The bathhouse consisted of three rooms: a pool with cold water, another with warm water, and finally a sauna. Even if there were other children there, I preferred to stay close to my father. He thoroughly scrubbed my body with a brush made out of dry leaves that had an extraordinary aroma—one that was incredibly powerful, especially in the sauna. The weekly bathhouse excursion made me feel very cared for and drew me even closer to my father.

Before they went to synagogue on the Sabbath morning, Eli was required to read the Torah portion of the week with his father. On the Sabbath everyone went to synagogue, Eli says. "It was a way of life that unified us. You had to conform because to do otherwise was a form of disrespect for the norm."

After lunch they rested, and when they got up Eli would sit with his father reading and exploring the pearls of wisdom found in *Pirkei Avot,* the Ethics of the Fathers. In the summer months, they frequently went for a walk in the fields, with the elder Zborowski teaching his son about nature and telling stories about his childhood marked by poverty and deprivation. Because his children were growing up amidst plenty, Moshe wanted to be sure they understood that there were others who were not as privileged as they. He also reminded the children that times and fortunes can change.

Anti-Semitism Escalates

The Jews of Żarki lived in their own insular community, as did the Christians. The members of both religions followed their own customs and traditions. Jewish children, in particular, rarely interacted with their non-Jewish neighbors. There was an ever-present uneasiness and mistrust between Jews and non-Jews that was part of the fabric of life in Żarki. Young children were especially guarded. Going home from school, they were afraid to walk through non-Jewish neighborhoods and would tend to wait for the older children to accompany them. This fear was exacerbated on Christmas. With excess amounts of liquor freely flowing in the veins of the Poles, the veneer of civility fell by the wayside, revealing basic feelings of hate. On this day, Jews would experience overt anti-Semitism in the form of beatings and damage to their homes. To protect themselves, Jews remained at home with the windows shuttered. Eli recalls this period:

Starting in about 1933, we began to feel the winds of anti-Semitism blowing over us from Germany. There were already signs discouraging people from patronizing Jewish merchants.

A supermarket owned by Poles had signs in the window that read, "Don't buy from Jews! Support your own people."

The Jewish community abided by these restrictions, accepting them without retaliation. In our hearts and minds we knew that these sentiments emanated from and were supported by the Catholic Church.

The Youth Movement

Given the discriminatory atmosphere, it was not surprising that hopes for a more secure life in a Jewish homeland took hold in Poland. From the time Eli was ten years old he was a member of Hashomer Hatzair—the Young Guard—a Marxist-oriented Zionist organization. His recollections provide some insight into how he resolved the dichotomy between his own background and the philosophy of the youth movement:

As odd as it might seem, most of the children involved in Hashomer Hatzair were from the more well-to-do homes. It made us feel that we were fighting for a better future for those who were not as well off. In a town like Żarki everyone was religious. You wouldn't dare desecrate any of the religious laws or customs—no one would dare to keep a store open on Shabbat; no one would dare drive a horse and wagon on Shabbat. The children who belonged were all observant Jews. The library, which had leftist books, helped us understand the social philosophy of Hashomer Hatzair. I read Karl Marx's *Das Kapital* when I was fifteen years old. It helped me dream of a future where people would be equal with each other. At the same time, my father, a very religiously observant person, would always reach out a helping hand to a beggar. There was, therefore, no conflict in my life with regard to this.

It was not only the social and political philosophy of Hashomer Hatzair that attracted Eli to the organization. He readily confesses that they had "the best selection of girls." One day, he was having such a good time with his friends that he lost track of the time and came home late. His parents were already very worried about him. Eli says,

"I thought my father would beat me, so I hid behind a chair. He really didn't want to hurt me, but, rather, to make a point. While I was hiding behind the chair, he was swatting the chair with a piece of leather."

Moshe Zborowski had always dreamed of emigrating to Palestine, but he felt that he could not go before his children finished high school. In Poland, high school was more rigorous and intense scholastically than college is in America. It was rare for a Jewish child to attend a public high school. Private school tuition was prohibitively high, and it was difficult to get accepted to public high schools. Since he was well able to afford the cost, and his children were bright, Moshe wanted them to have the opportunity to attend a fine high school.

The Tarbut School

In the fall of 1938, after his bar mitzvah—an event marked by being called to read the Torah in the synagogue followed by a celebration with vodka and *lekach* (sponge cake)—Eli left for Częstochowa to attend his first year of Hebrew high school. It was part of the chain of secular Hebrew-language schools associated with the Tarbut network in Poland, Romania, and Lithuania in the interwar years. The curriculum included Judaic as well as general studies. Because travel to and from the school was complicated, it was necessary for Eli to board with a family in Częstochowa. While he was proud and happy to be able to attend the private Hebrew high school, it was his first experience away from home. He recalls his overwhelming feelings of alienation and profound homesickness:

> My father had arranged for me to board with a fine family, but they didn't have any children my age. On the first Friday night when the man of the house stood up to recite *Kiddush*, I simply broke down. I had never been at a strange table for Shabbat. I began to cry because I was so homesick. The family was very nice to me, but I was not happy there. This prompted my father to look for other arrangements. The second home was more modest, but there were children my age, so I felt more comfortable. While the homesickness was not as intense, I still missed the familiarity of home—waking up in my own bed, my mother's cooking, walks with my

father on Shabbat, the freedom to run to my grandmother's house and my old friends On occasion a bus passed through Częstochowa on its way to Żarki. When I saw this bus, I was overcome with longing. Sometimes, I would just jump on the bus and go to Żarki without telling the family with whom I was boarding. A day or two later I would return.

A Final Fun-Filled Summer

The summer following Eli's first year of high school was joyous and relaxed. Because his high school included Jewish studies as well as secular subjects, Eli did not attend *cheder* that summer. For the first time he felt as if he was having a real vacation: "Due to the good weather, the clean air and the beautiful forests all around, our town Żarki became a resort destination in the summer. I enjoyed playing with the summer children, with whom I was very popular. This time, it was because I was the only child that owned a two-wheeled bicycle. When I arrived on my bike, the children gathered around me for turns to ride the bike. I liked all this attention and I was very willing to share the bike with them."

That summer there were many rumors of an impending war. To allay the fears, the president of Poland spoke convincingly about the strength of the Polish nation and reassured the people that the country was able to defend itself. In Eli's mind, war was fought between soldiers and he felt no personal threat. An optimistic, sociable teenager, Eli could not possibly have anticipated what was about to befall them.

Chapter 2 Notes

1. A *sukkah* is a temporary booth constructed for the holiday of *Sukkot,* which is celebrated in the fall of the year. The roof of the *sukkah* is covered with branches from plants which have grown in the ground. It is customary to eat one's meal in the *sukkah.* Some people also sleep in the hut.

2. Yeshiva—a Jewish religious academy.

3. *"Ma nishtana"* are the first two words of the traditional four questions that appear in the Passover *Hagaddah.* The questions, which inquire about "why this night is different from all other nights", are asked by the youngest child present at the Passover *seder.*

Map of the area around Żarki, based on Martin Gilbert, *Atlas of the Holocaust*, 4th ed. (London and New York: Routledge, 2009)

Chapter 3

WAR COMES TO ŻARKI

The big synagogue in Żarki

❦

War Comes to Żarki

Throughout 1938 rumors flowed through Żarki about the fate of Jews in Nazi Germany. In August, Germany cancelled residence permits for foreigners. Those who returned to Poland brought with them eyewitness accounts of the mounting anti-Semitism, of fascism, and of Nazi preparations for war.

The Polish government announced that Jews who had left Poland would not be permitted to return after the end of October. On October 28, Germany physically expelled the remaining 17,000 Polish Jews, putting them on trains headed for the border. There the Polish border guards turned them back. With nowhere to go, these unfortunate exiles, tired, hungry, and wet from the pouring rain, sought what shelter they could find in the surrounding villages. Eventually, 4,000 were admitted into Poland; the remainder were interned in refugee camps on the border. The expulsion from the Reich of Jews holding Polish passports was known as the Zbaszyn deportation, after the largest of these camps. The deportees spent months in the border area in limbo, because the Poles, like the Germans, were unwilling to accept them.[1]

Conditions in the refugee camps "were so bad that some actually tried to escape back into Germany and were shot," recalled Rosalind Herzfeld, a British woman who was sent to help those who had been expelled.[2]

A young woman among the refugees, Berta Grynszpan, sent a postcard to her brother in Paris, describing the situation and asking for help. Herschel Grynszpan was so unnerved by his sister's communication that he bought a revolver and, on November 3, went to the German embassy, where he shot a twenty-nine-year-old member of the diplomatic corps named Ernst vom Rath. When Grynszpan surrendered without resistance to the French authorities, a postcard to his parents, found in his pocket, provided the motive: "May God forgive me . . . I must protest so that the whole world hears my protest, and that I will do."

The murder of vom Rath by a Jew provided the pretext for a brief, terribly violent pogrom in Germany on the night of November 9, now known as Kristallnacht, or Crystal Night, for the broken glass of the windows of Jewish business establishments strewn over the streets.

In the aftermath, Jewish newspapers were shut down, cutting off the Jewish community's principal source of news and guidance. Burdensome economic and political restrictions were placed on the Jews. One hundred and ten synagogues were destroyed, and in the weeks that followed 30,000 Jews were rounded up and sent to concentration camps already prepared for them. Among them was Eli's uncle, his mother's brother, who was taken to the Buchenwald concentration camp. He subsequently managed to escape and found refuge in Shanghai, China.

The news of Kristallnacht and the events that followed failed to prepare the Jews of Poland for what was coming. They were in denial. Here is how Eli remembers it: "While we knew what was happening elsewhere, we never thought it could touch us. We thought that if it came to war, it would be fought between soldiers. We never thought it would touch civilians. We had some non-Jewish neighbors. And at first the threat was a war against Poland, not specifically against the Jews, so the non-Jews were also affected. But in my childish mind, war was not before me at all. I was thirteen years old at the time."

Nevertheless, Moshe Zborowski began to take precautions against the cataclysm he didn't quite believe would come. Accompanying his father on business trips, Eli observed that he frequently exchanged cash receipts for gold coins. "He was just setting the money aside in a very portable form, something we could carry concealed if we had to. I was only thirteen, but I realized this was something we had to do in case of war. I carried the gold coins on these trips. The fact is that the coins were key to our survival. Even after the liberation, we still had a sum that allowed us to get a new start in America."

In the summer of 1942, three years into the war, with the threat of deportation looming, Moshe took pains to secure these portable assets. He approached a gentile shoemaker whom he knew well through his leather business and arranged for him to make midsoles for the family's shoes. This piece of leather, which would be concealed between the inner and outer soles of the shoe, had cavities in which three gold coins could be hidden. Five pairs of shoes with midsoles were to be prepared, one pair for each child, as well as one each for Moshe and Zisel. Moshe personally directed the shoemaker throughout the night in the preparation of the shoes.

In addition, each member of the family had small gems sewn into the shoulder pads of their garments, and each wore a small drawstring bag with paper currency around their neck, concealed under their clothing. Thus, if they were unable to get back home or were separated from each other, each member of the family would have some limited means of survival.

Over the years, Moshe had set aside far more than thirty gold coins. He now had the task of hiding the rest, gold and jewelry, in or around the house. He contacted a roofer whom he knew, and asked him to make three waterproof canisters. Then he, Eli, and Mendel shoveled their supply of coal to one side and dug a hole in the cellar floor, where they buried two canisters containing coins. Breathing heavily and soaked with perspiration from their efforts, they filled the hole and replaced the coal over it, confident that no one would think to search there.

Knowing that Germans and Poles often searched for buried caches by poking a steel rod into the ground, Moshe decided to bury the last canister, with all the family jewelry, under the large stone slab in front of the door. When he had completed this task—and it was all the family could do to move the heavy stone off its site and back on—he felt he had done everything he could to protect his material possessions.

Meanwhile, that summer of 1939 the president of Poland assured his worried people that the country was strong enough to defend itself against any enemy. Poles were not afraid of German threats, he declared.

But overnight, the leisurely vacation atmosphere was transformed into full-fledged war, filled with danger, uncertainty, and restrictions.

Behind the Zborowski house stood a large storage building, constructed long before Moshe Zborowski so carefully built his home. Used to store his leather inventory, it had walls nearly three feet thick. In addition, the building was guarded by two large German shepherd dogs that lived in a dog house outside the entrance. The night of Thursday, August 31, the dogs began barking furiously, in a tense way Eli had never heard before. Other dogs in the neighborhood joined the dreadful chorus, apparently responding to the rumble of approaching heavy artillery that was still inaudible to the human ear.

Żarki lay on the very road along which the German army entered Poland, thereby beginning World War II, on Friday, September 1, 1939. In advance of the invasion, the Germans shelled and bombed selected targets. The Zborowskis had no radio, but one of Eli's uncles did, and he confirmed that war had broken out. But no one in Żarki knew what that meant for them; Żarki was certainly not of any strategic value in the defense of Poland.

The first bombs fell on Żarki on Saturday morning, one landing in the Zborowski front yard. It seemed that the Germans were trying to undermine morale through these random attacks on civilian centers. Eli recalls a gruesome incident that morning:

> My uncle Mendel and his family were getting ready to leave town to go east. Just as the family was ready to leave they sent their thirteen-year-old son, Lazer, back to their apartment. Lazer was named after the same grandfather as I am and born the same year. Just as he arrived home, bombs began to fall, concentrated on the Jewish sector. Lazer was hit by flying debris. He fell to the ground screaming for help, but nobody could get near him because of the fire. He was burned alive. This was my first experience of the war with the murder of a close relative. Sadly, it was not to be the last.

By early evening, German army vehicles were rolling into town. The Zborowskis sought shelter in the warehouse, joined by the Jonisz family, who lived next door. While they huddled within the stout protective walls the bombing intensified. When they finally emerged, they found that the front wall of their home had been badly damaged, but the house of their other next-door neighbors, the Hershlikiewicz family, had taken a solid hit, and several members of that family had been killed.

On Monday, the fourth day of the war, the Germans rounded up a great many people and took them into custody. By the end of the day, ninety had been summarily executed.

German soldiers burst into the Zborowski home and carried off whatever appealed to them. Zisel wept with fear and indignation, but Moshe, determined to calm her, said, "Just thank God that we are alive." Nevertheless, he was visibly frightened. Eli, who had always seen him as a composed, confident protector, would remember the incident for the rest of his life.

Within a few days, Żarki was a scene of utter devastation. Houses stood open to the weather, their roofs and walls blown away. Bodies lay in the streets unburied, along with the swelling carcasses of dead horses. The city was in ruins. Jews were commanded to clean up the streets. On Monday the German soldiers began shooting Jews randomly on sight, men, women, and children. Despite all they had heard about the treatment of Jews in Nazi Germany, the Jews of Żarki had never thought it could touch them.

Where was the Polish Army? Why weren't they defending Żarki? They had, in fact, decided to abandon the towns along the German border to their fate, withdrawing to the southeast to defend the area east of the Vistula River and await the support of French and British forces. What they did not know was that Germany and the Soviet Union had agreed to divide Poland, in the Molotov-Ribbentrop Pact. When the Soviets invaded Poland from the east, the entire Polish strategy was nullified. The government had abandoned towns like Żarki along the border without gaining any advantage whatever.

The Occupation of Żarki Begins

The Germans established rules freezing the prices Jews could charge for goods such as the leather Moshe Zborowski dealt in. Money became worthless under such restrictions. "My father, a leather wholesaler, had no place of business other than the warehouse in our backyard. When the Germans confiscated his warehouse, he was smart enough to hide some of the leather stored in the warehouse in ditches that he dug in the ground. This would become as good as gold later in the occupation."

It took about six weeks before the German occupation fully settled in. With time, the Jews of Żarki were obliged to adapt to a new reality. They were confined to an open ghetto centered around the Old Square. The borders of the Żarki ghetto were defined by signs warning Poles not to enter, and Jews not to leave, without the written permission of the occupying forces. Nevertheless, most of the Jews in the ghetto were still living in their own homes; communication and trade with the outside world continued.

Restrictions were posted throughout Żarki. Jews were required to wear a white armband with a blue Star of David, and their homes were marked with the word *Jude*. When the schools opened, Jewish children were not permitted to attend. Food purchases were restricted. As time passed, the restrictions on Jewish life tightened. Jews could not congregate in groups of more than three. This meant they could not form a *minyan*, the traditional quorum of ten men required for public prayer.

Throughout the years of 1940, 1941 and the first half of 1942, despite the restrictions that the Germans imposed, we somehow managed to live a kind of life that one can consider, under these circumstances, as bearable. We felt we could continue to survive for another year or two should the war continue. We kept in touch with the news of what was happening on the front. We knew that the Germans were attacking and moving deep into Russia. We heard the news about the victory of the Red Army over the Germans in Stalingrad. Altogether, it was a life that was still imbued with hope and meaning.

After creating the Żarki ghetto, the Germans established a *Judenrat*, an administrative council of Jews, headed by Yisrael Borenstein, to serve as an intermediary between the occupier and the Jewish community, and a Jewish Order Service to police the community.

Members of the Jewish Order Service saw themselves as serving the Jewish community rather than the Germans.

In later months and years, the *Judenrat* became the body to which the Germans gave orders to collect sums of money as a "contribution" from the Jews. They demanded hundreds of men for physical labor. Under threat to their own lives, the members of the *Judenrat* had to make heartrending decisions: who was to serve in the labor battalions; who was to be assessed for "contributions," and how much.

As vice chairman of the *Judenrat*, Efraim Monat was the liaison to the regional German administrative headquarters in Radomsko. One of his functions was to obtain travel permits allowing Jews to leave the ghetto for approved reasons. In early 1941, he began providing the Jewish underground in Warsaw with travel permits obtained through the Żarki *Judenrat*. In the final weeks of September and October, before the deportation of Jews to labor camps, Monat used his contacts to provide hundreds of Jews with travel permits that enabled them to escape. By the time the deportation began, there were only some 800 Jews remaining in the ghetto, out of an initial population of 3,500 to 4,000.

As if they didn't have enough of a plague from the Germans, in late 1941 Żarki suffered an outbreak of typhus. The Judenrat established a hospital to care for the victims, many of whom perished. During the summer of 1942, the *Judenrat* opened a soup kitchen to feed some 250 refugees who had fled to Żarki from other towns with few of their assets.

Despite the travel restrictions, people were fleeing from one town to another. Among them were many professionals: accountants, lawyers, teachers. As the children were barred from attending school, Moshe Zborowski engaged some of the Jewish teachers to tutor them. They taught whatever they could without textbooks or a formal curriculum. Eli's sister Tzila was tutored by a Christian teacher, along with two other Jewish girls. Jews were constantly being recruited for menial labor, but Moshe paid off those in charge of selecting work crews not to call upon him.

Youth Organizations

The Jewish organizations in Żarki went underground when the German occupation began, on the second day of the war, as they were clearly in violation of the occupation restrictions. Eli, as mentioned earlier, was a member of Hashomer Hatzair, the strongest youth group in Żarki.

Founded in the early years of the twentieth century, Hashomer Hatzair (the Young Guard) is the oldest Zionist youth movement still in existence. It is an international socialist organization, emphasizing kibbutz-style communal living, and training and preparation to establish collective agricultural settlements, or kibbutzim, in Israel. In the summer of 1941, it organized a kibbutz in Żarki where Eli visited frequently and engaged in agricultural labor. He had every intention of relocating to Palestine as soon as that was possible.

Later in the war, Hashomer Hatzair focused its attention on resistance against the Nazis. Mordechai Anielewicz, the leader of Hashomer Hatzair's Warsaw branch, became head of the United Jewish Fighters Organization (ZOB), the Jewish underground, and was the leader of the Warsaw Ghetto Uprising in 1943.

Through Hashomer Hatzair, Eli became a member of the ZOB, which brought together young people of all ideological persuasions. Members who had military experience trained younger members in military skills, handling weapons, the use of grenades, and similar matters.

Meetings were held frequently, in the forests and fields surrounding Żarki. "At these meetings we engaged in very humanitarian and ideological discussions. We had book discussions of the current leftist literature, and we talked about Israel and our hopes and dreams for a Jewish State, the meaning of a collective lifestyle on a kibbutz, and the need for agrarian training."

Hashomer Hatzair agrarian *hachshara* (training farm) in Żarki , June 1942.
Eli is sitting on top of the load of hay (third from left).
Courtesy Leah Hammerstein Silverstein,
United States Holocaust Memorial Museum

To protect its contents, the library was closed and locked. However, it continued to be available to leaders of the youth organizations, and through them, to their members. "The educational content of our meetings was very much enhanced by the availability of this wonderful library. The books we were reading were in Yiddish, in Polish, and some in Hebrew."

We read *Das Kapital* by Karl Marx. We also read about Ber Borochov's philosophy of combining Socialism with Zionism. Unfortunately, only one other person from my group survived, a boy named Moniek Fiszer (the same boy who had fallen with Eli's bicycle, breaking his nose).

Left to right: Eli, Lemel Feifkopf, Aron Steinbrecher, Icek Kartusz, and Moniek Fiszer in 1942. The boys are wearing white armbands with blue Stars of David that were mandated by the Germans. The only two to survive the Holocaust were Eli and Moniek Fiszer, for whom Eli had provided forged identity papers.

Eli and his best friend, Golda Szwarcbaum in Żarki in 1942. Golda perished in the Treblinka death camp.

Several Jewish underground newspapers were printed and distributed in occupied Poland. Typically, they were set by hand, mimeographed, or printed on small hand presses. To aid in secret distribution, the newspapers had to be small and brief. They reported on events throughout Poland, on the battlefields, and in occupied countries.

Hashomer Hatzair had an underground newspaper, prepared and printed in Warsaw and then brought to Częstochowa for distribution to nearby cities and towns. Eli was assigned to distribute the paper. When Moshe Zborowski learned that Eli had taken on this responsibility, he was filled with fear for his son's safety. He extracted a promise from Eli that he would stop, but he continued nevertheless, hiding his activities from his father.

In the first week of October 1942, the Germans began deporting Jews for what was euphemistically called "resettlement to the east." German police, assisted by Polish, Lithuanian, and Ukranian police in black uniforms, forced the Jews into freight cars. The doors were fastened shut and the train pulled away–and nothing more was heard from them. As most of the Jews had fled to the forest or, using travel permits obtained by the Judenrat, gone to nearby communities, only 800 remained to be deported. The Germans left a work force of about 50 Jews in Żarki, including Judenrat president Yisrael Borenstein and vice presidents Efraim Monat and Lejzer Steinberg.

ZOB members in Warsaw had observed that whenever Jews were packed into railroad cars ostensibly for transfer to the east, the same cars would return empty the next day, hardly enough time to get to an eastern destination. The railroad workers said that they delivered the cars to a town near Treblinka where the SS met the car and escorted it to Treblinka, and then returned the empty car. The ZOB sent members to interview the nearby residents. They said that at night they could smell burning flesh. This information was circulated in the illegal publications of the ZOB.

People read about Treblinka in the underground newspaper Eli delivered, but they still did not believe it. Eli was astounded. "If people in the United States did not believe the accounts of atrocities it's understandable, but people of my father's generation, despite being so close to it, didn't believe it either. It simply seemed unimaginable that this could be their fate."

The United Jewish Fighters' Organization trained young Jews like Eli to defend themselves. This raised the issue of weapons. While the ZOB had open communication with elements of the non-Jewish underground, and cooperated with them on many issues, they were denied the precious arms with which to defend themselves and their communities. The Polish underground, and especially its right wing, felt that the Jews were doomed, rather sooner than later. Thus, giving them weapons and ammunition was seen as a waste—the recipients would be killed, and their weapons would be confiscated by the Germans.

Within the ZOB, assignments were made by the older members, mostly men in their twenties. As Eli knew the countryside well, and all the neighboring towns, he was given the responsibility of seeking arms and ammunition.

The national organization often sent *shlichim* (emissaries) to observe the Żarki chapter's progress, and to bring them up to date on events. Some of these—Mordechai Anielewicz, Aryeh Wilner, Tosia Altman, and others—subsequently were leaders of the Warsaw Ghetto uprising.

Following the German invasion of Poland, the country was broken into three regions. A band along the western border was annexed by Germany. This brought the Polish-German border within one kilometer of Żarki. East of this region, the German-occupied part of Poland was designated as the Polish General Government. The Russians occupied Poland east of the Bug River, and it became part of the Soviet Union.

The *shlichim* (emissaries) from Hashomer Hatzair headquarters in Warsaw, and later from the ZOB Center, had missions in Zaglembia, an industrial area in southwestern Poland that was part of the German-annexed region. Żarki was frequently the point at which such missions crossed into Zaglembia. Eli arranged for a Pole who knew the area to guide Mordechai Anielewicz across this border whenever he visited. This person, often a professional smuggler, knew the territory intimately and was best prepared, traveling through field and forest, to circumvent the German roadblocks, checkpoints, and patrols.

In 1941 and the first months of 1942, the Germans began arresting Jews under various pretexts, sending them to the forced labor camp at Auschwitz. The Germans usually sent back the clothing and informed the family that the person had died, even if he was still alive, to spread fear.

Among those arrested in this way was one of Eli's uncles. "When my uncle's clothing came back, the package included his glasses. My father removed the glasses and told my aunt that her husband must still be alive, because the glasses had not been returned. In fact, people who were sent to Auschwitz two years later and survived told us after the war that my uncle *had been* still alive, albeit swollen with hunger. He ultimately did die in Auschwitz."

In addition to Jews, the Germans also arrested many of the Polish intelligentsia and sent them to forced labor camps. They sought to drain the country of its creative and intellectual resources and reduce the population to those suited to hard labor.

As the war progressed, it became clear that the Zborowski family's Zionist dream would have to be postponed. The future of the Jews in Poland was questionable and life in general was uncertain. Nevertheless, Moshe felt he ought to prepare his children with whatever information he had in case any of them survived and had the opportunity to go to Palestine. He gave them the names of three cousins who had already settled there and could be contacted for assistance should his children make their way to Palestine on their own. Many years later, Eli and his siblings were able to connect with these cousins.

Moshe Zborowski had a tremendous impact on his elder son. "During my entire life, whenever I had to make a decision, I recalled some advice, or saying, or behavior of my father. He has been a constant point of reference in my life, my polar star, long after his death. I often ask myself, 'What would my father say? What would my father do?' "

On September 21, 1942—Yom Kippur, the solemn Day of Atonement—the Germans began deporting Jews from Częstochowa. Moshe Zborowski feared it would not be long before they reached Żarki. Through the *Judenrat*, he obtained a travel permit to Kraków, well to the south, and six days later the Zborowskis left Żarki. It was the second day of Sukkot, a holiday traditionally so filled with joy that it is referred to in Jewish prayer and literature as the Season of our Rejoicing. The irony was not lost on Eli: there was certainly no cause for rejoicing on the Sukkot of 1942.

While their permit allowed travel all the way to Kraków, the family's journey ended in Pilica, a town whose 3,000 Jews had all been deported to Belzec, an extermination camp located in the Lublin district of southeastern Poland. Several hundred had escaped before the deportation, and some of them had returned to Pilica; they had been allowed to remain. The Germans often waited until there were enough returnees to fill a freight car before rounding them up. Meanwhile, it seemed like a relatively safe location.

On the last day of Sukkot, over 100 Jews were shot to death in Żarki on various pretexts; the remainder were forced to run to the Zloty Potok railroad station, where they were deported to the Treblinka death camp. Out of the initial Jewish population of 3,500, only 800 were deported, as more than 2,500 people had fled, some into the woods, some of them to the smaller villages, some of them with permits. The Germans kept a work force of fifty people behind to clear out valuable items from the Jewish homes. All these goods were taken to the synagogue to be catalogued and stored. Later, the Germans allowed a few people to return to clean the houses that had been stripped of all their valuables.

In mid-November, Moshe Zborowski was able to bribe the Germans, through the *Judenrat*, to include him among the returnees as a worker. Zisel and Eli's siblings stayed illegally, hiding in the attics of empty houses. The work permits turned out to be a trick. When the Germans eventually gathered enough Jews together through this ruse, they sent them to a ghetto and from there to the death camps. Jews had lived in Żarki for 600 years as an independent, vital community. This was truly the end of an era.

In the spring of 1943, Eli was sought out by Tzvi Brandes, an activist in Hashomer Hatzair and the leader of the United Jewish Fighters Organization in Zaglembia. Brandes knew Eli from his work as ZOB liaison to the ghettos of Żarki, Radomsko, and Pilica.

Brandes had concluded that there was no escape for Poland's Jews except to Palestine, via circuitous, risky routes. There was no established "underground railroad" to Palestine: Following one route, a group would make its own way from Poland through Czechoslovakia to Hungary, where its members might, or might not, find passage on a ship. And, if they did, they might be turned back by the British, who governed Palestine under a mandate from the League of Nations. It did not matter that the mandate included a directive to create "a national home for the Jewish people." The British turned away Jewish refugees seeking refuge in Palestine.

Brandes urged Eli to join the movement and attempt to reach Palestine, where he could join a kibbutz requiring heavy labor under the most trying circumstances. He asked Eli whether his father could provide the equivalent of $300 toward his attempt to reach Palestine. Moshe Zborowski said that he would only sanction this if Tzila, only thirteen years old, could also go, in which case he would provide $600. Brandes was unable to arrange for the girl's emigration, and Moshe would not allow Eli to go without his sister. As a result of this experience, Eli recognized and accepted his responsibility for Tzila. As it turned out, escape to Palestine by this route was hopeless. On July 17, Brandes wrote, "Our hope of reaching the Homeland has not been realized, to our deepest regret."[3]

Another new reality had commenced: the sad, often terrifying, saga of the Zborowski family in hiding.

Chapter 3 Notes

1. *Chronology of the Holocaust, 1933–1938* (Yad Vashem, 2004).
2. "Recollections of Rosalind Herzfeld," *Jewish Chronicle*, September 28, 1979, p. 80; cited in Martin Gilbert, *The Holocaust: The Jewish Tragedy* (London: William Collins Sons, 1986).
3. "Last Letter from Bedzin" (July 17, 1943), co-signed by Frumka Plotnicka, Herszl Szpringer, Tzvi Brandes, Kozhuch Israel, and Szlomo Lerner.

❧ Chapter 4 ❧

In Hiding

Eli in disguise and Kolacz
on a visit to the local photographer

ॐ

In Hiding

During the month the Zborowski family remained in Pilica, Eli made contact with several Jewish communities in the neighboring villages and began to act as an underground courier between the ghettos of Pilica, Częstochowa, and Radomsko.

When they returned to Żarki, Moshe Zborowski was assigned to a labor unit that was building a stable for the German police. Josef Placzek, the builder in charge of the construction, was the son of the contractor who had built the Zborowski home in 1928. As a result of the respect Moshe had shown for the contractor and the workers, both Josef and his father had the highest regard for him.

On January 5, 1943 the Germans rounded up all the Jews who had returned to Żarki after the deportation and ordered them to gather their belongings and assemble in the marketplace, presumably for transfer to the ghetto in Radomsko. In fact, upon their arrival in Radomsko, they were loaded on a train that carried them to their deaths in Treblinka.

The ghettos in Poland were created as part of the Nazis' unfolding anti-Jewish policy. Designed to isolate Jews, during the period of the Final Solution, the ghettos served to funnel victims to the Nazi extermination and labor camps. As the killing machinery was working at full capacity, it was necessary to concentrate the "raw material" for efficient, timely transportation. Jews from remote areas were brought to a ghetto located on a railroad line. When enough Jews had been assembled to fill a freight car or a cattle car, they were loaded and sent to a death camp.

Conditions in the ghettos of Poland were grotesque. As described by Nechama Tec, a noted sociologist and Holocaust scholar: "Ghetto inmates were entitled to fewer than 400 calories a day. Added to [the] effects of hunger were the severe problems caused by cramped living conditions, with seven to fifteen people in a single room. The absence of electricity, running water and adequate toilet facilities led to terrible hygiene and [consequent] epidemics."[1]

Zisel had spent a few days in Radomsko, and found conditions there intolerable. She decided to continue evading the Germans by hiding in various attics. When her family came to say goodbye, two of her sisters chose to stay with her. Her sister Sheindl, however, could not let their parents go alone to Radomsko. Despite warnings from the rest of the family that she would be unable to do anything for them once they arrived in the ghetto, she insisted. "If I can be with them just one more day, it will be worth the effort." In her mid-twenties, Sheindl was young and vibrant. On January 5, 1943, the day she arrived in Radomsko, the Germans liquidated the ghetto, ordering all the Jews to the railroad station, where they were loaded into waiting freight cars. Sheindl and her parents, along with a few thousand other Jews from surrounding towns and from the Radomsko ghetto, were immediately transported to the death camp, Treblinka.

Eli Returns to Radomsko

While the family was in Pilica, Eli made contact with Polish partisans, who agreed to take 150 youngsters into their group. The plan was to take fifty from the Częstochowa ghetto and a hundred from the Radomsko ghetto. The Jews in Radomsko were at greater risk of deportation because there was no industry there, while in the Częstochowa ghetto thousands of Jews were employed in German-run factories.

Eli returned to Radomsko, on January 4, 1943 to take out the youngsters, and stayed overnight. The next day, unknown to him, a few hundred Jews from Żarki, including some members of his family, were simultaneously being escorted by the Germans to the ghetto to join in the deportation to death in Treblinka.

When he awoke, he saw that the ghetto was surrounded by three cordons of armed police at intervals of ten meters; every fifty meters there was a black-uniformed guard—Lithuanians and Ukrainians.

Those black uniforms meant only one thing: death. Zisel was right: The final liquidation of the ghetto had begun. No one could leave the ghetto any longer; Eli's permit was useless. He decided to run through the police cordon and escaped unharmed in a hail of bullets.

While trying to catch his breath after his narrow escape, Eli suddenly remembered that a girl named Dora Rothenberg was still inside the ghetto. Dora was a member of the Żarki chapter of Hashomer Hatzair. He could not leave her there. He had to go back.

A young Polish woman was pushing a baby carriage along the street bordering the ghetto. Gradually, she became aware that a young man in a blue beret was walking close beside her as if he were the baby's father. Eli smiled at her but said nothing. When he was well out of sight of the heavily guarded front gate of the ghetto, he stopped to speak with someone inside. Soon, Dora appeared. She wanted to say farewell to her parents, but Eli convinced her there was no time. She managed to slip out of the ghetto, and they began walking back to Żarki, sixty-four kilometers (40 miles) away, in below-freezing temperatures, amid high snow drifts.

From time to time, Dora would ask, "How much farther?" And I would say, "See that little hill ahead? Once we're over that, we'll look down on Żarki."

And she would say, "We already passed two hills." And I'd reply, "No, no. I meant this one."

The last ten kilometers, I was exhausted. Now it was Dora's turn to encourage me. "Don't sit down," she said. To sit could have been fatal. In such cold weather, one can easily fall asleep and freeze to death.

In Żarki, Dora hid with her uncle, who, like Moshe, had a work permit to remain. Believing that she would be safer in Zaglembia, her uncle sent her on to another uncle who lived there. Enroute, Dora was discovered and arrested. As she was being taken away, she threw a letter addressed to Eli out of the wagon. The letter arrived with a torn photo of her. It was as if the person who found it had begun to tear it up, thought better of it, and instead saw that it got to Eli. Dora was deported to Auschwitz where she perished.

Dora Rothenberg (left) in the torn photo she threw from a wagon in an envelope addressed to Eli. On the back, she wrote:

I'm being sent to Auschwitz.
Instead of me,
You will have my photo

During the next seven months, Eli was occupied with work for the underground. He was continually on the move, acting as a courier and trying to obtain ammunition for the ZOB. In Żarki, he hid in the attics of empty houses, while his father, who had a work permit, brought him food at night.

Hide or Be Killed

Moshe asked Placzek to hide his wife and children. This would be an extremely dangerous commitment. Hiding Jews was punishable by death; entire families were publicly executed for this crime. But the Placzeks did not hesitate. Placzek built a room behind a false wall in his attic, and by the end of January Zisel, Mendel, and Tsila were securely concealed there. At the same time, Moshe found shelter for Zisel's two remaining sisters, Cywia and Rochel, and her brother Yossel, with a family named Kolacz in the nearby village of Bobolice.

Eli traveled continually through the area as a courier between the ghettos, bringing additional fighters into the underground, and acquiring ammunition and hand grenades wherever he could find them. Known for their courage and daring, many such couriers disappeared without a trace. Some were apprehended and sent to concentration camps; others were executed. These couriers performed another vital function. The ghettos isolated Jews from the local gentile population and also from other Jewish communities. Through the couriers, illegal lines of communication were established for the transfer of information, money, goods, arms and forged papers.[2]

Courier Service: A Close Escape

A factory baking in the sun is surrounded by a high security fence that runs alongside a narrow-gauge railroad track. Eli is crouching in the shadow of a broad elm tree on the other side of the track. His attention is focused on a spot where a dip in the ground leaves a space under the fence surrounding a factory. Hearing a low whistle, Eli glides quickly to the fence. A grimy hand appears with an envelope, and Eli exchanges the packet he is carrying with the unseen person inside the factory compound. As he rises and turns to leave, he barely avoids a collision with a Polish policeman patrolling the railroad track. He

clutches the package of forged papers and other illegal documents to his chest.

One of Eli's tasks as a courier was to distribute forged documents. This is a forged identity document that he provided to Dobra Borzykowski, a member of the ZOB, giving her the Polish name Jadwiga Gomuliska and listing her religion as Catholic. Dobra survived the war, and deposited her papers with Yad Vashem.

Kennkarte
(identity card)

Dobra Borzykowski

"All right, young man," says the officer, in a gruff voice, "Let's go down to the station house and take a look at that stuff you're carrying."

"I can't go there," replies Eli in his perfect Polish. "There will be an SS man on duty there. I'll be taken by the Nazis and killed."

"Not my problem," responds the policeman. He starts to reach for something on his belt—handcuffs, perhaps. Eli notes that the officer has a lapel pin with the flag of Poland on his official uniform.

"Hold on a minute, comrade," says Eli, producing his Polish passport. "We're both Poles, aren't we? I don't want any harm to come to you."

The officer is puzzled by the implicit threat. How could this unarmed teenager do him any harm? He continues to reach toward his belt.

Exuding self-confidence, Eli draws himself to his full height. "Look, I'm in the Polish underground," he begins, in a vaguely threatening tone. He turns to the surrounding forest. "They are watching us right now. If you take me to the station, you will not return home tonight. Your wife will be a widow; your children orphans. Who will take care of them?"

Just then, a German patrol walks by with two large police dogs. Seeing Eli in conversation with the policeman, they simply nod and pass on. Eli notes with relief that the policeman had made no attempt to turn him over to the Germans. A sign of progress!

Now the policeman's eyes also turn to the forest, trying to penetrate its dark recesses. It's just a job. He is not a brave man. He really doesn't give a damn if this tall Polish teenager keeps his envelope. Suddenly, he feels a surge of national pride. "Both Poles. It's true." He releases his grip on Eli's arm and walks past him. Eli watches as the uniformed figure grows smaller and finally disappears around a turn in the road. Eli smiles for the first time in several weeks.

That summer. while building the stable for the Germans, Moshe Zborowski developed a painful kidney ailment. Eli was serving as a courier between the Częstochowa ghetto and a unit of the Polish underground based near Pelica. This allowed him to pass through Żarki quite often.

I visited my father, coming home for a few hours during the night, to avoid detection by the Germans. Just warming up with my father, just hugging him and then I would leave before daybreak. He was so ill that he could not take care of the rest of his family, hiding with Placzek. If he ever failed to show up for work, he would probably have been shot by the Germans—and then who would take care of them? With tears in his eyes, he asked me to take charge of my mother, and my brother and sister, until he felt better.

Eli promised that he would do so, after first letting the ZOB know that he needed some time off after completing his current mission in Częstochowa. As it turned out, the Germans liquidated the Częstochowa ghetto only a few days later. Unable now to carry out his mission as a courier, Eli remained in Żarki, hiding during the day and sleeping with his father at night.

Moshe Disappears

On August 5, 1943, with the stable finished, the Germans announced that they would now deport the work crew of the last fifty Jews in Żarki, including Moshe. Eli could no longer remain with him; the time had come when he had to join Zisel and his brother and sister. In broad daylight, he had to leave the ghetto and walk through Żarki, where everyone knew he was Jewish, to the Placzek house. On his last ZOB mission, Eli had procured three priceless hand grenades, which he could not leave behind. Certain that he would be recognized, he disguised himself as a peasant woman, carrying a market basket containing the grenades. Moshe walked ahead very uncomfortable about Eli's cargo. As they passed through the marketplace, the door of a bar flew open, and the most vicious German officer in Żarki strode out. Moshe paled with fear, but the German didn't recognize Eli. It was the last time Eli would see his father. He kept walking purposefully, head held high, until he arrived at 49 Czestowchowska Street— Placzek's house—where he joined the family hiding in the attic.

The Jews working in Żarki were taken by the gendarmerie— German police—to the synagogue to await their fate, either deportation or a walk to the cemetery, where they would all be shot. Among them was Moshe's sister-in-law, Bela Monat. Moshe told her that he planned to flee to the home of Andrzej Kolacz, in Bobolice, where Zisel's sisters were hiding. He had chosen this as his destination because Placzek's house was in the middle of Żarki, where all the neighbors would have seen him entering the house. "Besides," he told her, "It will be safer for Zisel and the children if Placzek knows that I am still alive somewhere else." Even though he liked and trusted Placzek, he still took precautions.

The synagogue overlooked the Nysa Łużycka River. Moshe jumped from a window on the second floor into the river. Two young men, also members of the doomed work detail, were standing there.

"Let's go!" cried Moshe, as he stepped through the window and dropped into the river. The other two followed. They swam swiftly downstream, but Moshe, suffering dreadfully from his kidney ailment, could not keep up. A Polish client, whom Moshe had always treated sensitively, saw him jump. "Zborowski," he called out, "You are a good man."

Kolacz had never given the Zborowskis his street address. Instead, as a precaution, he told them that he lived "three houses beyond Dratvina," a well-known family in Bobolice. Two days after Moshe's escape from the synagogue, two Polish men came to the Dratvina home and demanded the Jews they were hiding. Mrs. Dratvina, who was buying the possessions of fleeing Jews for a fraction of their worth, denied that any Jews were on her property. In a Byzantine twist, pitting the morally corrupt against the morally bankrupt, the two men took all of Dratvina's Jewish plunder. It seems plausible that Moshe dragged himself from the river and turned to these two thieves for help. He would have asked directions to the Dratvina house, after which they robbed and killed him.

Life in Hiding

The attic room that Eli shared with his family was accessible only through a hatch in the floor. Using a rope and a basket, they brought food up from below and sent down their waste. Nearly every night, Placzek brought a ladder from his backyard and climbed up to be sure they were all right, and to see if they needed anything else. The Zborowskis provided money for food, both for themselves and for the Placzek family.

Placzek was the town fire chief, Eli recalled. "Wearing his uniform, he frequently went drinking with the German police. As a result, he usually had first-hand information about Jews who were caught and murdered. We never heard from Placzek any word about my father, and this further confirmed our suspicion that the Germans were not responsible for his death."

Placzek's heavy drinking was quite normal among Polish workingmen. But the late hours of his drinking bouts did not sit well with his wife, Maria. She suspected that he had another woman. When Placzek came home in the wee hours of morning, she threatened to call the police and tell them that he was hiding Jews. It was, of course, an empty threat. And she would have been endangering herself, since she had readily accepted them in her home.

Throughout the war Eli and the others were able to maintain some contact with his aunt and uncle, Cywia and Shlomo Jonisz, who were hiding with Kolacz. Every once in a while they were able to send letters to one another that were left at a designated place and then picked up. This was how Eli learned that his father had never made it to the Kolacz house. He continued to hope that Moshe would turn up after the war, however.

Although confined to the attic, Eli was not without reading material. The Germans had stripped the Jewish homes of everything of value, but apparently did not consider books to fall into this category. The Poles who followed after them, however, were glad to take the books. Not that they were eager readers, but there was a severe shortage of firewood, and books would keep a house as warm as logs. Eli read whatever he could get his hands on. He also kept a comprehensive diary that included encoded descriptions of his contacts and missions for the ZOB. Hand grenades, for example, were referred to as "eggs."

Isolation pained the family deeply. Their entire lives had been wrapped in the warm, intense culture and society of the Jewish community. Hearing of Jews in a labor camp in Częstochowa, they longed to join them, despite the hardships this would entail. Eli explains this by quoting an ancient Hebrew maxim: *tzarot rabim chatzi nechuma*— "shared distress is a partial consolation."

Risking Exposure and Death

One of Eli's cousins, a three-year-old girl, had been placed with a Polish family for safekeeping, and her parents were paying for the child's upkeep. When they ran out of money, they turned to the Zborowskis for assistance. Eli left the Placzek attic disguised as a woman and brought the money to the Polish family.

On another occasion, again wearing a woman's clothes, Eli met with Josef Kolacz in the open central marketplace of Żarki, again to transfer funds. Kolacz arrived with his horse and wagon, and Eli climbed onto the seat beside him. The marketplace was surrounded on four sides by retail shops and services.

"Take me to the photographer's shop," suggested Eli, smoothing out his dress, "and we can have our picture taken together." Kolacz agreed, and several weeks later picked up the photo, which is reproduced at the beginning of this chapter.

Reflecting on how dangerous this escapade was—all for a souvenir —Eli recalls: "After the war I met the photographer, who told me, 'Look, I recognized you because a photographer has a good eye.' He knew me very well, because he had photographed our family from the time I was a small child. I was willing to take this chance because I wanted to have a memento from this period."

One way to cope with the restrictions and indignities of living in hiding was to introduce a touch of normality by engaging in behavior from the past. From his childhood, Eli was an avid stamp collector. During his confinement in the attic, he frequently communicated through Placzek with stamp dealers to purchase albums and other philatelic supplies. Although these were sent to Placzek, the clerk in the post office knew this was Eli's hobby. Before the deportation, he would often direct a German soldier or policeman with similar interests to Eli to exchange stamps. After the war, the postal clerk said he had known Eli was hiding with Placzek because there was no one else in Żarki who ordered philatelic materials.

Time to Move On

In August 1944, after the family had been in hiding for eighteen months, and Eli for a year, Placzek came home from a drinking bout with the Germans and brought some very unwelcome news. The German officer with whom he was drinking had heard that Placzek was hiding Jews! Of course, he didn't believe it, he said, and they both had a good laugh.

For the Zborowski family, this was a clear sign that they could no longer remain with Placzek. They left that night, just after midnight, headed for the Kolacz home, where Zisel's family were hidden. Because of the curfew, they could not just walk through the center of town. No one was allowed on the streets, and they were clearly Jews. They decided, instead, to walk through the fields and forest around the perimeter of Żarki to reach Bobolice.

Maria Placzek opposed the idea. She and her husband had shared the risks associated with hiding Jews for a year and a half. She was very fearful that the Zborowskis would be caught and executed. This wonderful woman, who had threatened her husband that she would turn them in if he continued to drink into the late hours, cried and begged the family not to leave. She felt they should stay together, as the Russian army was drawing closer every day. In fact, at the time they left, Russia had already reoccupied half of Poland. As it turned out, one week after the Zborowski family left, a squad of Polish and German police descended on the Placzek house. With the house surrounded, and with snipers on the neighboring roofs, they burst into the house without warning and demanded that Placzek turn over the Zborowski family. His only child, a little girl named Jadwiga, began to weep. Eli had often helped her with her schoolwork. Fortunately, the family had destroyed all evidence of any Jewish presence as a precaution, even burning Eli's Hebrew books and his wool *tallit* (prayer shawl). Finding no evidence that the Placzeks had been hiding anyone, the police left without harming them. Placzek knew exactly where the Kolacz farm was, and two weeks after the incident he bicycled over and told the Zborowskis about it.

Through the Forest to Bobolice

For more than a year and a half, Zisel, Mendel, and Tzila had been confined to a small part of the attic, with barely room to sit or lie down. They had no opportunity for exercise. Mendel was fifteen. His body was growing, and for twenty months he had not had an opportunity to walk more than a few feet. Now they faced a challenge that would push their meager physical resources to the limit. While their destination was only seventeen kilometers away by road, the route they followed in order to avoid contact with German patrols was considerably longer.

Because we did not want to be detected, we walked in the fields. It was very difficult to walk because it was just after a rain and the wheat that normally stood up lay flat on the ground. Every time we put our feet down, our legs became tangled in the wheat.

Only a few hundred meters from the Placzek house, we had to jump over a small river in order to continue on the other side. Each of us had a rucksack with a few belongings, some of which might be needed to barter for food. When my brother jumped, his legs failed him. He tripped, badly spraining an ankle, and thereafter couldn't walk. At seventeen, I was now the head of the family; I had to carry him the rest of the way. Because I couldn't carry him and our two rucksacks as well, I walked a hundred meters with the two sacks and then went back and carried Mendel. And that is how we advanced for a while. But after sundown, I was unable to find my brother in the trackless forest. When I finally located him I decided we could no longer be separated. I don't know how, but from then on I carried my brother and two rucksacks. I never let him out of my sight after that.

At about five o'clock in the morning, people began to appear on the roads on their way to work. We became concerned about our safety; if we were seen, we would attract attention and perhaps suspicion because I was carrying Mendel on my back. After a while, Mendel said "Just leave me here. You go take care of our mother and our sister and whatever will happen will happen." But I decided that I would never leave him. The lesson I learned from my father about Tzila applied also to Mendel: he was my responsibility now.

Ahead of us stretched a new forest and I felt if we could reach it without being detected we would be safe. When we got into the forest, I could see that we couldn't continue like this. We were simply exhausted from struggling with Mendel and the rucksacks, and in such poor condition. I knew that Kolacz had a horse and wagon. I decided to leave the others in a concealed place and proceed ahead alone to our destination, returning with the means to carry us the rest of the way. I had been told to proceed to the ruins of the Mirów Castle, a well-known landmark that stood high above the valley floor. From there, it was only a few hundred meters to Kolacz's home.

I had with me the three grenades and a jacket from a Polish officer. I wanted to look like a Polish partisan. When I reached the Kolacz residence, where my aunts were hiding, I found the horse lying on the ground dying! I was so exhausted and tense that I fainted. After a couple of hours, Kolacz's fourteen-year-old sister, Stanisława, accompanied me to the forest. Because we didn't walk on roads, we had difficulty finding the place where I had left them. I had remembered some markers, like an old, burned-out castle. We finally located my exhausted family. For the rest of the trek to the Kolacz residence the girl took all three rucksacks and went ahead, while I followed slowly with my family.

At the Kolacz farm, the Zborowskis joined six Jews already hidden in a chicken coop, now so overpopulated that when one person wanted to turn over, the person next to him had to turn also. Shortly, the family moved into a hayloft in the barn, where they shared one thin blanket. Zisel and Eli slept on the outer edges, and the two younger children on the inside, to take advantage of their body warmth. Here they remained in hiding until they were liberated, on January 17, 1945.

Poles who risked their own lives were the exception. Yet they could be found throughout Poland, in every town and village.[3] Not only was there the risk of terrible retaliation if they were found harboring Jews, but shortages and rationing meant that the rescuers had to share their meager supplies. The four members of the Kolacz family divided their food and water with ten hidden Jews!

Among the residents of the Kolacz chicken coop was Eli's uncle, Joseph Dauman. Here is how he describes the situation:

Their one cow gave only a small amount of milk each day. There was no water well in that village, Bobolice. The nearest well was two kilometers away, in the village of Mirów, and in summer and in winter, rain or snow, the fourteen—later fifteen and sixteen year-old girl, Stanisława Kolacz, was carrying water pails to provide the family and us with water. One had to be careful that the neighbors should not wonder at the Kolacz family using too much water, a sign of perhaps hiding some people. The same fear was in acquiring food. Apart from the difficulties to buy food, we knew how careful the Kolacz family had to act when buying food, as well as bringing water to the house.[4]

Eli recalled the ever-present fear of discovery:
One day, some neighbors came into the house and saw the ten of us there. We were sure that they would denounce us. We had a meeting and developed a strategy to deal with this new development. Three of us went to the neighbor's house. Wearing my Polish officer's jacket, I was armed with a rifle that belonged to Kolacz. We called the man of the house out and I told him that we were Polish partisans who came occasionally to visit. We let him know that no one was to talk about this and if they did we would shoot him. We must have instilled the necessary fear, because they never breathed a word about us.

Officially, the war would continue until May 1945, but it ended in Bobolice on January 17. The Jews hidden with the Kolacz family heard the sounds of battle: aircraft, heavy artillery, grenades, and rifle fire. It was difficult to tell which was German or Russian or American. Kolacz shepherded them all into an underground cellar where he stored wheat. Suddenly, he called Eli to come outside. There, looming over Kolacz, stood a Russian soldier in white winter camouflage. To Eli, he looked like one of God's angels. Eli fell to his knees and kissed the Russian's boots. Eli recalls the confusion that fell over them now that they no longer had to focus on day-to-day survival: "We were still uncertain about what to do. We were afraid that the Germans would come back. We waited until nightfall and left the hiding place to run away. But to run *where?*"

In March, 1978 Yad Vashem recognized both Maria and Jozef Placzek as Righteous Among the Nations, and in May their daughter Jadwiga was similarly honored. Jozef and Apolonia Kolacz received the title of Righteous Among the Nations in 1978, and Andrzej Kolacz and Stanisława Pikula (formerly Kolacz) were recognized by Yad Vashem as Righteous Among the Nations in 1998.

Risks and Rewards

Research shows that most of us are risk-averse. Rather than take a chance on a whole loaf of bread, we will accept half a loaf. But the same research reveals that about a quarter of us take risks in stride; some even seek out risk.[5] Among the risk-takers, it is found that some achieve their highest objectives, while others crash and burn. The difference is that the winners use risk functionally; they take the reasonable risks necessary to achieve their goals. The others, the "wild men," take irrational risks, apparently for the thrill of it, and more often than not suffer the consequences.

Asked why he was willing to take risks that were not imposed on him, Eli responds, "It's all relative. Our underlying situation was filled with risk: I could be shot crossing the street. Under those circumstances, the things I did just did not seem to add much to the risk of daily living."

Perhaps the answer is that Eli had a somewhat higher tolerance for risk than others. In any event, risk has not been a stranger to him. Compared to serving as a courier, gathering ammunition, appearing in the middle of Żarki dressed as a woman, being photographed there, and maintaining a highly visible hobby—what could he fear from any business risk that he had carefully evaluated? Risk researcher Nick Tasler speculates that it was the rational risk-takers among our ancestors who expanded their world beyond the cave and its immediate environs.[6] His research also shows that rational risk-takers achieve their goals far more often than the risk-averse.

Within this framework, we may begin to understand the role that risk has played in Eli Zborowski's life. In every case, he had an objective that could only be achieved by accepting the risk that went with it. This pattern of goal-seeking is not innate; it builds recursively. With each such experience, the rational decision-maker gains confidence and becomes better equipped to balance risk against reward. Eli, for example, admits that having his photograph taken was a teenage prank. Today he would not value having a memento of his disguise so highly as to risk his life and possibly the lives of his family.

Willingness to accept risk is also a basic element of what we call courage. Ambrose Redmoon says, "Courage is not the absence of fear, but rather the judgment that something else is more important than fear."[7] This is consistent with the goal-seeking behavior in which Eli engaged after the war descended upon him at the age of thirteen.

Planting a tree in honor of rescuers in the Avenue of the Righteous at Yad Vashem Marvin, Tzila, Jadviga Placzek, Eli, Josef Kołacz in the early 1980s

In a ceremony honoring rescuers at the Beit Hanassi – President's Residence in Israel. Jadwiga Placzek, Eli, Stanislawa Kołacz -Pikuła

Chapter 4 Notes

1. Nechama Tec, "Jewish Resistance: Facts, Omissions and Distortions" (Miles Lerman Center for the Study of Jewish Resistance, U.S. Holocaust Memorial Museum, 1997), p. 7.

2.Ibid., p.10.

3. Martin Gilbert, *The Righteous: the Unsung Heroes of the Holocaust* (New York: Henry Holt, 2004) p. 103.

4. Joseph Dauman, letter to Yad Vashem, February 26, 1998 (Yad Vashem Righteous Among the Nations Archive, file 1322). Cited by Gilbert, ibid., p. 104.

5. Nick Tasler, The Impulse Factor: Why Some of Us Play It Safe, and Others Risk It All (New York: Simon & Shuster, 2008).

6. Ibid.

7. "No Peaceful Warriors!" *Gnosis: A Journal of the Western Inner Traditions* (Fall 1991).

Chapter 5

LIBERATION AT LAST

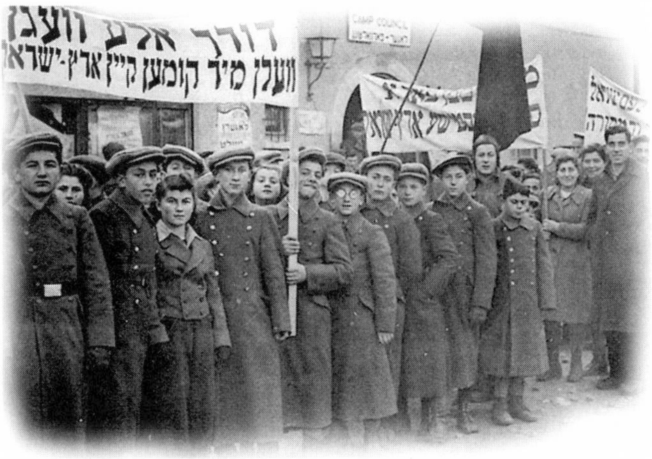

The Zionist Dream
"Through every avenue we will arrive in the land of Israel"

CHAPTER 5

Liberation at Last

Liberation on January 17, 1945 was a remarkable day. That it was a day of joy is certain; however, it was also a day that was filled with a potpourri of emotions. After six years of escalating danger and losses it was impossible for those who survived not to continue to feel threatened. Eli describes his mixed feelings:

> You cannot, today, possibly fathom the feelings that overcame us at the moment of liberation. It was really a combination of feelings that we experienced. We felt born again. But at the same time, we continued to dread the possibility of our imminent death. In many ways, we had feared the manner in which we would be killed more than death itself. I feared that our mother might see us tortured or that we, her children, would see her tortured. My greatest personal fear was of being killed in a barbaric manner. Apprehension overtook me mostly during the night when I couldn't sleep. I often had bad dreams about being attacked by dogs. Even when it appeared clear that we would soon be liberated, we still worried that the Germans would come back.

While Eli felt this very profoundly, he never verbalized it to anyone. Quite the opposite, he spoke only about what he and his family would do when their liberation finally came. Feelings of hope never really left them.

Even though the family did not know the whereabouts of Moshe, its husband and father, they were able to take advantage of the network of acquaintances he had made with the local peasants. After liberation, they went east and spent the night in the home of a farmer from whom Moshe Zborowski used to buy apples every October, which he then stored for the whole winter in the cellar of their home in Żarki. By the time they reached the farmer's home, the Russians were already arriving in larger units. Some of them stopped by the house of the farmer. Eli reports on a conversation with a Russian officer:

> I engaged one of the Russian officers about how far west of our town they had succeeded in reaching. The officer could see that I was more knowledgeable than the average peasant. He asked me how come I seem to know so much about the war effort. I told him that I tried by whatever means I could to keep abreast of the news. I also told him that I was Jewish. He then advised me not to talk about the fact that I am Jewish. I am not sure whether he simply wanted to protect me or perhaps he was also Jewish and he knew that Jews continued to be in jeopardy.

When the family reached the village of Bliżyce, farther to the east, they encountered hundreds of German prisoners. For years Eli had harbored fantasies in which the barbarism that the Germans inflicted on the Jews would ultimately befall the Germans. Yet, when he approached a group of German prisoners who had been rounded up by the Russians, a basic sense of humanity took over:

> As I looked at them more closely, I noticed that they were unshaven, unkempt and untidy. I assumed that they had been standing outdoors exposed to the elements for days. They certainly did not resemble the German soldiers who marched into our town with authority and arrogance, and decimated our homes and our lives. I was suddenly overcome with pity for them. I knew that they had not had food or water for days. I decided to bring out some water for them.

> Now, in retrospect this incident still leaves me with an unsettled feeling. I cannot really understand my motivations, except that in their disheveled and diminished state, I no longer saw them as menacing demons. Just one day before, I would have been pleased to see them killed. I would even have been

pleased to have the Americans or the Russians bomb an area in which I was located. I would have gladly given my own life in order to spill German blood—*Tamot nafshi im Plishtim* ("May I forfeit my own life with the Philistines"),[1] and here I was, taking pity on German POWs and bringing them water to quench their thirst!

One would expect that people who had experienced the cataclysmic events of the war might emerge bitter, angry, and vengeful. Yet, once liberated, Eli, continued to live by the values instilled in him by his parents—values that dictate compassion for the demoralized.

Return to Żarki

The trauma of the liberation and having to shoulder all the responsibility without her husband was so overwhelming for Zisel that she suffered a radical change in her appearance. Within ten days her jet-black hair turned almost white! When they arrived in Żarki,, their return was not heralded by joy. They were often greeted by Poles who knew them with the question, "How come you are still alive?" Of course the Poles could see that they were not dead, but this was not a cause for celebration, quite the opposite. The Zborowskis found that a Polish family had appropriated their home in their absence. Fortunately, this family stayed on for only a brief time and then surrendered the dwelling to its rightful owners.

The front of the house, damaged at the outset of the war, had still not been repaired, making a few rooms uninhabitable. Nevertheless, there was room for Zisel and her three children, as well as for Zisel's sister and brother. In addition, the officer commanding the Russian troops asked to sleep in the Zborowski house. He was apprehensive staying with Poles, but felt secure with Jews. It was not easy to determine the allegiance of Poles and Ukrainians. Many of them did not trust the Russians. After the Zborowski family left, the Russian commander was, in fact, killed by Poles.

When the family returned following the liberation, they were reluctant to go down to the cellar to see if they could retrieve the gold and jewelry that Moshe Zborowski had so cleverly hidden before they left. Fear of disappointment prevented them from doing this in the early days following their arrival. Only several months later did Zisel muster up the courage to begin looking for their hidden treasures. With fear and dread in her heart, Zisel instructed Mendel to remove the coal and start digging up the ground with a shovel. Sweat pouring down his brow, Mendel dug for what seemed like an eternity. He thought, "Perhaps I don't remember where the canisters were placed and I'm digging in the wrong spot." But just as he was about to give up hope, he heard a ringing sound as his shovel hit a metal object. Then suddenly the two containers appeared. Due to water seepage, they had, in fact, moved slightly, but they were there!

Zisel did not want it to be obvious that the ground had been disturbed, so they filled the hole with coal that Moshe had stored in the cellar and had not been used by the people who lived in the house during the war. Armed with this triumph, Zisel now had enough nerve to look for the jewelry that had been hidden under the stone slab in front of the door. Again, she enlisted Mendel's help. Because the slab was very heavy, Mendel spent an hour or so inching it away from the doorway. When the slab was successfully pushed aside, they found the third canister, with all the jewelry untouched, exactly where it had been placed. With tears of joy, Zisel hugged Mendel, who was both exhilarated and exhausted from the conquest.

Other than the retrieval of the gold and jewelry, the return to Żarki was a heartbreaking experience for the family. Eli recalls his feelings: "When I walked out into the street, I was filled with sadness. It was like a ghost town. There were no Jews in a town that used to be filled with Jews. I recognized all the houses that were now devoid of their previous residents—uncles, aunts, grandparents, and good friends Continuing to live here seemed unthinkable. I began to feel that the only hope was to go to Palestine."

Shortly after they returned to Żarki, they heard that 15,000 Jews had been liberated in Częstochowa. Perhaps Moshe Zborowski was among them. Eli decided to go to Częstochowa to find out and hitched a ride with a truckload of Russian soldiers who were going there. He later recalled a perplexing episode that took place along the way:

We were flagged down by a local Pole telling us that several German soldiers were hiding in the forest nearby. The commanding officer ordered the men to search the woods and in short order a German soldier was dragged out. The officer told his men that the Germans had burnt his village to the ground outside of Kiev killing his grandmother and that he would have great pleasure taking revenge on those that did it.

The task of translating the interrogation from German to Russian fell to me. I learned that the soldier was from the town of Bytom, not far from the prewar Polish border with Germany. He seemed very much like me; we were even born in the same year. His identity papers also included a photograph of a young lady, his fiancée. In response to the officer's fateful question: "Where was your unit active during the retreat?" the German indicated that during the retreat he was in the southern region of the Ukraine, placing him at the scene of the village in which the officer's grandmother perished. But the officer never heard this, because I impulsively altered the soldier's story in translation. I reported that the German soldier's unit served in the region of Belorussia, well north of the Ukraine.[2]

In reflecting on his intervention on behalf of the German soldier, Eli admits that "to this day, I don't know why I did it, and to this day I do not regret it." As in his previous encounter with German soldiers in distress, he suddenly saw them not as Germans but as human beings. Sadly, Eli did not find his father in Częstochowa.

Sustained uncertainty and fear pervaded the Zborowski family's life in Żarki. With no apparent provocation, one day grenades were thrown into the house through the window. Zisel decided that it was no longer safe for them to stay there, so she packed up the children and left for Sosnowiec. Of the 4,000 Jews who lived in Żarki before the war, no more than seventy survived.

It was hard for the family to confront the reality that Moshe Zborowski would not return. He had been so dominant a figure in their lives—pious, decent, compassionate, responsible. He not only provided them with comfort and a sense of security, but through his actions set the tone for their religious and moral behavior.

Eli reflected on his father's life:

My father was orphaned as a teenager. He was poor and frequently didn't have anything to eat. In the evenings he would sit and learn in the *beit medrish* (study house) with his rabbi. On occasion, the rabbi's wife was kind enough to bring in some tea for the students. In the summertime, my father would wander through the fields and eat whatever seemed edible in order to relieve his pangs of hunger. He shared these stories with us for two reasons: first, that we should not think that life will always be easy for us, and second, because he felt that one should always look ahead and prepare for the possibility of more difficult times.

When he was twenty, he was already engaged to my mother. He married her one year later, and when he was twenty-two, I was born. From the time I was just a little boy, I recall that on my grandfather's *yartzeit*—the anniversary of his death—my father would attend the *shtiebel* where my grandfather prayed during his lifetime rather than the one he customarily attended. He did this out of respect for his father's memory and to teach us about the importance of adhering to the biblical commandment to "honor your father and your mother."

My father always planned ahead for our day-to-day security and safety as well as for major events. Each summer, he bought a winter's supply of coal. He also bought several hundred pounds of potatoes at one time which we stored in the cellar. But the foresight that had the greatest impact was securing hiding places, in advance, for the family during the war. He would frequently quote from the Talmud: "Who is the wise man? He who can see what tomorrow will bring."

Fearing that her husband had been murdered, Zisel consulted with a rabbi in Sosnowiec about when to observe her husband's *yartzeit*. The rabbi concurred that if Moshe was alive, he would have already returned. He suggested that they observe his *yartzeit* four or five days following the date on which he disappeared. The family selected the fifth day of the Hebrew month of Av.

Moshe Zborowski and all the others who perished were denied the dignity that traditionally accompanies a Jewish death. There was no *shomer* to chant psalms and attend the body from the time of death until burial, no *tahara* ritual of washing, purifying, and dressing the deceased on white shrouds, no burial in consecrated ground, no *shiva* mourning period for the seven days after the burial, and no opportunity to reconcile oneself to the death of a loved one who disappeared. Denied these sacred rituals, Eli's mourning for his father continues unabated to this day.

Possibilities of Aliyah

Several Hashomer Hatzair kibbutzim in Poland functioned under the German occupation, but the only agrarian one was in Żarki. Shortly after the liberation, while Eli was still in Żarki, a delegation of five people came from Warsaw to see if they could rescue any material or documents about the kibbutz. Eli was acquainted with some of them from his work as a courier during the war, and when they heard that he had survived they came to see him. Among them was Lodza Silverstein, who had been a member of the agrarian kibbutz in Żarki. Others were Israel Sklar, the head of Hashomer Hatzair in Warsaw, and Tuvia Borzykowski, head of the Hechalutz and Dror Zionist youth movements. The visitors shared some information that gave Eli hope of making *aliyah* to Palestine:

> They told me about the work of the Bricha[3] in assisting people to reach Palestine by leaving Poland via Romania. These people already had experience with the illegal *aliyah* that had been organized in Lublin. Through them I made contact with Warsaw. Later I went to Częstochowa and there I met two friends from school who survived. They put me in touch with a group of young people my age who lived together because their families had perished during the war. Since there were already people making *aliyah* from Lublin, I suggested that we would like do the same. This gave them hope.

One day, two girls from that group went with me to Warsaw to introduce ourselves to the people who came to Żarki and to declare that the group of youngsters in Częstochowa were prepared to make *aliyah.* They said they would let us know.

In the meantime, the route for *aliyah* through Romania fell apart. The Bricha was no longer able to bring Jews from Warsaw to Romania. Since it was quite uncertain whether the group from Częstochowa would be able to get to Palestine, Eli and his friend Moniek Fiszer decided to join the Polish army. They went to enlist in the big city of Zawiercie. There they came across another Jewish boy their age, Amos Turner, and the three of them joined the Polish army in hopes of fighting the Germans. Eli describes his conviction and the ensuing conflict:

> I felt very strongly that I wanted to be part of the final defeat of the Germans. I wanted to do my share. When I took off my street clothes and put on a uniform I was still wearing my *tzizit* (fringed ritual undergarment). I took them off because we were required to give up all of our civilian clothes. This is probably the last time I wore *tzizit.*
>
> We started with a six-week extensive training program. At the end of the training program, the three of us were then selected to attend an officers' school in Łodz. It turned out that it was an officers' school with a political bent. I was much more educated than most of the Polish village boys, who had barely completed elementary school. This was the reason for transferring us to the officers' school instead of to the front lines to fight, which is what we would have preferred.

The sergeant responsible for their training frequently made anti-Jewish remarks. He said that Jews stood back while others went into battle. He also accused Jews of behaving in a more privileged manner by putting butter on their bread, whereas everyone else only had bread.

On May 9, 1945 the war ended. Eli and his friends had not even had a chance to fight. They felt discriminated against, and since the war was over they no longer had any purpose in serving in the army.

In the subsequent days there were parades to celebrate the end of the war, and the soldiers were given a few days off to join in the festivities. There was an electricity in the air. The streets were full of marching bands with hundreds of spectators joining in the merriment. Despite the revelry, Eli was overcome with an uncontrollable sadness:

Amidst all the celebrating, I broke down and cried. I had returned to my hometown after the liberation and I had seen the devastation. At that point, I couldn't be happy, because I felt that Żarki had become one large Jewish cemetery. At first, I couldn't even express my sorrow at not seeing beloved family and friends that perished. It was only at this moment of celebration at the end of the war that I realized the totality of the destruction and annihilation. These were not tears of joy, but of desolation. True the war was over, but at what cost to the Jews?

Eli made up his mind to leave the army. One could not leave without permission, of course, so he told his commanding officer that he had to visit the eye doctor. When he got out, he gave his permit to his friends, each of whom used it to leave the army base. The three of them left the base and headed to the home of a sister of one of their army mates. They shed their uniforms, changed to civilian clothes, and made their way to Warsaw to join the kibbutz organized by the leaders of the Zionist youth for the young people of Częstochowa. In their minds, they were not deserters, because they had joined the army voluntarily and then left voluntarily.

Life in the Kibbutz in Warsaw

The Hashomer Hatzair kibbutz occupied space in a building that housed the United Zionist Leftist Party, which encompassed several left-wing organizations. Eli was one of a group that worked to remove rubble from the place where it was thought that the Ringelblum Archives were hidden.[4] Lacking shovels and other tools, they dug with their hands. The effort turned out to be futile because the material was buried very deep down and would have required more manpower and equipment to be successful.

There was a wonderful *esprit de corps* among the kibbutz members in Warsaw. They felt that they had a responsibility to help one another. The boys lived mostly on bread with a marmalade made out of beets. The girls ate this too, and an occasional egg. Although food was meager, there was great satisfaction in being together, united by the common cause of making *aliyah*.

When the opportunity for *aliyah* emerged, in June and July of 1945, they were told that they could send only half of the kibbutz at this time. Eli and his friends were first on the list to go. Wanting to keep his commitment to look after his sister Tzila, Eli asked permission to take her with him. This request was granted and Tzila came to Warsaw, while their mother remained with their brother in Sosnowiec.

The group from Warsaw went to Sosnoweic, where they stayed for a few days and picked up others from kibbutzim in the neighboring areas. By now the group numbered more than a hundred people. Since *aliyah* was illegal, their papers were made out with the names of Greek children who were returning to Greece. They were told that if they were stopped at the border, they should be silent and take care not to reveal their identity by speaking Polish. Eli, then twenty years old, describes what ensued:

> We traveled in freight cars that had no seats, so mostly we were lying on the floor. On the train there were both boys and girls. To sleep, we certainly didn't change to pajamas, we just stayed dressed. If any of us had a coat, it was used as a blanket. When I got a chance to be lying next to a girl, I was naturally very pleased. But that was all. There was no contact. However, there was one girl who was really interested in more. She wanted to have sex with me. I was afraid that she would become pregnant. When I didn't respond to her advances, she said, "I can see that you haven't been around!" She really pushed to arouse me sexually, but my head managed to control the other parts of my body.

The journey was marked by a great deal of uncertainty and many starts and stops. As they were illegal immigrants crossing several borders, it became necessary to change their identity frequently. From

Sosnoweic, they went to Prague. The leaders of the Bricha in Prague obtained passes for the group as Belgian children. In Pilsno, before the crossing to the American-occupied zone in southern Germany, the Russians checked the trains. They stopped the group and kept them there for weeks. Eli recalls, "We were not guarded and we could ostensibly run away. But run where? So we spent our time talking to the young people who were traveling in the other freight cars."

One of these cars carried more than a hundred youngsters in their middle teens, a few with slightly younger siblings, who were part of a kibbutz. They had lost their families during the war, and the *madrich* (leader) who was responsible for them had mysteriously disappeared. Eli offered to help them in whatever way he could. Shortly thereafter, following a discussion with his organization, he took charge of this group and became their new *madrich*. "My role was to tend to their overall needs," he said. "I assumed responsibility for finding food to feed them, locating a place to sleep and looking after anyone who didn't feel well. Nobody gave me any instructions. I identified their needs and met them as well as I could. I simply used my own intuition and my own judgment."

The magnitude of the crisis created by leaving these wartorn orphaned teenagers alone on a train was of gargantuan proportions. The next stop on the journey was tentative at best. Each of the youngsters had lost family, friends, and home. Many were malnourished and suffered from a variety of illnesses. All the basic anchors of life had disappeared, leaving them grief-stricken and dazed. Without a moment's hesitation, Eli perceived the gravity of the situation and quickly stepped in to alleviate the crisis, demonstrating what John C. Maxwell says in *The 21 Indispensable Qualities of a Leader:* "Crisis doesn't necessarily make character, but it certainly reveals it."[5]

Their journey began with a short stopover in Landsberg, in the American Zone of Germany, and finally they arrived in the displaced-persons camp in Feldafing. A small group was brought to St. Otilien in Bavaria.

Chapter 5 Notes

1. Samson's last words in Judges 16:30, as he crushed the pillars bringing down the temple of Dagon upon himself and the Philistines.

2. "Eli Zborowski, Of Things Past," *Lifestyles Magazine* profile, 2001.

3. The Hebrew word *bricha*, which can be translated as "escape," was the name of the organization that arranged illegal *aliyah* for Jews in postwar Europe from the time of liberation until the establishment of the State of Israel in 1948.

4. The Ringelblum Archives are a collection of sixteen hundred archival units (approximately 25,000 pages) that were retrieved from the Warsaw Ghetto. Inspired and guided by Emanuel Ringelblum, the material was written, collected, and organized to record the daily struggle of the Ghetto inhabitants.

5. John C. Maxwell, *The 21 Indispensible Qualities of a Leader: Becoming the Person Others Will Want to Follow* (Nashville: Thomas Nelson, 1999), p. 3.

❧ Chapter 6 ❧
AMONG THE DISPLACED

Eli escorts officers of the American occupation forces on a tour of
Feldafing, the displaced persons camp

࿇

Among The Displaced

Eli and the 116 kibbutz youngsters for whom he had assumed responsibility embarked on a journey with many detours. While the ultimate
destination was always Palestine, numerous obstacles stood in the way
of the fulfillment of this dream. It was one which Eli pursued with passion, demonstrating true qualities of leadership. As Alan Deutschman
has observed, "The final proof of leadership isn't having new ideas,
it's pursuing an idea obsessively—with every action, in every moment, with everyone watching—for many years or even for several
decades. That's when you're a real leader."[1]

This spirit of perseverance continued throughout the period of dislocation during which he had to negotiate the needs of the orphaned
teenagers in his charge. Eli established a kibbutz to care for the youngsters. Kibbutz Ma'apilim (illegal immigrants into Mandatory Palestine) was named in tribute to Eli's former *madrich,* Tzvi Brandes, the
heroic leader of the ZOB. With the help of the Bricha in transporting
people over the borders during the night, Eli and the 116 children ultimately arrived in Munich in the fall of 1945. From Munich they were
sent to a displaced-persons camp in Landsberg.

Wherever he went, Eli looked for other youngsters who had been
left orphaned and homeless by the war and invited them to join his
group. In a hospital in St. Otilien in Bavaria, he met a thirteen year-
old girl, Manya Knobloch, who had survived a concentration camp.
Manya, now in her mid-seventies, with homes in New York and Israel,
recalls that time:

> I met Eli a few months after the liberation while I was in
> a hospital in St. Otilien which had been a monastery and was

converted to a hospital by the American occupation forces. Eli had come with a transport of children who were orphaned and had managed to miraculously survive, some by working in menial jobs on farms.

I became part of Eli's group of children as long as they were in St. Otilien. Until his group's arrival, I was the only child in St. Otilien. I was excited and very happy about participating in activities with other children. I would have liked to continue on with them to their next destination, but I was sick and still too weak to leave the hospital.

We had an orchestra in the hospital that gave a concert occasionally in order to lift our spirits. During the intermission, Eli, who was about twenty years old at the time, went up on the stage and addressed the audience in various languages— Yiddish, Hebrew, Polish and German. His message to us was that we had a future and that we can rebuild our lives.

I looked up to Eli as a teacher and a mentor. He was totally devoted to the good of the Jewish people. I was then, and am still now, full of admiration for him. Even when he encountered obstacles, he succeeded in every project he undertook.

In Germany there was already a Jewish Committee established to take care of the displaced persons arriving from East European countries. However, there were political differences that did not sit well with Eli:

The leadership was primarily Lithuanian Jews who were members of the Poalei Zion· which was the Social Democratic Party, Mapai. We, on the other hand, were oriented to Ichud Smol—a much more left-wing group whose goal was to settle in Palestine as pioneers in kibbutzim on agrarian land. They wanted to absorb our young people into their youth organization called Noam—Noar Meuchad, the United Youth. At that time (September 1945), when there were no Jewish children in Germany, we were in a position of strength as a result of the young people in our care. At my initiation and insistence, we negotiated with the leadership and reached an agreement.

We joined with them and changed the name of the organization to Nocham—Noar-Halutzi-Meuchad, United Pioneer Youth. The newly named organization grew rapidly as more groups and youngsters kept arriving from Eastern European countries.

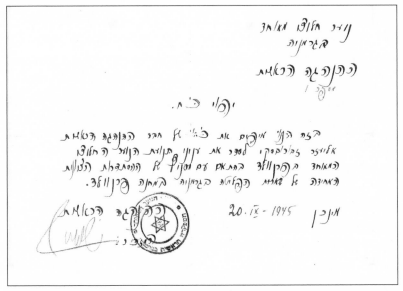

This certificate documents the role that Eli (Eliezer) Zborowski played in establishing the Zionist Youth Organization in Germany in September 1945 when he was nineteen years of age. The certificate carries the seal of the organization, *Noam Hameuchad,* "The United Youth."

This was the first certificate issued by the United Pioneer Youth in Germany. It authorizes Eliezer Zborowski, a member of the Executive Committee, to take care of all issues of youth organization in conjunction with the Zionist Organization branch in the Ferenwald DP camp. September 20, 1945

Life in the Displaced-Persons Camp

Displaced-persons camps played a crucial role in the lives of Jews fleeing postwar anti-Semitism in Poland, Czechoslovakia, Hungary, Romania, and Russia. Bereft of home and family, there were as many as 200,000 Jews wandering through Germany and Central Europe. Known as the *She'arit Hapleta,* a biblical term that means "the Surviving Remnant,"[2] they were plagued by illness and exhaustion. Their homelessness created the need for a colossal relief effort.

At the outset, the efforts of the Allied military authorities to deal with the *She'arit Haplata* were quite inadequate, for they had endured horrific hardships. "Curfews were imposed and the DPs were given limited rations. They often were housed in camps with non-Jewish Poles and other Europeans, some of whom were Nazi collaborators."[3]

Daily life in the camps was difficult. As reported by Yisrael Gutman, "The DPs lived in crowded conditions, usually large barracks, with no private space or family rooms; their diet was monotonous and scanty; their clothing was shapeless. . . . They tended to be short-tempered and distrustful of strangers, and even regarded their friends and the committees and institutions around them with suspicion."[4]

In the summer of 1945, President Harry Truman commissioned Earl G. Harrison, dean of the University of Pennsylvania Law School, as the American envoy to the Inter-Governmental Committee on Refugees to survey the DP camps. Harrison reported: "As matters now stand, we appear to be treating the Jews as the Nazis treated them except that we do not exterminate them. They are in concentration camps in large numbers under our military guard instead of the S.S. troops."[5]

Harrison's findings resulted in immediate and far-reaching modifications. Harrison recommended that Jews should be housed in exclusively Jewish camps. Initially the camps were administered by the United Nations Relief and Rehabilitation Administration (UNRRA) along with such organizations as the American Joint Distribution Committee (JDC). In 1946, a congress of the *She'arit Hapleta* elected a Central Committee of Liberated Jews in the American Zone. Self-governance empowered the survivor population. Even as they waited for affidavits to emigrate to other countries, they rose from the ashes of the Holocaust and began to transform their shattered lives. The survivors quickly asserted their vitality and energetically began establishing social and cultural institutions—schools, clubs, youth groups, cultural events, libraries, and political movements.

Feldafing: The First All-Jewish DP Camp

In Landsberg, Eli and his charges did not get the support they needed, so he began to look around for another camp. This led him to Camp Feldafing. It was close by and had more politically diverse Zionist groups and organizations, including Mizrachi, the religious Zionist movement; the Bund, the secular socialist movement; and representatives of a Jewish Communist organization. Feldafing welcomed them; they became part of the camp

At first the term "camp" made Eli and the others uneasy, and they didn't quite know what to expect. When they arrived they saw that there was a guard at the entrance gate. One could not come and go at will. People leaving had to show identification and indicate their destination. Identification was similarly required upon return. For those who had already been liberated, this procedure seemed overly regimented but was offset by the advantages it offered.

Feldafing, a Bavarian village, was opened as a displaced-persons camp by the United States Army in 1945. Formerly a camp for German soldiers and for Hitler Youth, it consisted of seven large two-story buildings, about a dozen temporary buildings, and several large villas. It was the first all-Jewish DP camp in the U.S. zone and had the distinction of being administered by the first elected Jewish camp committee. In 1946, about 4,000 Jews lived in Feldafing.

Under the leadership of the camp committee, educational and religious life flourished in Feldafing. In 1946/1947, there were already secular elementary and high school systems as well as a number of religious schools, including a Talmud Torah (religious elementary school), a yeshiva (religious academy), and several seminaries. The camp population organized an orchestra. In addition to the camp committee, there was a rabbinical council that supported its religious office. There was also an extensive library and several newspapers. The Organization for Rehabilitation Through Training (ORT) ran a nursing school and provided vocational instruction for adults at an evening school.

Eli's priority in Feldafing was to take care of the teenagers. He was assigned an entire floor to house them. This enabled him to arrange separate sleeping quarters for boys and girls. The camp committee provided rations and other items, but there was never enough for all of their needs. For example, there were forty boys and the committee provided only twenty pairs of shoes. Eli had to either determine which youngsters did not need shoes or go back and ask for more. Some of the shoes were leather, while the others in the allotment were made of treated fabric and did not provide as much protection. Because he wanted to serve as a role model for the children, Eli took fabric shoes for himself, thereby "sharing the struggle vital for anyone who aspires to leadership."[6]

The emotional needs of the teenagers were often more difficult to meet. Eli tried to be sensitive to the thoughts and feelings of his young charges. He poignantly describes the conflicts this created:

> The girls in the group were especially starved for affection. As orphans they would have loved to be embraced by a father figure or an older brother. I would have liked to oblige, but I felt that it would be inappropriate. I was careful to behave in the most discreet manner. I tried not to get too attached to any of them. There was one girl who became very fond of me. I was concerned about this and was therefore very pleased that she was one of the first ten youngsters who were selected to join the Bricha path to Palestine. My sister was also selected as part of this group.

The youth group Eli worked with was the first of its kind to arrive in the American Zone of Germany. In recognition for his work with the young people, Eli was invited to become an executive member of the Central Committee of the Liberated Jews in the American Zone, located in Munich. He was their authority on youth and as such was assigned a room in Munich so that he could stay over and attend meetings. Because he was under the age of twenty-four, he could not be a full representative. In order to obtain full powers, he changed his birthdate to indicate that he was born in 1921 instead of his true birthdate, which was 1925.

The kibbutz, Ma'apilim, for which Eli served as the *madrich* was in every sense identified with Hashomer Hatzair. His leadership was greatly valued by the directors of the youth movement. They invited him to attend a *kinus* (convention) convened in Landsberg for the heads of all the Hashomer Hatzair kibbutzim. It took place in midwinter in 1945 when it was difficult to reach Landsberg. Eli recollects the hardships of the trip as well as the joy of meeting a long-lost relative:

It was cold and windy with a foot of crusty snow on the ground. Wearing my flimsy fabric shoes and trudging slowly in the snow, I made my way to the outskirts of the city to find some means of transportation. I flagged down a military truck that was traveling in that direction.

Zelig Shushan, the Hashomer Hatzair emissary from Eretz Israel to the *kinus,* came to my room in Munich looking for "Eliezer," with no last name. He introduced himself to me and we traveled together from Munich to Landsberg to attend the *kinus*. In conversation with him, I discovered, to my great surprise, that his wife's maiden name was Esther Zborowski. She came from Zawiercie, a town near Żarki, and was my cousin—one of the relatives in Israel my father told me about before he disappeared. This was to be the first of a long association I was to have in Israel with this part of my family.

I managed to arrive in time for the *kinus* and to attend a full day of sessions. The following day I came down with a very high temperature. I was drenched in sweat and felt very weak.

The next morning I was taken to the hospital in Landsberg where I languished for days with an unrelenting high temperature. I was so debilitated that the doctors told me that I was "with two feet and one hand in the grave. Only one hand pulled you out of the grave." I was so sick that I became delirious. At one point I saw a doctor who was the son-in-law of the doctor from our town. He had been sent to Auschwitz and his clothing had been sent back to his family in Żarki. Therefore, we assumed that he had perished. In my delusional state, when I saw him, I thought I had died and that I was reunited with him in heaven.

While I lay ill, my sister, who was about to embark for Palestine, came to say good-bye. When she saw how sick I was she wanted to stay with me. I told her that it was totally out of the question. I said, "How could you possibly forgo this opportunity to make *aliyah?*" I insisted that she should go as planned, even though I was sick. When I felt better, I returned to all my activities in the camp.

As the first all-Jewish DP camp, Feldafing was host to several world-renowned visitors. In September 1945, General Dwight D. Eisenhower personally inspected living conditions at Feldafing. His visit was a direct result of the Harrison report. Visits such as this served to boost the morale of the population of Feldafing and its central committee. In October 1945, David Ben-Gurion, then chairman of the Jewish Agency, visited the Frankfurt-Zalsheim DP camp. Together with an officer of Polei Zion, Eli Zborowski, then only twenty years old, represented the newly established Zionist youth organization, Nocham, as part of a delegation that received Ben-Gurion. During the journey from Munich to the Zalsheim DP camp, Eli recounted, "Ben-Gurion sat in the front of the limousine and I sat in the back. At that time I did not think this was anything special. I felt like I was simply meeting another Jew. During the trip we had a heated political discussion because I was an advocate for a United Zionist Workers Party."

Refugees were constantly arriving from concentration camps and from hiding. To accommodate them, the Americans established additional camps, including one in Föhrenwald, the largest Jewish DP camp, and the last to be closed. At the opening, Eli was assigned to accompany Meir Yaari, the founder of Hashomer Hatzair.

In the summer of 1946, one of the older members succeeded Eli as leader of the kibbutz he had brought to Feldafing. Most of the group eventually made *aliyah.*

Members of Kibbutz Ma'apilim
An Album

Kibbutz Ma'apilim in tribute to Tzvi Brandes, Feldafing 1946. Eli is standing in the top row, second from the left. The sign at the bottom is the Hashomer Hatzair motto, *Chazak V'ematz* —"Be strong and Courageous"

Miriam Citron (left) and Rivka Pinkus (right) with Eli in the center, prior to the girls' making *aliyah* in 1945.

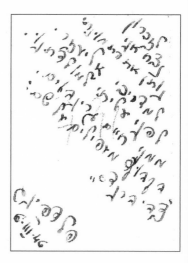

Aryeh Schwartz, in Hebrew:

"To my dear leader Eliezer, for eternal remembrance on the day of *aliyah* to our land. I hope to see you soon. Be strong and courageous! Feldafing, March 6, 1946"

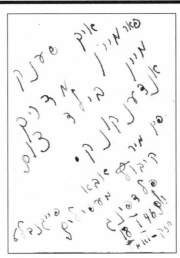

In Yiddish: "I give my picture to my leader as a remembrance from me, Abba Feigenblat, Kibbutz Ma'apilim , January 18, 1946. Be strong and courageous!"

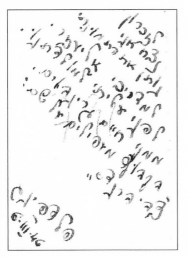

In Hebrew: "As an eternal remembrance, I give this picture as a gift to my leader, Eliezer, prior to making *aliya* to our homeland. From me, Chaim Greenbaum, Kibbutz Ma'apilim in tribute to Tzvi Brandes. Feldafing, March 6, 1946."

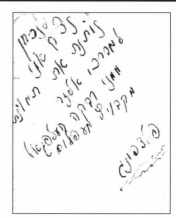

In Hebrew: "For eternal remembrance, I give this picture to my leader Eliezer, from me, Rivka Helfgot of Kibbutz Ma'apilim, Feldafing."

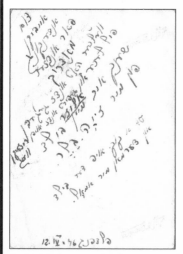

In Yiddish: "As a lasting remembrance for our leader Eliezer, who has taught us so much and has guided us on the right path. I give you a gift of my photograph. From me, Tzivia Baler. Look at my picture and remember me from time to time. Feldafing, April 12, 1946."

Looking For and Finding Family

Eli was already in Germany when the rest of the Zborowski family left Żarki after grenades were thrown into their house, forcing them to recognize that the place they had always known as home was no longer safe. A day before Rosh Hashana, the family—Zisel, Mendel, and Zisel's sister Rachel and brother Yosel—went to Sosnowiec and a few months later to East Germany. Because there were no telephones, Eli had not had any contact with them in some time. This was a period during which everyone who had fled from their hometowns were on the lookout for other family and friends who might have survived the war.

New arrivals in Feldafing from Leipzig in what was now East Germany spoke about the many families that were fleeing Poland to Germany. In March 1946, Eli met someone at Feldafing who had come from Leipzig. Eli described his mother, brother, and aunt and uncle. The newcomer told Eli that although he did not know their names, he thought he had seen a family in Leipzig that might fit the description. Eli decided to make his way to Leipzig. Years later he described his odyssey in detail:

Hearing this, I put together a few things in a musette bag, including several packs of cigarettes that I could exchange for food. On a map, I could see that I would have to cross a border between the American and Russian occupied zones. My objective was to get to a town that was close to the Russian zone and then to get help crossing the border from the local townspeople. At the train station, the Russians maintained strict control by asking everyone for papers. I was in mortal fear of being caught because I heard that those who attempted to cross borders without the proper documentation stood the danger of being sent to Siberia. Since I was without the necessary papers, when I saw the border officials coming toward me, I slowly drifted over to the section of the station where people had already been queried, and thus evaded the interrogation. There I was able to board the train to Leipzig.

When I arrived in Leipzig, I was faced with the dilemma of where to go. I decided to try the Jewish Committee. What I did not know at the time was that when my family arrived in Leipzig they were afraid of being sent back to Poland, so they registered under the name Steinbrecher because it sounded German.

Since my inquiries at the Jewish Committee bore no fruit, I didn't really know what to do next. In the absence of any other alternatives, I went to visit the zoo. As I was walking around, I encountered a Russian soldier. We began to talk and I found out that he was also a Jew. I encouraged him to shed his uniform and to come back with me to Feldafing and to join our group that had plans to go on *aliyah.* He said he would gladly do this, except that he had a grandmother and a little cousin who survived the war who were dependant on his pension as a soldier and that he could not abandon them. We decided to take a walk and then get a mug of beer.

There were many people in the street. If I saw people who looked Jewish, I addressed them with the code name *amchu*—our people—which identified people as Jews. Once people identified themselves as Jews, I described my family, hoping that perhaps someone had crossed their paths. I also told them where I was staying so that in case they came in contact with them, they would know where to find me.

As I continued on with the Russian soldier, I suddenly heard someone running behind us in an attempt to catch up with us. Lo and behold, it was Mendel and my uncle Yosel! It was totally unbelievable that I was able to find them! How improbable a task this was from the beginning! Imagine that I had traveled hundreds of miles from Feldafing to Leipzig, a city of a million people, without any money or proper papers to cross borders, to look for a family without an address and registered under a different name! It was totally miraculous!

Again without resources or the necessary documents, Eli took his mother, brother, uncle, and aunt back with him by train to Feldafing. When soldiers boarded the train to check papers, Eli hid the four in the lavatory. He finally got them across the border and brought them to Feldafing.

Here again we see the role that risk-management has played throughout Eli's life. Studies show that risk-takers can be divided into two groups.[7] *Functional* risk-takers measure the risk against the potential reward. They say no to undue risks. *Dysfunctional* risk-takers, on the other hand, place no limit on the risks they will take. They go for broke, and often wind up broke or broken. Eli Zborowski's behavior reveals him to be a classic functional risk-taker. In this instance, for example, he felt he could evade the Russian patrols. Had he evaluated the risk as excessive, he might have simply left the station and sought another opportunity to reach Leipzig.

When the family arrived in Feldafing, Eli was faced with the challenge of finding them accommodations. This was no easy task, but by this time his demonstrated leadership skills had earned him the reputation as a person of stature. He used his influence to get them one very large room. They were happy to have living quarters, but they had very little food and no facilities for cooking.

Establishing a Beit Hanoar— a Youth Home

Refugees continued to arrive at Feldafing. Among them were orphaned children. In some cases the children were brought by adults who were not their parents but came from the same town as the parents who had perished. Many of the children, ages eleven to fifteen, wanted to be accepted into the kibbutz but were too young. Their presence in Feldafing raised a number of questions: Who would care for them? Where would they be housed? What activities and services were needed in order to meet their physical , emotional, and educational needs?

Michael Korda, editor-in-chief of Simon & Schuster, has written that "success on any major scale requires one to accept responsibility. . . . In the final analysis, the one quality that all successful people have is the ability to take on responsibility."[8] This truth is clearly illustrated by Eli's unhesitating acceptance of responsibility for the children. His concern for the youngsters prompted him to organize a Beit Hanoar, or Youth Home.

> Based on the need I perceived, I decided on my own to do this. I managed to obtain from the Committee a space to house forty to fifty children. Once I was in charge, I had to find support for the endeavor. I found a teacher among the general

population of Feldafing and invited him to live with us so that the children could receive some education, as schools had not yet been developed in the camp. One woman with an eleven year-old child volunteered to join us so her child could be with other children, My mother, who was already in Feldafing, also gave a hand. As time went along, I devoted myself mostly to the Beit Hanoar because the kibbutz youth were taken care of and were preparing to make *aliyah*.

The JDC and UNRRA supplied care packages and services for the children. As adult refugees arrived in Feldafing from various parts of Europe, some recognized children in the Beit Hanoar from their hometowns and unofficially adopted them. In some instances, a relative turned up and took a child to live with them. Like the kibbutz youth, most of these younger children also emigrated to Palestine.

Beit Hanoar

Beit Hanoar members at Feldafing DP camp in 1947. Eli is at the top center of the pyramid wearing a jacket and an open-neck shirt. His mother, Zisel, wearing a black dress, is second from the left.

A post card of appreciation from a fatherless youngster in the Beit Hanoar. The child's dedication of this photo tells Eli in the most endearing manner in Polish that she views him as a surrogate. The inscription says:

To my dear "Father"
Your little daughter
Feldafing, February 19, 1946

Dating and Marriage

In 1947, Eli was invited to go back to Poland to be involved in the Bricha—the organization that oversaw the illegal *aliyah*. He was occupied with Bricha activities during the second half of 1947 and a good part of 1948. During this period, members of the socialist Bund who had once denounced the idea of *aliyah* now turned to the Bricha to see if it would help *them* make *aliyah*. The Bund was one of the organizations that had accepted Eli and his youth kibbutz into Feldafing in 1945. When the Bricha did not respond favorably to their request, Mordechai (Matvei) Berenstein[9] and Gurewicz, the leader of the Bund, asked Eli for help. After the establishment of the State of Israel, in 1948, the Bricha ceased operations.

At age twenty, Eli was already dating girls. He limited himself to girls who were not members of the kibbutz or the Beit Hanoar. He felt it was not wise for him to become involved with a girl for whom he had a professional responsibility. For Eli, looking for a girl was synonymous with looking to create a family. He did not care to date anyone simply for a good time. He wanted a girl with a good background, one with whom he could share his interests, his values, and his desire to build a family.

Eli dated one girl whose mother was a good friend of his mother, Zisel. At the time, he was traveling back and forth to Poland, where he worked for the Bricha. He would sometimes be gone for two or three months at a time. While Eli was away, this girl befriended a boy with a motorcycle. She would cheerfully ride on the back of the motorcycle with him in public. Eli found this humiliating and embarrassing. He became jealous and broke off the relationship.

Eli returned to Feldafing to be with his mother for the High Holidays in 1947. While he was there, his mother told him that she would soon have an opportunity to send a package to his sister in Israel with a girl whose family in Israel was working to get her a visa. His mother said that the girl lived with an uncle in Feldafing and had another uncle in Israel whom she was planning to join. Zisel was very impressed with this girl.

During the intermediate days of the Sukkot festival that same year, Eli joined a friend for an evening out in Munich. At the railroad station in Feldafing on the way to Munich, he noticed a group of girls also waiting for the train. One of the girls seemed to match his mother's description of the girl who had agreed to take a package to his sister in Palestine. When they boarded the train, Eli elbowed his way toward the girls. He wanted to strike up a conversation so that he could find out whether she was, in fact, the one of whom his mother had spoken so highly. This was indeed the girl. Her name was Diana. When they arrived in Munich, Eli and Diana went their own ways. The encounter with Diana left Eli in an emotional upheaval. He suddenly lost his enthusiasm for socializing that evening and simply turned around and got on the train back to Feldafing.

I was totally smitten by Diana and could think of nothing else. I had no idea where she lived, but I had an overwhelming urge to see her again. The next morning I went down to the center of the camp where people often gathered in the hope that I would bump into her. I milled around in the crowd for a few hours and since I didn't spot her in the crowd, I decided to return to the outskirts of the camp where my mother lived. Suddenly, Diana appeared at a crossroads! I was thrilled, but I felt that I had to contain my feelings. I politely offered to walk her to her house.

Following that encounter, I invited Diana to go to Munich to see a movie. Because I had been a kibbutznik, a scout, I did not own a tie. I borrowed one from a friend because I wanted to impress her. After two or three dates during which we indicated that we cared for each other and had common goals in life, I gave her a goodnight kiss. Feeling that it was too soon in the relationship for that display of affection, Diana slapped my face. Even though Diana thought my behavior was inappropriate in that instance, we continued to see each other. After three weeks we had already declared our love for each other.

During their courtship, Diana Wilf and Eli shared their wartime experiences with each other. During an *aktsia*—a raid in the ghetto—Diana hid with her mother and brother in the attic of their home in

Drohobycz. They witnessed the cold-blooded shooting of their husband and father. Within a week, her mother and brother also perished at the hands of the Germans and their Ukrainian collaborators. That day Diana was taken in by the family maid and spent fourteen months hidden under a sofa.

Diana survived the war, but for her the liberation was bittersweet. In reflecting on that time, she said, "You would think it was the luckiest day of my life, but it was not. Why? Because there was no one for me to share my happiness. Now that the danger was over, I realized that I was totally alone."

There was a tremendous thrust among refugees to rebuild their lives. The reuniting of families went hand-in hand with the creation of new ones, as evidenced by the astounding number of weddings that took place in DP camps.[10] Zisel's single brother and sister, who were only six and nine years older than Eli, were among those who were eager to move on with life. One day they came and told Zisel that they wanted to become engaged to people they had met in the camp. As she began making preparations for the engagement party, Eli announced that he too wished to become engaged to Diana. Zisel was hesitant, because she wanted to be sure that Eli would keep his commitment. Eli's next task was to share this with Diana:

> I went to see Diana and I told her what I had in mind. This was in the morning and the party was planned for the evening. She looked at me in disbelief. "What! Are you crazy? How will I explain this to my uncle?" Her uncle went to Munich each day to look for business and only returned in the evening. I reminded her that we had already declared our love for each other, so there was no need to wait. I suggested that the two of us agree that we are getting engaged and that she would tell her uncle when he came home. In the event that he wouldn't agree, then she would not come to the celebration. In the meantime, she decided to bake a cake as her contribution to the party. That evening when her uncle returned, she told him about our plan and the two of them came to the party. That was our engagement.

At this time, Eli was still traveling back and forth to Poland. Diana moved in with a surviving uncle in Poland for several months so that they could see each other more often. After a year's engagement, Zisel said that if they were going to travel together, it would be more appropriate if they were married. The wedding took place in Feldafing on December 7, 1948. It was a very small affair attended by fewer than ten people. Eli recalls his honeymoon and the work he did to enable Jews to leave Poland:

> The Bund arranged to have an American military limousine at my disposal. This enabled us to cross the border. We went over to Salzburg, Austria. There I received papers that indicated that I was repatriating back to Poland. We returned to Poland in a freight car along with non-Jewish Poles who were returning to the country. This was my honeymoon!
>
> My work in Poland with the Bund was to help Jews leave the country over the mountains into Czechoslovakia where I arranged for them to take a train to Bratislava. There, former Bricha members took them over the border to Vienna.

These maneuvers were not legal and were carried out in middle of the night. After a few days, the Polish officials began to look for the Jews who did not show up for work. When they went to their homes, they found everything intact. The Jews, eager to leave, did so without even a suitcase so that they would not be detected. They had no specific destination. Most of them came first to Feldafing with aims of ultimately emigrating to America, Australia, or Israel.

Eli's last assignment in Poland was at the end of May 1949. The time he had spent there was very productive. He had enabled key people to leave the country, including some generals who were Bundists and the president of the National Jewish Community. In this work, Eli's contact was Dr. Marek Edelman, a former commander in the Warsaw Ghetto Uprising, whose unrelenting Bundist principles dictated that he remain in the country in which he was born.[11]

Zisel, eager to join her daughter, emigrated to Israel in the late summer of 1949. Diana and Eli returned to Feldafing briefly and then moved to Munich with his brother Mendel. They waited to hear from

Zisel about her adjustment before they made a decision regarding their next move. During this transition period, Diana developed severe asthma that became seriously aggravated when they were in Israel. When an opportunity to emigrate to the United States opened up, they applied and were accepted. Because Diana was already in her third trimester of pregnancy, she was spared the long, arduous ocean voyage and was allowed instead to fly. When they arrived in the United States, they were told by the JDC that their invitation to the United States had come from the Jewish community in Cincinnati, Ohio, which would provide them with funds and a variety of resettling services. Eli wished to remain in New York and decided to forfeit the help offered by the JDC. Prior to striking out on their own, they stayed briefly with two newly arrived aunts of Eli's who lived in the Bronx.

Eli and Diana shortly after their arrival in New York

Chapter 6 Notes

1. Alan Deutschman, *Walk the Walk: The #1 Rule for Real Leaders,* (New York: Portfolio, 2009), p. 166.

2. *Life Reborn: Jewish Displaced Persons 1945–1951* (International Conference, United States Holocaust Memorial Museum, Washington, D.C., January 2000).

3. Ibid., p. 3.

4. Yisrael Gutman, *She'arit Hapleta, 1944–1948: Rehabilitation and the Political Struggle* (Jerusalem: Yad Vashem, 1990), p. 519 (Hebrew).

5. Ibid., p. 3.

6. Deutschman, *Walk the Walk*, p. 86.

7. Nick Tasler, The Impulse Factor: Why Some of Us Play It Safe, and Others Risk It All (New York: Simon & Shuster, 2008).

8. John C. Maxwell, *The 21 Indispensable Qualities of a Leader: Becoming the Person Others Will Want to Follow* (Nashville: Thomas Nelson , 1999), p.111.

9. Mordechai Berenstein was the father of Masha Leon, popular columnist of the *Forward.*

10. *Life Reborn, Jewish Displaced Persons, 1945–1951* (Washington, D.C.: United States Holocaust Memorial Museum, 2000), p. 5.

11. Dr. Edelman died in Poland on October 2, 2009 at the age of ninety.

Eli and a *shaliach* from Israel
Miriam Citron, Rivka Pinkus, Ruth Haskel
December 11, 1945

❧ Chapter 7 ❧

TAKING CARE OF BUSINESS

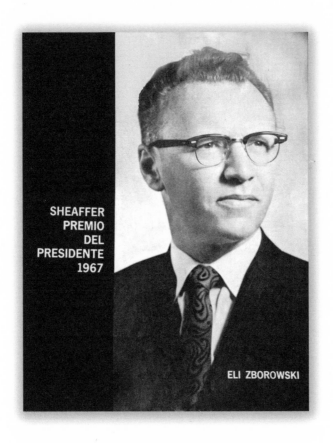

SHEAFFER
PREMIO
DEL
PRESIDENTE
1967

ELI ZBOROWSKI

Eli Zborowski, President
Sheaffer Latin America

CHAPTER 7

྾

Taking Care of Business

When Eli, with his expectant wife, Diana, arrived in New York, he hit the ground running. It never occurred to him to find a job working for someone else. His training, at his father's side, was in selling, and he would sell for himself. But what could he sell? He had no credit, and little cash.

He didn't know much English, but he quickly became adept at using the New York subway system. The fare was ten cents. For a dime, an enterprising young man could leave his home in the Bronx and in a half hour be within walking distance of any business in the city. Eli decided, therefore, to locate his business in the center of New York. With a map and a ruler, he determined that 42nd Street and Fifth Avenue was his target. Eli decided to look for some kind of business he could undertake from there.

Selling Camera Parts

While in Munich, Eli had done business with Israel in the area of fine German cameras—Leica, Roloflex, and others. He decided to look around to see what he could sell in the photography field. He quickly found that since the war there had been little contact with Europe, especially Germany There were many repair shops looking for parts. This was a business that he could get into. The parts that were needed were of nominal value—many could be bought in Germany for only a few cents. Perfect! Eli began to order parts from Germany and sell them to camera repair shops.

Within a few weeks, Eli had organized a company called Overseas and Continental, with a logo of two hemispheres. He signed up for a mailing address at 545 Fifth Avenue for only $10 a month, and printed stationery with a corporate letterhead. Overseas and Continental subsequently rented a desk in an office in the same building for $25 a month.

Overseas & Continental envelope, 1952-1953

Eli recalls: "From the Yellow Pages, I could identify the location of each of the repair shops. I walked from repair shop to repair shop to find out what they needed and then, since the parts cost so little, I ordered 10 times as much. Before long I had inventory and could fill orders from the stock I had accumulated. I was making between 100% and 300% on these parts."

For five dollars, he bought a used typewriter that was missing an *R*. Whenever he typed a word that had an *R* in it, he wrote it in by hand. The person from whom he was renting desk space showed him how to format a business letter. Then Eli began to learn conversational English by reading the newspaper, and he bought a *Secretarial Handbook* to learn business English.

It wasn't long before Eli realized that there was a problem with his business plan. Despite the high markup, the parts he sold were still priced at only a few cents each. As a result, it proved impossible to earn more than $50 a week! One of Eli's strengths, critical at this juncture, was knowing when to abandon one path and find another. He needed to find a more lucrative business.

Manufacturing and Selling Jewelry

Eli often stopped in at the Żarki *landsmanshaft*, an association of Jews from Żarki. There were thousands of *landsmanshaftn* throughout New York, mostly established during the great Jewish immigration at the end of the nineteenth century and early in the twentieth. They helped the immigrants integrate into American life, and served as social centers where Jews connected by their ties to specific towns could seek and provide mutual assistance to each other.

On one such visit, Eli met a man named Sam Hersly. In Żarki the family name had been Herszlikiewicz, but clearly it had to be changed in America. Sam had a job making and selling jewelry. He had actually learned his jewelry-making skills as a prisoner in a German concentration camp! Eli suggested that they go into business together. Eli offered to buy the necessary equipment; Hersly would create the goods, and Eli would sell them. At first, Hersly was reluctant. He preferred the certainty of a weekly salary to any business opportunity that Eli could offer him. It was finally agreed that Hersly would keep his day job and manufacture jewelry at night and on weekends. The two *landsmen* formed a partnership and called their firm Duet Jewelry Company because there were just the two of them. Every evening they made jewelry together until 1 or 2 a.m. in Hersly's apartment on Christie Street. Worn out and exhausted, Eli filled a briefcase with gold jewelry and traveled via subway from the Bowery back to his home on 169th Street. He caught a few hours' sleep, and at eight in the morning headed back to the heart of Manhattan to sell the merchandise he and Sam had made.

Foreign Currency Exchange

After several months, Eli realized that this business could not support two families. He left the firm, but Sam Hersly continued. Today Duet Jewelry Company thrives in New York, making and selling fine jewelry.

In the United States it was entirely legal for anyone to purchase foreign currency, whether from a bank or a foreign currency exchange. In contrast, throughout Europe after World War II, currency could be purchased only from a bank, and then only with a license from the government. As a result, currency exchange was limited to commercial transactions and was fully recorded. Individuals, whatever their need, had to turn to the free market, where they paid a hefty markup.

Yoineh Landesman, a man Eli knew from Munich, approached him with a proposal. Landesman was an intermediary for diamond dealers in Antwerp, an association that involved many foreign currency transactions. He proposed to open a foreign exchange firm with Eli. He had many foreign contacts who needed currency, and he wanted a partner to run the day-to-day business.

Eli had some trepidations. That evening, he discussed the proposal with Diana:

> I said that I was hesitant to have this man as my partner; in some ways, I felt we were too different from one another. Diana's response was, 'So, do you have something better? Look, he is a businessman, he is older than you and he has contacts. Why don't you go into it? You have nothing to lose." And that was exactly the encouragement that I needed!

So Eli went into business with Landesman. They called the company Lazol and took office space at 505 Fifth Avenue, consistent with Eli's early conviction that the corner of 42nd Street and Fifth Avenue was the center of the New York business world. He had graduated from a mailbox for $10 a month to a desk for $25. Now he and Landesman would share a real office for $75 a month. Although the agent offered them a second office for only $25 more, Eli stuck to his budget: $75 was all the new business could afford. The two partners would sit at desks facing each other, with a secretary at the front of the office.

As the chief operating officer, Eli was the contact with the firm's clients. Following the principles he had learned traveling with his father, he soon established a solid reputation for honesty and integrity, critical in a business where all the transactions were in cash. When Eli gave his word, clients knew he would honor the agreement.

One day a client named Klein, with whom Eli had done business only by telephone, came to the office and asked to see Mr. Zborowski. Eli said, "I'm Mr. Zborowski." "No," said Klein, "I want to see your father." Eli told him that his father was long dead. Klein said that from speaking with Eli on the telephone, he thought he was dealing with a much older man. He left shaking his head; he couldn't believe that so young a person could be so knowledgeable and trustworthy. Shortly after this, he returned—to offer Eli his daughter in marriage! Eli informed Mr. Klein that he was already married.

At the end of every day, Eli tallied all the cash on hand before closing the office. One day he found that the balance was $1,200 over what he was supposed to have.

> I tried to figure out what had happened and who it could have been, and I couldn't account for it. I took the $1,200 and I put down the date and the customers I had that day, about five or six, and I put it in the safe. I called up the customers of that day and told them that *I* was short money. Everyone counted the money they gave me and assured me that it was the correct amount.

A few weeks later, one of the firm's clients appeared in the office. He was a broker who did not have his own business. He said he had a headache because he was short $1,200. I went with him to the safe and I took out the accounting for that day and I gave him the $1,200 overage that I had secured with a rubber band around it. Believe me, I felt so good that I found the person to whom the money belonged. The man might only have made $5 on a transaction and he thought he had lost $1,200.

Doing Business in Brazil

One of the firm's clients was an exporter named Pinchas Gross, who was relocating to Brazil. In March, 1955, he offered to go into partnership with Eli: Gross would order merchandise to sell in Brazil. He would take firm orders for a wide range of products; Eli would buy and ship the goods. Gross would sell them, remitting the full revenue to Eli, and they would share the profits. He ordered all kinds of things, pens, needles, textiles, sweaters, sunglasses, underwear, slippers—just about anything. Even before Eli was prepared to ship the first order, Gross had requested several hundred thousand dollars worth of goods. Eli decided to visit São Paulo to study the market and assess these orders.

Satisfied that the orders were genuine and the customers reliable, Eli agreed to extend credit to Gross, limited to $15,000 per shipment. "I made this agreement immediately. My firm belief was that if I treated a partner honestly and fairly, he had no justification to work behind my back."

That is how Eli began exporting goods to Brazil. The number of customers ordering merchandise from the company began to increase. Eli closed Lazol, his foreign currency operation, and started a new trading firm called All America Export/Import Company.

One of the most popular products Gross sold was the Parker 51 fountain pen, Parker's showcase product. It had a gold cap—enough gold to tie the price of the pen to the price of an ounce of gold. When the price of gold fluctuated, the price of the pen followed suit.

Parker pens were the most profitable item they sold. No duty was required on shipments weighing less than a kilogram. This permitted Eli to ship a large number of high-value Parker pens without paying duties, and to price the merchandise aggressively.

One problem remained: the firm did not have enough capital for the growing business. Orders were coming in for a wide range of products: needles, textiles, sweaters, sunglasses—but more orders were for fountain pens than anything else. Eli needed to expand his ability to ship the merchandise on credit. He came up with a solution that required exquisite timing.

Eli approached a vice-president of the commercial bank where his firm had a checking account, a Mr. Schiffman, who knew him well, and requested credit against uncollected checks: checks deposited to his account would be treated as cash. Schiffman approved the request. Eli would place an order with Parker at 3:00 p.m., paying with a check after the bank closed. Then he picked up the order at the shipping terminal on 42nd Street and Eleventh Avenue at about 11:00 p.m. The next morning, he gave the merchandise to a messenger to take to

Idlewild Airport—now John F. Kennedy International Airport. There the messenger flew to Brazil with the merchandise, and personally delivered it to the All America office. In this way, Eli cut the time between receipt of an order and its delivery to less than twenty-four hours.

Many people in Brazil received remittance checks from the United States. They sold these checks to a foreign exchange firm at the free-market price. In São Paulo, Gross converted the sales receipts for the Parker order into American dollars by buying remittance checks at a discount from the currency exchange firm. He put these freely negotiable checks in an envelope and headed for the airport. There he would find a traveler bound for New York who was willing to do a favor for him and carry the envelope. Next he telephoned Eli, describing the courier's clothing and appearance. On his arrival in New York the courier would be met by Eli, who thanked him for his assistance and took the envelope. Within a few hours, the checks from Brazil were deposited in Eli's bank account, providing the funds needed when the check he had given to Parker cleared. Despite the risk, none of the voluntary couriers ever absconded with Eli's receipts!

The sales of pens grew steadily. However, there was a lot of competition from other importers. Eli decided to ask the Parker Pen Company for exclusive distribution rights in Brazil.

Forging a Closer Relationship with Parker

The vice-president responsible for exports was George Parker, grandson and namesake of the company's founder. He received Eli cordially. After Eli explained that he wanted exclusive rights to sell Parker products in Brazil, Parker responded, "How can I do that? We have a distributor in Brazil."

Eli pointed out that Parker had nothing to lose: he was outselling the distributor even without the exclusive rights. Furthermore, Eli would provide him with a forecast for the entire year. With this forecast, Parker could manufacture pens throughout the year at marginal cost, whenever the company had excess capacity.

Parker refused. As Eli reached for the doorknob, Parker called him back.

"Look," he said, "I can't do that to my distributor in Brazil because he's been with us for so very long. However, I can offer you exclusive rights to sell in French Guiana." Eli's principal knowledge of French Guiana was that it was the site of the penal colony known as Devil's Island, where Alfred Dreyfus had been sent after his conviction as a spy. Clearly, this was no market for high-end fountain pens! Both parties understood that the real market for the pens would be Brazil.

Having exclusive rights in French Guiana did not fully achieve Eli's objective in Brazil. He pressed for more: he wanted a special discount on the pens, so that he could generate even greater sales volume. Parker hesitated, afraid that Eli would sell the pens outside Latin America, underselling Parker's agents around the world.

"I told him, 'Manufacture pens that you can recognize. Make the gold cap two millimeters shorter. If these show up outside of French Guiana, you can take the exclusivity away from me.' And I got a super-special price for the Parker 51. No one could compete with me."

At the end of that year, Parker needed to sell off excess inventory of several models. The company offered Eli the opportunity to buy any part of these overstocks, valued at $600,000—nearly $5 million today—for 25 percent off. After examining the list, Eli asked how much larger the discount would be if he took the entire excess off their hands. Astounded at the offer, the Parker representative gave him a much deeper discount.

There was a catch: Because the pens were a branded product, Eli was not permitted to sell them below the regular Parker price. Eli had long ago learned from his father that terms could be exchanged for price. In this instance, he offered the pens to buyers on credit terms of 50 percent down, and the balance in three to six months. Because of the discount he had obtained from Parker, he made a small profit on the initial payment alone! Although collections were often tardy, all his customers came through with the second payment.

After a few years, Landesman left the firm, and Eli became the sole owner of the All America Export/Import Company. A year later, he asked his brother Mendel, now known as Marvin, to join him as a partner in the business. Eli recalls fondly the opportunity this provided to further build on their shared history in a close working relationship.

Eli (at the far right) meets with Sheaffer Pen Co. executives in Fort Madison, Iowa in 1965

Eli welcomed Marvin's dependability and devotion to the business. They continued to work together until their retirement.

Clearly, Eli's affiliation with Parker Pen was working well. This had been a turning point in his business career. But his success with Parker in Brazil had not gone unnoticed; Eli was about to reach the next turning point.

Developing a Relationship with Parker

Sheaffer and Parker were the two dominant companies in fountain pens. One all-gold Sheaffer model sold for over $4,000. Sheaffer pens have been used by presidents, generals, and governors to sign many historic documents. The United Nations Charter was signed with a Sheaffer pen, as was the Japanese surrender agreement—by both Gen. Douglas McArthur and Japanese officials aboard the USS *Missouri* in 1945. The final Japanese peace treaty was signed in 1951 with Sheaffer pens, as was the truce agreement that ended the war in Vietnam. Eli was about to become part of this glorious history.

Eli recounts the courtship: "The Sheaffer Pen company had a factory in Brazil. They wanted me to do business with them, and the vice president for international sales and the head of export frequently visited me in my New York office. And whenever I was in Brazil, I visited them. They took me out, and they were constantly asking me to do some business for them. I said, 'I cannot, I have Parker—it makes no sense!'"

Finally, in 1961, Sheaffer came up with a concrete offer to be their exclusive distributor in Mexico. They trusted Eli to do as well for Sheaffer in Mexico as he had done for Parker in Brazil.

Eli returned to Parker and told them of the offer. Perhaps he hoped that Parker would counter the Sheaffer bid and give him Parker in Mexico. In any case, he wanted to retain his valuable relationship with Parker by being totally open and aboveboard with them. In the end, Parker accepted that Eli would represent Sheaffer in Mexico, as long as he would continue to be exclusively their de facto Brazilian distributor.

In February 1962, Eli went to Acapulco to discuss the terms of their relationship with Sheaffer's representative, Karl Dinnauer. They wanted to put him up in a third-rate hotel over the fish market, called the Fish Hotel. According to Dinnauer, this was the only space available.

Eli recalled that when his grandfather, who was a judge (*dayan*) in a rabbinical court, came to a town, he always took a seat in a front row of the synagogue, quickly establishing his place in the pecking order. If he was to negotiate a relationship with Sheaffer, Eli felt, he certainly was not going to sleep over a fish market.

> On the way there we passed the first-class Hotel Las Brisas. I asked for a room, and the room clerk said, "There are none available." I drew a $50 bill out of my wallet. He looked around left and right and said, "Sit down for a minute." I gave him the $50 bill, and he pulled out a bunch of keys and took me around to select the room that I wanted. Then he showed me a group of villas across the street that offered the same services as the hotel. Under a grove of trees was a villa used by Jacqueline Kennedy. I said. "Not bad." For a $50 tip, I got the villa next to Jackie Kennedy's!

Eli went back to the Fish Hotel and met with Dinnauer and Sheaffer's Mexican distributor, who had been selling Sheaffer products since before World War II. He owned a factory in Mexico, where he manufactured and bottled the Sheaffer Skrip brand of ink. He was ready to give up the distributorship if Eli would buy the factory as well. Dinnauer made it clear that Sheaffer favored the deal.

It was common for people from Mexico to avoid paying the import duty on top-quality pens by crossing into the United States to make the purchase. If this practiced continued, it would cost Eli sales to which he was entitled. He told Dinnauer that his acceptance was contingent on the inclusion of a strip along the U.S. side of the border. With this license included in his franchise, he planned to open a store in El Paso, Texas, to capture these sales. This turned out to be a very profitable business opportunity.

Eli returned to New York with a signed agreement to purchase the whole Mexico operation. The terms were 50 percent down and 50 percent within a year. Eli paid within six months, and for many years he owned the land and the factory. In one trip, Eli became the Sheaffer representative in Mexico and owner of an ink-bottling plant.

For several years, Eli represented both Sheaffer and Parker, but it was very difficult. Because he was such a large customer for both, they trusted him with new models and advance information. It was hard not to share information from one with the other, so Eli parted amicably with Parker.

Over the next few years, Eli sharply increased Sheaffer sales in Mexico. Sheaffer wanted him to take over its factories in Brazil and Argentina as well, because they were not yielding adequate profits, but Eli was not yet ready to take on this additional responsibility.

In 1966, Textron, Inc., one of the earliest conglomerate corporations, bought the Sheaffer Pen Company. Textron wanted nothing to do with the South American operations. On a handshake, Eli agreed to buy the two companies in Brazil and Argentina, with an exclusive license to all Sheaffer business in South America. Four years after the meetings at the Fish Hotel, Eli Zborowski was the owner and president of Sheaffer Latin America! Several years later, Textron promised that if it ever decided to sell, he would have the right of first refusal for the worldwide Sheaffer Pen Company.

Building Sheaffer Latin America

Eli became deeply engaged in factory operations. The average wage of his workers was about 1,000 pesos a month—$80. They had to bring their own lunch or buy it outside the factory, costing them not only money they could ill afford, but also working time. Eli decided to open a plant cafeteria. He charged a nominal one peso for a full meal, because he felt it would help the workers to maintain their self-pride, rather than accept a free meal. The one peso was deducted from their monthly salary. It was their only good meal of the day. When devaluation reduced the peso to four cents, the price of a meal remained one peso. A woman who came in and prepared the meals charged ten pesos for each meal, and Eli charged one. When she increased her price to twelve pesos the price of the meal remained a symbolic one peso.

Eli explains:

> This came not only from my experience with Hashomer Hatzair, but also from my father. We had a Jewish guard who slept in our warehouse. Evenings, he joined us in the house, especially in winter when it was warm inside. He sat at the same table with the rest of the family. Unlike many families in Żarki, we had both bread and meat on the table at the evening meal. Of course, Friday night we had fish and other delicacies. On Shabbat my father always brought home one or more beggars from the synagogue to join us at dinner. This respect for all people is what I was taught. This is how I grew up. It was natural for me.

The factory in Mexico, with about 180 employees, became known as a very good place to work. Women approached Eli, asking him to hire their daughters just out of high school. And the employees were very loyal. A supervisor in the Mexican factory named Zoila informed Eli that the factory manager was stealing parts from the plant and paying employees to assemble them at his home after work. When Zoila took inventory, the manager asked her to record these parts as sold. Eli fired him immediately. He had such faith in the woman's loyalty that he assigned her to supervise the annual count of inventories in both El Paso and New York.

Going for the Gold: Sheaffer Pen Company

In 1987 Sheaffer executives alerted Eli that Textron had decided to sell Sheaffer. They very much wanted him to own the firm, and suggested that he might be able to negotiate a direct purchase for about $80 million.

Textron had added other factories and product lines to what it now called the Sheaffer-Eaton Division, notably Eaton Fine Papers and the At-A-Glance line of calendars and appointment books. They put the entire division out for bid, and Eli submitted an offer of $120 million. He turned to the investment banking firm of Bear Stearns for assistance in financing the purchase and presenting his plan for the company

Eli wanted to spin off most of these other lines. Eaton, the largest subsidiary, was losing money. Nevertheless, despite an offer from Irving Stone, president of American Greetings Corporation, to purchase the product line, Eli decided to keep Eaton because he felt he could turn it around and get much more for it in a few years.

Eli had other plans for enhancing the Sheaffer business:

I had also intended to use the trade name Sheaffer, which was respected worldwide, for other products. Years before, I made a similar recommendation to Parker, when the transistor radios came out and I started to sell them in Argentina. I told Parker if they would sell transistor radios under the Parker name, it would be a winner. They believed it would diminish the name of Parker, which they felt had to be synonymous with the pen. If I had had the trade name Sheaffer, I would've used that name for whatever is good to sell. So that's what I had planned for Sheaffer.

Bear Stearns decided to bring Eli's project to Pacific Western Bank in Los Angeles. They accompanied him and introduced him. Eli presented his plan for Sheaffer, and then, as he recalls: "The people from Pacific Western questioned me for a whole day about how I would handle the operation, and how I would repay the loan. They were stone-faced. I couldn't tell whether I was missing something or whether their attitude was positive. We left the meeting certain that we had struck out."

In fact, Eli had hit a home run: Pacific Western offered him a $120 million loan, with the proviso that he must provide additional working capital of $20 million.

Eli was about to invest $20 million that he did not have. He turned to the Reichmann brothers, founders of Olympia & York, then the largest property development and management firm in the world. Like Bear Stearns and Pacific Western Bank, the Reichmanns found Eli's plans convincing. He could put up $8 million on his own. They agreed to provide $12 million, in exchange for a 40 percent share of the company.

Eli returned to New York, certain that the Sheaffer-Eaton Division of Textron would be his. At 1:00 a.m. he received a call from Textron: They had received a bid of $135 million, but there were some issues with the bid. If Eli could come up with just $5 million more, the company would be his.

The bank loan was final. He could not go back to the Reichmann brothers for so large an increase in their commitment, and his $8 million investment was all he could offer. He had to pass on the deal he wanted so badly.

Textron sold the Sheaffer-Eaton Division to Gefinor, SA, a Swiss financial firm. Ten years later, Gefinor sold the Sheaffer Pen business to Bic USA for $50 million. Had Textron been willing to sell it to him at this price in 1987, Eli would today be the owner and president of Sheaffer Pen Company.

End of an Era

Eli had been associated with Sheaffer for thirty-five years. He manufactured Sheaffer pens to their specification, exactly the same products that were sold in the United States. During that time, he had steadily increased sales. His factories were running near capacity, and by 1997 he employed 750 very satisfied, loyal workers, many of whom had held their jobs for a decade or more, in Mexico, Brazil, and Argentina. Sheaffer Latin America had become a significant factor in the continent's economy. Then something happened that even Eli had not anticipated.

Sheaffer Latin America held its exclusive sales and manufacturing rights under a five-year agreement that was regularly extended by Sheaffer. Bic, however, had factories everywhere that Sheaffer Latin America did. They saw no value in Eli's making products that could be made in Bic factories. In accordance with the terms of the license agreement, Bic gave Eli twelve months notice that it did not plan to renew his license.

According to Julius Berman, Eli's close friend, attorney, and confidant, "This man is brilliant. He is able to think three steps ahead, and that's the key in business—in making decisions. He knows that nine months or a year from now, this and this will happen, and he will be prepared for it." But this time, Eli stumbled. It is as if he failed to comprehend something so far removed from his, and his father's, way of doing business, taking into account the human beings who would lose their livelihoods, the long-term affiliate who would have to shut down his enterprise after nearly four decades. Eli continued as if nothing had happened. He continued selling on standard credit terms. He continued shipping merchandise and replacing the inventory.

Bic advised customers of Sheaffer Latin America that after the termination date, the company would no longer be licensed to make or sell Sheaffer products. As the date approached, major customers began paying slowly, and some just stopped paying for their orders. Eli recalls: "After a highly productive, mutually beneficial relationship with Sheaffer, extending over thirty-five years, I was left with nothing but air. I owned the factories, the machinery, and the land, but I could do nothing with them."

Sheaffer Latin America had come to an end.

Fordham Plaza

Eli's friend David Chase, a real estate developer from Hartford, Connecticut, had a long record of success building large office projects. Also a Polish Holocaust survivor, he was known as a risk-taker in Hartford, where he constructed large buildings on pure speculation. He believed that new buildings have the power to energize and strengthen the communities surrounding them, thereby becoming far more rational investments than they at first appeared. In 1984, he approached Eli with a proposal.

Chase wanted to build a new office building on Fordham Road in the Bronx—his first major venture in New York City. According to the *New York Times*, this would be the largest speculative office project ever undertaken in the Bronx.[1] It was to include 400,000 square feet of rentable space and a 500-car garage on a three-acre plot across from Fordham University. The plan turned on being able to rent general office space for $25 per square foot in an area where the going rate was

$8 to $12. Quoted in the same *New York Times* article, Stanley Gardner, head of Chase Enterprises, admitted the risk: "We don't have the foggiest idea whether we can make a go of it!"

The building would be a first-class location, designed by the leading architects Skidmore, Owings & Merrill. The central concept was to attract tenants from Manhattan, where rents were substantially higher for quality space. New York State committed to leasing 140,000 square feet, and the city took another 30,000. In the remaining space, 140,000 square feet would be dedicated to small professional firms, such as lawyers and accountants, by providing amenities that included common meeting rooms, a law library, and regular transportation to the County Courthouse. Attracting such tenants was uniquely feasible because the site was only a short walk from stations of both the Metro-North commuter railroad and the IND subway.

David Chase needed to raise $60 million in cash or loan guarantees to move ahead with the project. He turned to Eli, who brought in the Reynolds Construction Company, the American subsidiary of Solel Boneh, Ltd. Solel Boneh, the largest builder in Israel at the time, was highly regarded worldwide. Chase sought to put its solid credit behind the project.

Eli agreed to join with Chase in the $60 million venture, which they incorporated as Fordham Renaissance Associates. The partners in the venture were Chase Enterprises, Reynolds Construction, and EZB Fordham, a company Eli had formed to handle his real estate transactions. Various city, state, and federal agencies provided nearly half the funds needed. After mortgage financing was obtained, the entire financial exposure of Fordham Renaissance Associates was only $5 million.

Fordham Plaza topping-off ceremony, 1985. Bronx Borough President Stanley Simon; New York Governor Mario Cuomo; Eli.

Cellular Telephones

When Sheaffer Latin America was shot out from under him, Eli did what any good trooper would have done: he found another mount and returned to the fray.

In 1997, cellular telephone service was just taking off in South America. A major obstacle, however, was that international cell phone manufacturers were reluctant to enter this market. They feared the political instability; they worried about the restrictions governments placed on foreign goods; and they had no idea how to deal with the risk of currency fluctuations and devaluations. In short, they simply did not know how to operate in South American markets.

Into this breach stepped Eli Zborowski. After nearly four decades of doing business in South America, he had a great deal of experience with these issues, especially financial negotiations and currency. All the manufacturers were eager to sell in Latin America. Eli found a partner in Brazil, and they formed All-America Telecommunications to sell their products through AT&T and Verizon, the principal providers of cellular service in South America.

Eli was widely recognized as a successful businessman with an excellent credit history. He bought telephones from the manufacturers with the help of sixty-day letters of credit from Safra National Bank, and sold the telephones in South America on thirty-day terms. The first company to sell cellular phones in Brazil, All-America released an enormous pent-up demand. As a result, several manufacturers decided to build new factories there, sidestepping most of their previous concerns. Eli's expertise was no longer needed. He left the firm. His Brazilian partner continued, but now refurbishes cell phones manufactured in Brazil.

The America-Israel Chamber of Commerce

A successful entrepreneur with strong links to Israel, Eli was a valued member of the America-Israel Chamber of Commerce; in 1984 he was elected National President.

The AICC was created to boost the Israeli and American economies by helping to develop business relationships and exploring new market opportunities in the two countries. Utilizing their expertise and networking connections, members of the Chamber volunteer their time to evaluate the needs of potential partners, provide market feedback, and identify interested investors. In its 56 years of operation, the AICC has become one of the world's most effective bi-national business organizations

The Chamber served as the principal American liaison for Israel's Ministry of Commerce and Industry. For example, during the development of a free trade agreement between the United States and Israel, Eli led the Chamber in urging its passage in Congress.

His prominent role in the Chamber's activities brought Eli into contact with business and political leaders in both countries.

When Ariel Sharon came here as the head of the Ministry for Trade and Industry, I accompanied him and his late wife Lillian. We had a wonderful time traveling together. I stayed with him in Washington and we appeared together before several committees. I recall being uncomfortable with some of Sharon's language which I thought was not as diplomatic as it might be.

After four years as president of the Chamber, Eli felt that he could no longer serve in that capacity, as he had to attend closely to building the American Society for Yad Vashem, which he had started in 1981. In 1991 he was presented with an award from the Chamber for "Dedication and Leadership as President."

American/Israel Chamber of Commerce and Industry meeting in Detroit.
Eli is seated on the dais, second from the right. He served as president from
1984 – 1988.

American/Israel Chamber of Commerce and Industry Dinner at the New
York Hilton Hotel, New York City, December 10, 1987.

Eli Zborowski, National President; Aron Kahana, President, Israel Discount
Bank; Eliezer Lerner, Presidemt, UMB Bank and Trust Company, NY; David
Novick, President, Bank Leumi NY; Uzi Vardizer, President, Bank Hapoalim,
Western hemisphere; Michael Arnon, President, Ampal, Dinner Chairman.

Now eighty-five years old, Eli still spends a full day, five days a week, at work in his office. Retirement does not appear to be an option.

Eli Zborowski has not been primarily motivated by money. He doesn't need a mansion: he lives in the same house he built in 1968. He has no yacht or other expensive toys. Far from seeking to impress others with his wealth, he still follows his father's modest precepts. And he has devoted at least as much of his life in unpaid service to Yad Vashem and to the American Society for Yad Vashem as he has to any commercial venture.

Chapter 7 Notes

1. Alan S. Oser, "For a Hartford Developer, A Challenge in the Bronx," *New York Times*, December 16, 1984

❦ Chapter 8 ❦

FAMILY, FRIENDS
AND COMMUNITY

Lilly, Diana, Eli and Murry

CHAPTER 8

Family, Friends, and Community

Eli and Diana were among the many refugees arriving in the United States who faced resettlement challenges and problems. There was, first of all, a new language to learn, an especially difficult task for those who were already adults when they arrived. The Jewish community was welcoming, but as Americans they thought differently and did things in ways that were new and strange. Added to that was the need to find work and to make a living.[1]

Perpetuating the names of *kedoshim*—martyrs—was of paramount importance to survivors because it was a concrete way to sanctify the memory of loved ones. The birth of their first child in 1952, three months after they arrived in the United States, was the beginning of Eli and Diana's primary dream—to build a family and to honor the memory of those who had been brutally murdered. The child, now known as Lilly, was named Leah after Diana's mother, who perished in the Holocaust. The joy of welcoming a newborn into the world, however, was intermingled with the struggle of adjustment in a new country.

Eli and Lilly in 1953

The family, including Eli's brother, Marvin, rented a small apartment in a working-class neighborhood in the Bronx. While Eli set about trying to find a way to support his family, Diana stayed home to care for the baby. Childcare was new and somewhat overwhelming, and she had no mother, older sister, or good friend to turn to for support. From time to time, an aunt of Eli's came by to help her. As Diana did not breast-feed the baby, Eli would come home in the evening to make formula.

One of their first purchases was a television set. It kept Diana company and also enabled her to become accustomed to the sound of the English language. Television sets were a rarity in their Bronx neighborhood, and Lilly recalls: We were the first family in our apartment house to have a TV. It was assumed that if I had exposure to television, I would learn English. However, as a child, my excitement at having a TV came from the fact that our home became a huge attraction for all the neighborhood children. Every afternoon, they gathered in our living room and sat on the floor with their eyes riveted on the set as they watched *Howdy Doody.*"[2]

Moving to Forest Hills

In 1955, a son, Moshe Shlomo, named for both his grandfathers, was born. Shortly afterward, Eli and Diana bought their first home in Forest Hills, a two-story attached house located near the Young Israel of Forest Hills Synagogue. Eli was eager to enroll Lilly, now three, in a preschool program so that she could begin to socialize with American children. He could not find a weekday nursery school, but he heard that the Young Israel synagogue, then located in a storefront, offered a Sabbath afternoon program each week. Lilly's attendance at this program led to a transformation in the life of the family and ultimately in their involvement in the community.

As Eli explained, "The Sabbath program began at three o'clock in the afternoon. I was told that I could leave her and come back in an hour and a half to pick her up. I didn't leave, but stood behind the door and watched and listened as the children sang *Shalom Aleichem* (a traditional Sabbath song) and danced around. It made me feel so warm and so good that I decided to join the Young Israel of Forest Hills."

Once he joined, Eli began to attend shul every Sabbath, an experience that impelled him to start reclaiming his tradition. Eli was reminded of his father's words to him when, as a teenage member of Hashomer Hatzair, he began to stray from religious practice: "As long as you are in my house you will observe the Jewish law. When you grow up and come among other Jews, I want you to know how to behave as a Jew. If you do not know the proper behavior, people will say that your father didn't teach you, and I don't want to be guilty of that."

As a result of the training he received from his father, Eli was able to reenter Jewish religious life with ease. An appreciation of the culture of Torah and mitzvot (the commandments) had never left him. As time went on, they became a source of comfort and joy, especially when he could share them with his children. He says: "The greatest pleasure I have had in life is walking to synagogue on Sabbath morning with my two children, holding a child with each hand. I prayed that my father in heaven would be witness to this extraordinary achievement—another generation of Jewish children committed to *Yiddishkeit*."

Eli was not a father who got down on the floor to play with his children. He never took them to a Yankee game, watched sports with them on television, or played baseball in the backyard. Yet, both Lilly and Moshe Shlomo, known as Murry, have very fond memories of doing things with him.

Today Lilly Zborowski Naveh is an ophthalmologist living in Israel with her husband and three children. Some of her earliest memories center on going to synagogue with her father. But most outstanding in her repertoire of recollections are the daily "business lessons" she received from him:

When my father came home in the evening, he would always recount his day's activities to my mother. She knew everything that was going on in his business life and was involved in all the major decisions. As Murry and I got older, we joined them at the dinner table and became part of the narrative he shared with my mother.

In the evening, he would open the Business Section of the *New York Times* to the stock page and teach me the meaning of all the abbreviations. Before long I was able to identify the highs and lows of the day for a variety of stocks. I was only in elementary school at the time and all this knowledge set me apart from my friends. Since I got a pretty good business education growing up, I am now able to give very basic financial advice to colleagues who were not nurtured on the essentials of business in their formative years.

Murry, too, fondly recalls attending synagogue with his father.

I would walk with him to shul every Sabbath morning and then again to *mincha* and *ma'ariv* (the afternoon and evening services). We would engage in conversation on the way to and from shul. He would talk to me about a variety of things—his father, work-related issues, plans for his business, or the politics of the organizations he was involved in. This went on from the time I was about six until I was almost in my twenties.

I sat next to him in shul. Unlike the rest of the kids my age, I chose not to go out to play with the other boys. There was a youth service, but I never went because my place was next to my father.

I remember Sabbath meals because we all ate together. When we came home from shul, my father took off his street shoes and put on a pair of comfortable leather slippers that he wore only for relaxation. As we lingered over our Sabbath meal, my father would quiz me and my sister on our knowledge of geography and math. I still remember learning from him about grams and decagrams (10 grams). Nobody uses the term decagram unless he deals in gold. He would also tell us stories about life in Żarki. He taught us the lessons of life through these stories.

In the early years of his business career, Eli stored inventory in the basement of his home and utilized the willing labor force of his wife and children to package merchandise. This was a productive activity that gave the family a feeling of all pulling together. Murry, who worked with his father in business for many years and now, the father of four children, lives in Israel, recalls being one of the workers:

Our job was to package sweaters. The label on the sweaters featured two kittens—one white, the other black. In order to make it fun for us, he would refer to me as the *veis ketzeleh*—the white kitten—because I was blond and blue-eyed and to my sister as the *shvartz ketzeleh*—the black kitten—because she had dark hair and dark eyes. I also remember that there were Parker pens that had to be packed by the dozen with a heavy rubber bands—six up and six down.

On Sundays the family would drive to the Lower East Side of New York to shop and on occasion to visit one of Eli's clients. The day was topped off with lunch at Ratner's, which was viewed by the children as a wonderful tradition and a great treat.

The Meaning of the Holocaust to the Children

Many survivors were reluctant to share their wartime experiences with their young children. They felt that disclosing the extent of the degradation and humiliation they had suffered would undermine the youngsters' sense of security. The Zborowskis were unusual in the survivor community in that they did talk about their wartime experiences. Lilly says, "There was never a time when I didn't know. There was no moment of discovery about what they went through. It was always there. My father was more talkative than my mother, and some of what happened to my mother I know from my father. There was pain, but no element of secrecy." Yiddish words like *der krig* (the war) and *di greeneh* (the greenhorns) became part of the children's vocabulary.

Such stories deeply affected many children of survivors, causing them to be more vulnerable to trauma, stress reactions, and unrealistic fantasies.[3] Eli's continued longing for his father is reflected in his children's imaginations. Lilly recalls a recurring dream:

I knew that my grandfather had disappeared following an attempted escape from the Germans. His body was never found. As a very small child my bedroom was just over the entrance to our row house. If I had gone to sleep at eight o'clock and someone came to the door at nine, I would hear the movement and voices, because I was not yet sound asleep. I always had the fantasy that my grandfather had returned and was standing at the door. Now, in retrospect, I realize that this was not a normal thing for a kid to be thinking.

Murry also fantasized about his grandfather's return. From the time he was a little boy until he was well into his teens, he believed that his grandfather had fled to Israel during the war and would recognize Murry in the street the next time he went there.

The Forest Hills neighborhood where the Zborowskis lived was populated by a large number of survivors and their families. The community was so insular, Lilly says, that she "must have been fifteen years old before [she] realized that the majority of American Jews had never experienced the war." Lilly and Murry's friends were also children of survivors who tended to reinforce each other's anxieties and fears about what happened during the war. Murry talks about the "play" in which he and his friends engaged:

The wartime stories were scary. When my father asked me what I wanted for my sixth birthday, I told him I wanted a tank with a gun so I could shoot the Germans.

A few years later, I came across some books in our house about Bergen-Belsen. When I opened the books, I saw all the photographs of the concentration camp. These images were impossible for me to comprehend. I didn't ask my father about them; instead I showed them to my friends. At that point, they took me to their houses and showed me the books that they had in their homes. Many of them had older brothers and sisters who filled them in on some of the history. I didn't really know whether or not this was part of my parents' experience. Since I didn't know all the details, I created a personal family history that was ever changing, and not altogether based in reality.

Murry and his friends felt that their parents' experience might be repeated, and that they needed to develop a strategy for dealing with it. The fear of being unprepared overwhelmed them. To overcome this, they talked about where they would hide, where they would get weapons, and how they would fight.

Even though Eli and Diana had suffered enormous losses during the Holocaust, a sense of hope and optimism pervaded their lives. Lilly talked about the profound lesson she had learned from her parents and their circle of friends: "Every time there was a bar or bat mitzvah or a wedding, these people were joyous. They used these milestone events to proclaim to the world that they had children, they succeeded and despite what befell them, they have learned to celebrate their continued existence." Murry recalls that on these occasions his father would surprise people with his ability to glide across the dance floor to the music of a waltz or a fox-trot!

In sharing stories of the Holocaust with his children, Eli rarely presented himself as a victim. In addition, he often telegraphed a tone of great humanity in terms of his relationships with Poles. Murray relates that his father spoke about how their Polish neighbors in Żarki jeopardized their own lives to save the Zborowski family. "My father emphasized the courage of those who rose above evil at a time when morality was virtually extinct. He rarely had harsh words to say about the human race and about the cruel and callous things that he endured."

Eli and his grandchildren

Erez Zborowski, Ariel Zborowski, Boaz Zborowski, Ori Gutman, Tamar Gutman, Eli, Maya Naveh in 2005

Murry's Family
Ariel, Erez, Zohar, Boaz in 2005

The Family Patriarch

When Moshe Zborowski disappeared, Eli assumed the role of family patriarch. His concern and his desire to be of assistance reached beyond his nuclear family to include uncles, aunts, nieces, nephews, and cousins, wherever they lived. He anticipated their needs and offered a generous and helping hand to those who asked for support. Within the family he was respected and admired, and as a person one could turn to for encouragement and advice. His niece Yaffa Zilbershats, who teaches international law at Bar-Ilan University in Israel, tells of the family's excitement at a prospective visit from Uncle Eli:

My earliest memory of my Uncle Eli emanates from visits he made to us from the United States in the 1950s. Going to the airport from our home in Tel-Aviv was a whole excursion. So that the entire family could be there to greet him, we used my father's car and borrowed another car from a relative. In those days, there were still no major highways and we had to travel on many local streets. Since known arrivals were infrequent and flights were late, we packed sandwiches and apples for the trip. Our anticipation and excitement was unimaginable as we waited on the porch of the small airport. When the passengers began to deplane, we felt we were greeting people from another world, and my Uncle Eli was our personal representative from this world.

In 1964, when Yaffa was eleven years old, she was invited by her uncle Eli to go to summer camp in the United States. As the oldest of his siblings, Eli felt he had the responsibility of broadening the horizons of all the children in the family. He thought it would be beneficial to provide Yaffa, and later her brothers, with an American Jewish camping experience. That was the year of the World's Fair in Flushing New York, and Yaffa was also treated to a tour of the entire exhibition.

Perhaps the most profound recollection of this trip came when Yaffa visited her uncle's office at 505 Fifth Avenue. The office was divided into two parts. There were the front offices, which included Eli and his brother Marvin's personal offices, and a long corridor that led to rooms where they kept the inventory of merchandise. In addition, there was a separate room filled with papers, posters, and newspapers.

When they entered this room, Eli explained that this was a collection of Holocaust-related material. Yaffa's grandparents and her aunt Shaindl, for whom she is named, all perished in the Treblinka death camp. She remembers very clearly what happened next: "He took me by the hand and spoke to me with words that were very powerful and definitely shaped the vision of my life going forward: He said to me: 'God has helped me and I have *parnoseh*—money to live on. Now I have to make sure that my life will not be distorted by having only the goal of making money for myself and my family. There is a big, big danger that one day an enemy of the Jews will stand up and announce that there was no Holocaust. I have to devote my life to ensuring that will never, never happen.' "

Her uncle's words had a tremendous impact: "I was only eleven years old and the words of this man I so revered moved me deeply. I came away feeling that devoting oneself exclusively to making money is of no value. While we have to work and save in order to provide for our families, we must also strive to give back to society. That day, I became aware that commemorating the Holocaust is of the utmost importance to the Jewish people and the world."

Today Yaffa is a scholar of international law—a field that has been significantly shaped by events stemming from World War II and the Holocaust. It has raised worldwide consciousness about the evil of war crimes and about the importance of universal protection of human rights. Yaffa says, "As a child of a survivor and as a legal scholar it is crucial for me to understand how the legal field developed as a consequence of the Holocaust."

Throughout her life, Yaffa has seen Eli as a second father. She has repeatedly consulted him at crossroads in her life, and he has always been the first person to whom she has turned for advice.

Over the years, Eli has been devotedly helpful to family members living in Israel. Through the commercial ventures he started in the United States, he established a business for his sister Tzila and her family in Israel. Today this expanded enterprise imports expensive watches and Samsonite luggage among other products that are sold throughout Israel.

At the outset of World War II, Moshe Zborowski gave Eli the names of cousins who had emigrated to Palestine. Coincidentally, Eli met one of them, Zelig Shushan, in 1945 at a convention in Landsberg. Years later, Eli helped one of the Shushans' sons meet the expenses of adopting a child. Feeling an ongoing sense of responsibility for the child's welfare, Eli has established a bank account for him to which he makes deposits every time he is in Israel.

Home, Hospitality, and Friends

Having established meaningful roots in Forest Hills, the Zborowskis decided to buy land and build a house in that neighborhood. They moved into their new home in 1968, the year of Murry's bar mitzvah. In honor of this event, Eli established the Moshe Zborowski Gemilat Chesed Fund, which is discussed in the next chapter.

From the outset, he and Diana were eager to share their pride in their new residence. It was a well-known fact in the community that one could turn to the Zborowskis to open their home for parlor meetings and organizational luncheons. It was also a gathering place for family milestones, for their children's friends, and for South American business associates longing for a home-cooked meal.

The Zborowskis' annual post–Yom Kippur break-fast was legendary. It started out in the early years with just a few close friends and expanded as their circle increased and as families grew and multiplied. It is not surprising that several generations of friends speak glowingly about having been part of this experience.

Barbara Gutfreund Arfa, the daughter of Eli and Diana's best friends, Salo and Regina Gutfreund, both survivors, remembers the kindness and hospitality: "The moment Yom Kippur was over, Eli would hurry home and get his car so that he could ferry all the guests to his house. Diana set a sumptuous table with everything your heart could desire—there was every kind of smoked fish and salads as well as wonderful desserts. The table was set with elegant china and linen, and Eli and Diana were the most warm and welcoming hosts. Their home was like a cocoon for survivors and their families. With them we felt safe and protected."

In the absence of the extended families that had perished in the Shoah, survivors clung to each other for the comfort and support normally provided by close kin. Barbara's daughter, Caroline Arfa Massel, who has gone on to become the chairperson of the American Society for Yad Vashem's Young Leadership Associates, remembers the break-fast with great affection:

We always stayed with my grandparents for Rosh Hashana and Yom Kippur, so going to the Zborowskis was a tradition. The feast that Diana would spread on their dining room table was always so beautiful. The meal started with chocolate babka and orange juice. To this day, when I host the break-fast, we must start with a piece of chocolate babka on everyone's plate and orange juice. Of course, I think Diana's was home-baked and mine is not. I have known the Zborowskis from the time

I was born. They were like another set of grandparents to me. Whenever I went to their home, I was lavished with attention.

The survivors' social world was characterized by strong friendships and loyalties. There was among them a determination to go on living despite adversity. Some even seemed to gain confidence and self-respect simply from the knowledge that they had lived through a terrible time which in turn gave them a sense of invulnerability.[4] On most Saturday nights and for vacations, the Zborowskis were joined by Joseph and Lusia Distenfeld, Jack and Lola Rozmaryn, and Salo and Regina Gutfreund. Caroline Massel provides some recollections of the Zborowskis' social life:

My grandparents and the Zborowskis went to the Plaza Hotel's Palm Court every Saturday night to shmooze over coffee and cake. Sometimes, Julia and Isidore Kartin, also survivors, would join them. When I was about twelve, I remember staying with my grandparents one weekend, and I was invited to go along. On that Saturday, Talia Toledano, the Kartins' granddaughter was visiting and so she came along as well.

Their seating arrangements followed the same pattern each week. They either took one long table with the men sitting at one end and the women at the other or two tables, one for men, the other for women. I remember that I found it curious that they chose separate seating because my grandparents did everything together as did each of the other couples. My grandmother explained that the women wanted to talk to each other and the men wanted to talk business. She said, "I talk to Papa all the time, I don't need to talk to him when we go out."

In revisiting this experience two decades later, Caroline thinks it remarkable that these survivors felt comfortable enough with themselves and their position in society to carve out a life that included spending an evening at one of New York's finest hotels. She sees strength and nobility in their struggle. She says, "While continuing to remain loyal to the memory of the dead they were simultaneously committed to self-renewal and to living."

Eli, Tzila and Marvin, August, 1963

Chapter 8 Notes

1. William B. Helmreich, *Against All Odds: Holocaust Survivors and the Successful Lives They Made in America* (New York: Simon & Schuster, 1992), p. 59.
2. *Howdy Doody* was the first and the most popular children's television program in the 1950s
3. This phenomenon, known as "intergenerational syndrome," is based on research done by Dr. Rachael Yehuda, reported in Ben Sherwood, *The Survivors Club: The Secrets and Science That Could Save Your Life,* (New York: Grand Central Publishing, 2007), pp. 178–179.
4. Helmreich, *Against All Odds*, p. 272.

❧ Chapter 9 ❧

COMMUNAL LEADERSHIP

Honorary Grand Marshal of the Salute to Israel Parade
with Yehuda Bloom,
Ambassador and Permanent Representative of Israel
to the United Nations, 1978-1984

CHAPTER 9

ॐ

Communal Leadership

Synagogue Presidency

The Young Israel of Forest Hills Synagogue had only been in existence for three years when Eli and Diana became members. Before long Eli's leadership ability became evident and he was invited to join the board. As a board member he actively participated in discussions, indicating his distinct interest in developing programs for the youth of the congregation. Soon thereafter he was appointed a vice-president; in 1964 he was elected president, and he was re-elected again for three more terms.

The beginning of Eli's four-year tenure as president was a tumultuous time:

> When I took over the presidency the synagogue was running a deficit, and there was a great deal of anger among the members. The Board had previously obtained promissory notes from them to guarantee a loan for the new building. They assured these members that all mortgage payments would be met out of membership dues and donations; the notes were merely a formality. In fact, the Board failed to make payments, and the bank drew on the personal notes. The membership was up in arms over this.

In an effort to make peace, Eli listened carefully to all the factions and attempted to arrive at a compromise. He acknowledged to the congregants that money was owed to them and promised that the board would do everything in its power to pay it back. In the spirit of

Benjamin Franklin's adage that "energy and persistence conquer all things," Eli set about devising a number of fundraising projects that would improve services and encourage members to become invested in the welfare of the synagogue.

Creating change by altering the way his membership thought, felt, and acted was essential.[1] Eli's first initiative was to launch a campaign to build permanent wooden pews. Prior to this, people sat on folding chairs when they came to pray. The permanent wooden benches afforded greater comfort and could be individualized with a small brass plaque for a fee. The members to whom the synagogue owed money were offered credit toward personalized pews or memorial plaques. Eli's next endeavor was to increase the membership. Aaron Levit, who was appointed an officer of the board, was assigned this task. Each week, he stood at the door to greet people as they entered the synagogue and encourage them to become new members. Both of these projects were highly successful and enabled the synagogue to liquidate its debt.

Finally, Eli revamped the traditional *Kol Nidre* appeal.[2] Instead of the appeal that night, Eli organized a committee of members who began to solicit donations a month in advance of Yom Kippur. In lieu of the regular appeal, the names of people who pledged were read aloud before the congregation. In subsequent years, they simply put up a poster with the names of those who made donations. As a sign of their own personal support for the synagogue, Eli and Diana donated a large bronze commemorative tablet on which individual small plaques could be affixed for a fee in memory of deceased relatives who perished during the Holocaust.

Rabbi Marvin Luban, who was the senior rabbi of the Young Israel of Forest Hills for twenty-six years, worked very closely with Eli. Luban says that Eli "set the tone for future presidents. He was an absolute dynamo—it's hard to imagine how vital he was . . . he was spirited, charming and a phenomenal leader who got other people to join in his commitment and to work toward achieving the goals he set for the synagogue."

During Eli's presidency, Julius Berman, a prominent New York attorney who at present is chairman of the Conference on Jewish

Material Claims Against Germany, became a member of the Young Israel of Forest Hills. He recalls how the congregation viewed Eli:

From the very beginning it became obvious to people in the congregation that he was leadership material. We felt confident that he would lead us in the right path. Once Eli decided to do something, he did it with a passion. Many of the congregants were Holocaust survivors and they needed a leader. Eli rose to the occasion and they embraced him. I don't know

Friends gather at the Young Israel of Forest Hills Annual Dinner honoring the Gutfreunds in 1984. *Left to right:* Eli & Diana Zborowski, Regina Gutfreund, Sam & Stella Skura, Salo Gutfreund

what percentage of the congregation were survivors, but it appeared that they ran the show.

Eli was always concerned that because there was such a strong representation of middle-aged people that younger congregants would feel the *shul* was a closed shop. Therefore, when vacancies became available, Eli would look for one or two younger people to invite to serve on the board.

Under Eli's leadership, the Young Israel of Forest Hills became a vibrant, growing synagogue. Every Sabbath, despite his pronounced accent and limited command of the English language, Eli stood up proudly and delivered the week's announcements. Julie Berman smiles affectionately at the memory: "We had a running joke at Young Israel through the years. Eli had so attuned us to hearing English spoken in the manner that he conveyed it that when American-born successor took over the position and made announcements in straight English, we kidded that we couldn't understand him because we had become accustomed to the way in which Eli delivered his announcements. In retrospect, I think Eli was barely cognizant of his broken English. When he stood before the congregation, he did so with the utmost assurance because he had a mission to convey that transcended language."

The First Yom Hashoah Commemoration in the United States

The parameters of the Shoah were fully known and publicized by 1943, and protest preceded commemorative observance in this country. The *New York Times* for April 20, 1944, reported on a protest meeting held in the Warsaw Synagogue on the Lower East Side. A thousand people crowded the building to give testimony of the Warsaw Ghetto's heroism. From there they marched to City Hall to plead for Mayor Fiorello LaGuardia's help for the plight of European Jewry.

The observance of Yom Hashoah, Holocaust Day, has its roots in the Warsaw Ghetto Uprising, which began on April 19, 1943. After the war, the uprising became the symbol of Jewish resistance and commemoration. In the 1950s the commemoration became a more formalized communal event and was usually held as close as possible to actual date of the uprising, April 19th.

While Eli attended these events and was active in encouraging others to do so, it was with some degree of misgiving. He wondered, "Why do we commemorate only the Warsaw Ghetto? Why not my town of Żarki, or Częstochowa, or Kraków, Vilna, or Lvov? There was also Kovno and Budapest and so many others." Having been in the underground, Eli was mindful that there were other resistance movements that got no mention, like the one in the Zaglembia region headed up by his Hashomer Hatzair leader, Tzvi Brandes. He was pained by the fact that the commemoration focused only on the Warsaw Ghetto and did not represent the range of Holocaust experiences.

In 1951, the Israeli Knesset (parliament) enacted a day of commemoration, *Yom Hashoah Ve'Hagevurah*, a Day of Remembrance, in which we commemorate the martyrdom and resistance of the victims of the Holocaust. The Knesset designated the 27th day of the Hebrew month of Nissan as an annual day of memorial tribute to all the Jewish martyrs and heroes of the Holocaust. One of the reasons for having selected the 27th of Nissan is that it never falls on the Sabbath, a day when Jews are not permitted to mourn.

In the early 1960s Eli became very enthusiastic about joining with the State of Israel in commemorating the Shoah on the date established on the Hebrew calendar. He felt strongly that this was the most appropriate way to observe the day, because it bound Jews all over the Diaspora with the State of Israel, thereby creating unity and centrality of purpose. In 1964, in his role as vice-president of the synagogue, prior to being elected president, Eli shared the idea with Rabbi Luban, and they agreed that the event would take place at the Young Israel of Forest Hills. They convened a small committee of survivors to plan the first Yom Hashoah commemoration ever held in the United States on the 27th day of Nissan.

Eli had a distinct vision for the scope and sponsorship of the program. He believed that the events of the Shoah demanded that Jews of all political persuasions and all streams of Judaism, including those who viewed themselves as secular or cultural, should join together. The purpose of the *yachdut*—the unity—would be to bear witness to the catastrophic events of the Shoah while simultaneously reaffirming hope for the survival of the Jewish people.

Propelled by conviction and confidence, Eli personally visited the heads of all the major Jewish organizations in the New York area to enlist their sponsorship of the first Yom Hashoah Ve'Hagevurah event. His enthusiasm was infectious; all the organizations ultimately agreed to sponsorship. But Eli encountered several obstacles to obtaining this unanimous support. A few instances stand out in his mind:

It was sometimes difficult to get all the factions together. For example, I invited Agudath Israel to join us, but they refused because we had Reform congregations among our sponsors, which they considered too liberal in their practice of Judaism. So I then turned to the two survivors who were part of the Agudah presidium, Rabbi Haskel Besser and Benjamin Fishoff. I convinced them that we cannot have any difference between one Jew and another when it comes to the cause of remembrance. I finally received their consent for sponsorship.

Promotion of the event took several forms. A flyer was created that featured a duplication of the torch that appeared on the Israeli stamp issued in honor of Yom Hashoah. The flyer included all the pertinent information regarding time, date, place, and program highlights. It also listed the sponsoring organizations and the names of their two representatives. Several days prior to the event, Eli positioned himself in front of the main subway station in Queens to hand out flyers to all who passed by. At his own expense, he also placed advertisements in the Yiddish *Forward* and *Der Tog-Morgan Zhournal, The Day–Morning Journal*.

On the next page is the advertisement that appeared on April 8, 1964 in *Der Tog-Morgan Zhournal* announcing the first synagogue-based Yom Hashoah commemoration.

That first event, on April 8, 1964, corresponding to the 27th day of Nissan, was a resounding success! An overflow audience came to hear guest speaker Rabbi Herschel Schacter, who had been a U.S. Army chaplain during the war and participated in the liberation of Buchenwald, and Sidor Belarsky, the preeminent interpreter of classical cantorial music, Yiddish folk songs, and ghetto songs.

This ad appeared in the Yiddish language *Der Tog-Morgan Zhournal — The Day-Morning Journal* on April 8, 1964.

Important Commemorative Evening
in memory of the six million victims
Today, Wednesday, the 8th of April, 8 in the evening
The 27th day of the month of Nissan
Guest Speaker
Rabbi Hershel Schacter
in a Program of Ghetto and Camp Songs
Sidor Belarsky,
Rabbi Menachem Mendel (Marvin) Luban, Yeshiya (Charles) Bick,
Marvin Cohen, and Cantor Avrom Shverd

A special commemorative plaque in bronze dedicated by
Mr. and Mrs. Eliezer Zborowski
In memory of the victims of the Holocaust

YOUNG ISRAEL OF FOREST HILLS
YELLOWSTONE BLVD. & BURNS ST., FOREST HILLS, N.Y.

A proclamation, developed in the State of Israel and calling for unity in remembrance, was read:

יום הזכרון לשואה ולגבורה

PROCLAMATION[3]
DAY OF REMEMBRANCE—YOM HASHOA V'HAGVURAH
FOR JEWISH MARTYRDOM AND HEROISM
APRIL 8, 1964—27 DAY OF NISSAN

WHEREAS, the Knesset of the State of Israel and Jewish Communities throughout the world have proclaimed the 27th Day of Nissan, corresponding this year to April 8,1964, as a Day of Remembrance of the Martyrdom of 6 million of our people who perished in the European Holocaust and as a Day of Tribute to Jewish Heroism; and

WHEREAS, it is our obligation to perpetuate and keep alive the memory of our Martyrs—*Kedoshim* and pay Tribute to our Heroes; and

WHEREAS, we remember the communities, synagogues and the "public, cultural, educational, religious and benevolent institutions which were destroyed in an attempt to erase the name, the faith and the culture of Israel; and

WHEREAS, we pay Tribute to the Heroism of JEWISH SERVICEMEN, to the UNDERGROUND FIGHTERS, to the heroic stand of the besieged FIGHTERS OF THE GHETTOES who rose and kindled the flame of revolt in honour of their PEOPLE; and

WHEREAS, the ancient Jewish dictum "Thou shall tell thy son" offers meaningful assurance for Jewish survival in the tradition of our people; and

WHEREAS, our brethren in Israel and Jews throughout the world will gather on this assigned day to commemorate the Holocaust and pay Tribute to Jewish Heroism;

Now therefore, we—the undersigned—representing our organizations and The Jewish Community, proclaim the evening of Wednesday, April 8th and Thursday, April 9th, 1964, corresponding to the 27th Day of Nissan, as a Day of Remembrance and Observance.

We call upon all Jews to assemble in their synagogues and other appropriate places of assembly to commemorate the heroic deeds of our people in the European catastrophe.

This day must become one of National Observance and Commemoration in our homes, in our synagogues, in our schools and any other places of Assembly.

We call upon Rabbis and Community Leaders to make this day a Day of Observance for the entire community and to make it a permanent Day of Observance from year to year.

Keep the Day of Martyrdom and Heroism holy.

REMEMBER THE 6-MILLION.

Light a memorial candle to their memory in your home on Wednesday evening, April 8th, 1964.

Dr. Alvin Schiff of the New York Board of Jewish Education, who was present at the memorial, said, "I remember the kindling of the six lights by six survivors to commemorate the six million Jews who perished. This established a feature of all subsequent Yom Hashoah programs."

Reflecting on this historic event many years later, Rabbi Luban observed: "While in retrospect it seems so self evident, at the time, this Yom Hashoah program was unprecedented. There were survivors who wanted to blot out the ordeal that they had faced, which yet tormented their sleep, and was engraved on their flesh. . . . Who would come to such a gathering? And could we arrange a program that would be in consonance with the ideals of those that perished? We first began to appreciate the wisdom of Eli's suggestion, when we saw the outpouring of people from all walks of life, and the stirring of deepest emotion at our first Yom Hashoah Memorial."[4]

Following the first success at the Young Israel of Forest Hills, Eli devoted himself to persuading leaders of other communities to host similar events in their hometown synagogues. He used the occasion of the family's Passover vacation at Grossinger's, in the Catskill

Mountains in New York State, where many leaders gathered for the holiday, to launch this campaign. Eli came armed with thousands of flyers announcing the date of Yom Hashoah and the importance of marking it with a commemoration in their synagogues. He made it his business to attend every religious service so that he could talk up the significance of the program. Barbara Arfa, along with her parents, Regina and Salo Gutfreund, accompanied the Zborowskis to Grossinger's for Passover. She has vivid memories of the distribution of the flyers:

> The main dining room, seating 1,600 guests, was beautifully appointed with magnificent crystal chandeliers, white starched tablecloths and fine china. People began to gather in the lobby for lunch about twenty minutes in advance of the meal. The doors that had large glass windows were never locked, but guests respected the need for the waiters to set the tables without any disturbance. Each day, Eli was among the early arrivals, but unlike the rest of us, he came with armfuls of flyers.
>
> There was a small window of opportunity for flyer distribution. One had to wait until the waiters had finished their tasks and had returned to the kitchen. Just before the doors were officially opened to allow guests to enter, Eli would open one of the doors slightly and slip in to start placing flyers on each of the 1600 seats. He often enlisted the help of his son Murry and on one occasion, I too helped out. Eli didn't ask permission from the management to do this because it probably would not have been granted. Being Eli, he was smart enough not to ask. The purpose was simply to get the job done.

Murry, then a teenager, remembers feeling resentful about having to perform this task. He says, "While my friends were going out to play tennis or for the famous walk to the lake, I was stuck giving out leaflets about the Holocaust." When he complained to his mother, she responded calmly, "Just do it!" And when he said, "*Why?*" she said quietly, "Because you can."

John Maxwell, who writes on the subject of leadership, says that "true commitment inspires and attracts people."[5] And so it did. The commemoration started by Eli at the Young Israel of Forest Hills encouraged other synagogues to do likewise. By 1968, other houses of worship were beginning to have their own Yom Hashoah memorials. Some members of the Young Israel of Forest Hills feared that this would adversely affect the attendance at their synagogue. Eli allayed their fears by sharing his convictions with regard to the priorities: "The most important issue is not our own attendance, but the fact that more and more synagogues begin to adopt Yom Hashoah as an annual event." He felt that it would remain a day of remembrance only if synagogues, the quintessential symbol of Judaism, would take ownership of this hallowed day along with their communities. In a letter in the *Forward* on October 2, 2009, titled "Queens Shul's Shoah Commemoration Was Ahead of the Times," Eli was quoted as saying: "As a survivor of the Shoah who has long been committed to the cause of remembrance, I am grateful to see that Yom Hashoah commemorations have now become an annual event—institutionalized in houses of worship throughout the world."

* * *

The last year of Eli's presidency (1968) coincided with his son Murry's bar mitzvah. In honor of this occasion, Eli established the Moshe Zborowski G'milat Chesed Fund in memory of his father, for whom Murry is named. The fund, based in the synagogue and dedicated to acts of loving-kindness, as indicated by its name, provides interest-free loans to those in need. Salo Gutfreund was the first administrator of the fund. It is currently administered by Steven Savitt, an attorney who is a vice-president of the Young Israel of Forest Hills.

Eli inaugurated the fund to perpetuate his father's legacy of assisting the poor. "On Fridays, when my father came home from the mikvah," Eli has explained, "he would send me with envelopes of money to distribute to friends in need. He wanted the money to reach them before the Sabbath so that their day of rest would not be spent worrying about financial commitments they would have to meet early in the following week."

In appreciation of his service to the synagogue, Eli was invited to be the guest of honor at the annual dinner at the end of his presidency. He accepted, on one condition—"that all the money raised in excess of the previous year, would be set aside as an endowment to buy property across from the shul to build a youth center."

As with most other goals he set for himself, Eli succeeded with this one as well. He left the presidency with $70,000 in the endowment fund.

American Zionist Youth Foundation

In the early 1960s, Charles Bick, an activist member of the Young Israel of Forest Hills, became involved in organizing the American Zionist Youth Foundation (AZYF), an umbrella organization for all the Zionist youth groups in the United States. Bick invited Eli to join the board of trustees of this pioneering effort. Eli gladly accepted. This gave him an excellent outlet for his strong Zionist convictions which he had not had an opportunity to actualize since his youth in Poland and as a youth leader in the American Zone of Germany between 1945 and 1948.

The AZYF worked in cooperation with the Jewish Agency's Youth and Chalutz Department, a body that directed its services toward youth and Zionist education in the Diaspora. AZYF represented the department in the United States and promoted Israel-oriented programs, such as Zionist education on college campuses, trips to Israel for young people, and sponsoring Israeli *shlichim* (emissaries) to Zionist Youth organizations and American summer camps.

A major project of AZYF was the Salute to Israel Parade, which takes place annually in the spring in New York City. Inaugurated in 1964, the parade is the largest single gathering in the world in support and celebration of Israel and its people. Eli became chairman of the parade. From the beginning, the parade reflected his philosophy of inclusiveness. It enables communities to come together in a nonpartisan, nonpolitical show of unity and solidarity with their brothers and sisters in Israel. It attracts participants from all across the country. In addition to the tri-state area of New York, New Jersey, and Connecticut, groups come from Boston, Washington, Baltimore, and as far away as Los Angeles.

Participants representing Jewish day schools, synagogues, youth groups, and Hillel organizations march in groups with T-shirts and costumes reflecting their identity. The parade traditionally features beautifully decorated floats, lively marching bands, street performers, clowns and jugglers, scores of motorcycle riders bearing Israeli flags, celebrities, dignitaries, and politicians from the United States and Israel. Each year it attracts 100,000 marchers as well as hundreds of thousands of spectators. It conducts a year-long educational effort geared toward the participating marching groups.

Ruth Kastner, the professional responsible for the parade during the years that Eli was its chairman, comments on his leadership style and efficacy:

> Under Eli's leadership, the Parade became a much bigger operation. He initiated a Chai Club for those who agreed to pledge $18,000 to help defray the cost of the Parade.[6] At first he involved people he knew professionally and in business. When he secured a number of pledges, he reached out to people he didn't know and impressed them with the cause. He was responsible not only for the Parade's growth and expansion, but for enhancing the reputation of the Salute to Israel Parade throughout the country.

> Eli was a Chairman "par excellence." He taught me what true leadership should be and how things should be done. I learned from him how to approach people; how to talk to people; and how to be both gentle and firm at the same time. He was a gatherer—bringing together different factions of the community for a common cause.

> His leadership was truly inspirational. He was not just a spokesperson, but deeply involved in the operation. He was a wonderful mentor who allowed me to develop as a professional. While he wanted to keep abreast of progress, he did not micro-manage my activities. He was very accepting and generous with his time and always available for my questions and concerns.

Eli was ultimately appointed chairman of AZYF. As both an ideal-ist and a realist, he used his business acumen to help the organization grow and flourish. During the golden age of his leadership, AZYF's fifty staff members included field workers throughout the country, educational consultants responsible for an array of special projects.

American Federation of Jewish Fighters, Camp Inmates and Nazi Victims

Lou G. Siegel's kosher restaurant, located on Broadway at 37th Street in New York City, was for many years the central address for Jewish organizations to conduct business. The massive menu of tradi-tional Jewish food, plus the specials of the day, recited without a mo-ment's hesitation by waiters who had served the same customers for a decade or more, left the clientele satiated and filled with goodwill. It was not surprising, therefore, that Eli chose Siegel's as the venue for the first planning meeting to establish an umbrella organization of survivors. Eli was impelled to form this organization because he felt that after the war it was important "to set aside all our differences and to work together for common causes such as fighting anti-Semitism, searching for war criminals and speaking in one voice about the im-portance of remembrance."

Gideon Hausner, formerly Israel's attorney general and chief prosecutor in the Adolf Eichmann trial and now chairman of the Yad Vashem Council, was in New York at the time, and Eli used the op-portunity of his availability to convene the meeting at Siegel's in May of 1970. In calling the meeting, Eli sought broad-based representation of survivors. Among those present were Eugen Gluck from Romania; David Weiss from Hungary; Sidney Shtern from Carpatho- Russia; Sewek Robins, president of the Jewish Fighters; Sam Skura, president of the Zaglembia Survivors Organization; Ben Geizhals, president of the Cracow Survivors; Solomom Zynstein, Labor Zionist Survivors Organization; Alex Friedman, Czechoslovakia survivor; Ben Meed, Joe Tekulsky, and Robert Born, Warsaw Ghetto Resistance Organiza-tion (WAGRO); and Tuvia Bielski from Belarus, who had organized the largest armed rescue of Jews by Jews during World War II. The Bielski partisans have been immortalized in Defiance, a book by Ne-chama Tec which has been made into a movie by the same name.

Sam Gruber, Rabbi Israel Miller, Eli, and Tuvia Bielski, head of the largest armed rescue of Jews by Jews during the Holocaust. (1976)

At the meeting, with Gideon Hausner present, the American Federation of Jewish Fighters, Camp Inmates and Nazi Victims was established with Eli as its founding president. It was the first umbrella organization of Holocaust survivors in the United States. Eugen Gluck, a concentration camp survivor, recalls: "Eli was the originator and force behind it. Most of us were preoccupied with establishing ourselves and making a living, and the idea of this organization seemed a little remote from our day-to-day concerns. But Eli was so determined and persistent about it. He felt so strongly. He was always in the forefront and when he took on a project, he never let it fall by the wayside."

While most survivors firmly believed in the need for an umbrella organization, WAGRO, the Warsaw Ghetto Resistance Organization, opposed it. Its members felt that they would lose their autonomy and would not properly be able to advocate their mission. They feared being swallowed up by the larger organization. After assurances were given that the autonomy of separate organizations would continue to be supported, WAGRO agreed to join the Federation, a body that could speak for all survivors.

The projects and achievements of the American Federation of Jewish Fighters, Camp Inmates and Nazi Victims were numerous and varied. It commissioned, from Yad Vashem, and organized the first traveling exhibit of the "History of the Holocaust." The exhibit featured photos and documents that were displayed on college campuses and at schools, as well as in synagogues and community centers all across the country. The exhibit was a dramatic and vivid educational experience for thousands of Americans who until then had been unaware of the dimensions of the Holocaust. The exhibit was supplemented by the services of the Federation Speakers Bureau.

David Rivlin, Consul General of Israel, at the New York City opening of the exhibit *Holocaust and Resistance*, 1972

American Federation of Jewish Fighters, Camp Inmates and Nazi Victims First Annual Dinner on December 12, 1976 at the Waldorf Astoria, New York City. Diana and Eli Zborowski were the honorees: Sam Skura, Eli, Diana, Joseph Tekulski

The following letter from a high school principal in New York is typical of the many received in 1977:

Our students will never forget the words or the message delivered by Mr. Sam Skura. All the words that come from the most eloquent history teacher or the most comprehensive textbook can never replace the impact of hearing a survivor of the Holocaust. . . . Students who have heard the words of a survivor will never forget what the Holocaust was and what needs to be done to prevent the tragedy from happening again. . . . We are most grateful to the American Federation of Jewish Fighters, Camp Inmates and Nazi Victims.

In the area of remembrance, the Federation supported all the commemorations of ghetto uprisings to remind the world that there were heroic moments in the midst of the tragedy—Jewish resistance movements that electrified the world. At the initiative of the Federation, the Day of Remembrance, Yom Hashoah V'Hagvurah, was placed on the calendar of all major Jewish organizations and cultural institutions. Every year the Federation distributed thousands of educational kits prepared by Yad Vashem. For example, for the observance in 1981, more than 26,000 posters, booklets, and program packets were distributed. Some 300 Holocaust and Resistance exhibits were sent to organizations, institutions, and groups throughout the country. Special praise was expressed by the Department of Programs of the United Synagogue of America for the Federation's role in providing information on how to organize and observe this day of remembrance. It cited the Federation "as the organization which brought Yom Hashoah to public prominence."

Cooperation was a key word in the life of the Federation. Jewish organizations were delighted that there was a vigorous organization of survivors ready to join forces with others in serving the community.[7] The Federation was instrumental in organizing rallies and demonstrations for the survival of the Jewish people and was the first organization in the United States to register the names of Holocaust victims on Pages of Testimony for permanent inscription at Yad Vashem in Jerusalem.

In 1976, the organization held its first annual dinner at the Waldorf Astoria Hotel in New York City. For their tireless efforts on behalf of the Federation, Diana and Eli Zborowski were selected as guests of honor. Greetings from major Jewish leaders throughout the world were published in the Dinner Journal, among them Katriel Katz, Israel's ambassador to the Soviet Union; Stefan Grayek, the founding president of the World Federation of Jewish Fighters, Partisans and Camp Inmates; and Dr. Alvin Schiff, executive vice-president of the Board of Jewish Education of Greater New York.

Addressing the more than 300 guests at this gala event, on December 12, 1976, Eli said:

We are survivors of the darkest days in man's existence. We live in the present with its many challenges and struggles. But we still live with the past. Yesterday's tragedies will be with us tomorrow and for all the tomorrows after that . . .

We who survived, we who physically and emotionally lived through it, have a special challenge and obligation to forever remind the world of the events of the 1930s and 1940s . . .

We have learned that whenever and wherever Jews are denied human rights, the whole world suffers. . . . On this our First Annual Dinner, we wholeheartedly pledge that we will continue our educational work so that the Holocaust will never be forgotten and will never occur again, and so that Jews will live in freedom and with dignity.[8]

Eli has played a key role in many organizations dedicated to the preservation of Jewish memory. He was appointed by Mayor Edward I. Koch to the New York Permanent Commission on the Holocaust. He was appointed by President Jimmy Carter and reappointed by President Ronald Reagan to the United States Holocaust Council, which oversees the operation of the Holocaust Memorial Museum in Washington, D.C. His involvement with the Conference on Jewish Material Claims Against Germany will be explored in Chapter 11, "On the World Stage."

Guest of Honor
Kether Shem Tov Award

ELI ZBOROWSKI
Young Israel of Forest Hills
Forest Hills, New York

Distinguished Jewish Leader,
Defender of Zion, Builder of Torah,
Standard Bearer of the
Jewish Tradition

Rabbi Shimon said: There are three
crowns, namely the Crown of Torah, the
Crown of Priesthood and the Crown of
Royalty, but the Kether Shem Tov—the
Crown of Good Name—excels them all.

Invitation to the Orthodox Union National Dinner in 1982, announcing Eli
Zborowski as the Guest of Honor and the recipient of the *Kether Shem Tov*
(Crown of Good Name) Award.

Charles Drukier, Eli, Julius Berman
Orthodox Union Annual Dinner in 1982.

ELI ZBOROWSKI'S AWARDS and HONORS

Year of the NEGEV Award – State of Israel Bonds
   Presented on December 9, 1962

In Grateful Recognition of our Esteemed Member and Past President
of Young Israel of Forest Hills – 17th Annual Banquet
   Presented on January 13, 1968

Israel's 25th Anniversary – Israel Silver Jubilee Award
Young Israel of Forest Hills Division
   Presented on May 23, 1973

Award for Outstanding Participation in the State of Israel Bonds
   Presented on November 24, 1974

Yeshiva University Heritage Award
   Presented to Diana and Eli Zborowski in 1975

Kether Shem Tov Award
Orthodox Union National Dinner
   Presented on February 22, 1982

Albert Einstein College of Medicine of Yeshiva University Award
To Diana and Eli Zborowski – Founders
   Presented in 1983

Outstanding Leadership Chairman of the SALUTE TO ISRAEL
PARADE
   Presented in 1984

Leadership and Commitment Award Groundbreaking
at the United States Holocaust Memorial Museum
   Presented on October 16, 1985

Benefactor Award on Behalf of the Yad Vashem Remembrance
Authority
Diana and Eli Zborowski, Benefactors, Valley of Communities
   Presented on October 30, 1985, Yad Vashem, Jerusalem

Israel Appreciation Award – State of Israel Bonds
The Elie Wiesel Holocaust Remembrance Award Dinner
        Presented on December 19, 1987

Israel President's Club Award
        Presented on December 10, 1989

In Honor and Gratitude for being instrumental in establishing
The Canadian Society for Yad Vashem
        Presented on October 27, 1991

International Society for Yad Vashem Remembrance Award
Presented to Diana and Eli Zborowski
        Presented on October 27, 1991

American Israel Chamber of Commerce and Industry, Inc.
Award for Dedication and Leadership as President from
1984-1988
        Presented on November 13, 1991

Emunah of America – Remembrance Day
        Presented March 9, 1995

Commendation Letter from the President of Israel, Ezer Weizman
        Presented on November 5, 1995

American Society for Yad Vashem – Clarion Award, 2000

Honorary Doctorate – Yeshiva University
        Presented on May 24, 2001

Eli Zborowski Day – Borough of Queens
Presented by President of the Borough of Queens, Helen Marshall
        November 15, 2002

Lifetime Achievement Award to Eli Zborowski
In Appreciation from Yad Vashem, Jerusalem
        Presented November 19, 2006

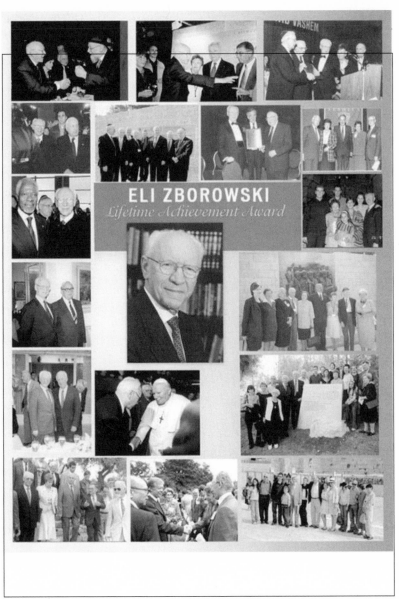

25th Anniversary Dinner of the American & International Societies for Yad Vashem, November 2006

Chapter 9 Notes

1. Alan Deutschman, *Walk the Walk: The #1 Rule for Real Leaders* (New York: Portfolio, 2009), p. xi.

2. Yom Kippur, the Day of Atonement, is ushered in with the *Kol Nidre* prayer. Following the prayer there is traditionally an appeal for money to support the synagogue. Since one is prohibited from handling money on the holiday, cards are distributed with fold-over tabs to indicate the size of the donation.

3. Translated from Hebrew by Dr. Alvin Schiff

4. Excerpts of Rabbi Marvin Luban's message in the Journal of the First Annual Dinner of the American Federation of Jewish Fighters, Camp Inmates and Nazi Victims, December 12, 1976. Many of the messages and essays in this publication were in Yiddish.

5. John C. Maxwell, *The 21 Indispensable Qualities of a Leader: Becoming the Person Others Will Want to Follow,* (Nashville: Thomas Nelson, 1999), p. 18.

6. The Hebrew word *chai* means "life." The numerical value of the letters is eighteen.

7. Ibid.

8. Excerpts of Eli Zborowski's message in the Journal of the American Federation of Jewish Fighters, Camp Inmates and Nazi Victims, December 12, 1976.

❧ Chapter 10 ❧

HOLOCAUST EDUCATION

Establishment in 1975 of the Eli and Diana Zborowski Interdisciplinary Chair for Holocaust Studies and Research, at Yeshiva University.

Eli, Diana and Lilly with Rabbi Dr. Norman Lamm,
President, Yeshiva University

CHAPTER 10

Holocaust Education

Survivors who came to America soon after the liberation were eager to put the past behind them and get on with building a new life. They tended not to talk about their painful wartime experiences to their American neighbors and friends; how could someone who had not confronted the brutality and humiliation possibly understand? Furthermore, Americans, although ready and willing to help them get settled, were far less enthusiastic about hearing their harrowing stories of survival. As a result, the agonizing memories remained shrouded deep within their souls.

Linking Up with Yad Vashem

Unlike most survivors, Eli felt strongly that remembering the past was vital to the future of the Jewish people. He was not deterred in the least by the fact that nobody was doing anything in terms of Holocaust education at that time. However, he needed advice on how to proceed. This prompted him to make an appointment to see Dr. Alvin Schiff, who was then the supervisor of the Department of Day Schools and Yeshivot for the Jewish Education Committee of New York and later became the executive vice-president of the New York Board of Jewish Education. Dr. Schiff remembers that meeting in remarkable detail:

I met with Eli in the board room of the Jewish Education Committee of New York on 58th Street. I recall that we were sitting catty-corner from each other in one corner of the big conference table. I couldn't help but be impressed with his commitment. He spoke to me in his broken English with lots of Yiddish phrases. We really communicated with each other—we were definitely kindred spirits.

I shared with him some of the difficulties I had had in trying to introduce Holocaust education into the curriculum of the Hebrew day school in Far Rockaway in the early 50s. There were a number of parents who objected. They said it was not good to expose the children to the horrors and the violence. I countered this by reminding them that the children are exposed to this on television every day. But there was no convincing them.

Still, Eli wanted to try to initiate community-wide programs regarding Holocaust education. I suggested to him that this kind of endeavor, if it is to succeed, cannot be a one-man operation. He can be an innovator and a motivator, but he must be able to communicate his message to other leaders if he wants it to spread. I recommended that the next step would be to seek out "something great on the horizon and to attach your wagon to that star." I proposed that perhaps he should link with Yad Vashem.

Eli did link with Yad Vashem. In 1970, through the efforts of Katriel Katz, chairman of the Yad Vashem Directorate, Eli commissioned a traveling exhibition on the history of the Holocaust for dissemination throughout the United States. Dr. Yisrael Guttman, then a research assistant and now a pre-eminent Holocaust scholar, wrote an explanatory booklet to accompany the exhibit. In addition, a notable scholarly work published by Yad Vashem, *Polish-Jewish Relations During the Second World War*, by Emmanuel Ringelblum, was distributed by the American Federation of Survivors. On May 4, 1974, Dr. Yitzhak Arad, chairman of the Yad Vashem Directorate, wrote a letter thanking Eli for spearheading this effort.

In the early 1970s, Eli was appointed by the Conference on Jewish Material Claims Against Germany to represent it as a member of the Yad Vashem Directorate. He ultimately founded the American Society for Yad Vashem in 1981—an organization that will be discussed in detail in Chapter 12.

The Eli and Diana Zborowski Interdisciplinary Chair in Holocaust Studies

Eli's vigorous outreach efforts in planning and organizing the first Yom Hashoah commemoration in the United States at the Young Israel of Forest Hills in 1964 led to his becoming a familiar and respected figure in the Jewish communal world. His offer to sponsor the first Yom Hashoah event at Yeshiva University (YU) in 1969 was enthusiastically received. The program, open to the entire YU community and the public, focused on the lessons of the past and the sober implications of the Holocaust for the future. Eli's support of this event for many years enabled students to hear from important scholars and personalities in Jewish affairs. Guest speakers included Elie Wiesel, Herman Wouk, Arthur B. Morse, Rabbi Dr. Irving Greenberg, Rabbi Herschel Schacter, Katriel Katz, and Prof. Lucy Dawidowicz.

Through his involvement with the American Federation of Survivors, it became evident to Eli that there was a burgeoning interest in Holocaust studies. But where would teachers and scholars be trained to fill this critical need? In the early 1970s, questions of this kind prompted him to seek an institution of higher learning that would be willing to develop a professorial chair in Holocaust Studies that he would endow.

Rabbi Israel Miller, vice-president of Yeshiva University and a passionate advocate for the interests of Holocaust survivors, facilitated the project. In the spring of 1973, Rabbi Miller arranged a meeting with Dr. Samuel Belkin, the president of Yeshiva University. This led to the creation of the world's first permanent professorial chair in interdisciplinary Holocaust Studies. It was named in honor of Eli and Diana Zborowski for their visionary support.

Rabbi Israel Miller, Vice-President, Yeshiva University; Diana
and Eli Zborowski; Dr. Samuel Belkin, President, Yeshiva
University at the Heritage Dinner in 1975 when the Eli and Diana
Interdisciplinary Chair for Holocaust Studies was announced

Dr. Herbert C. Dobrinsky, who was present at the meeting and
now serves as vice-president for university affairs at Yeshiva University, reflected on his first encounter with Eli:

My impression of him was that of a very unusual man,
different from other survivors. As a result of his vision and his
tenacity, Eli distinguished himself not only as a businessman,
but in scores of communal endeavors. He was an intellectual
who came not just with sentiment, but with a plan. And his
plan was to raise awareness of the Holocaust through Yom
Hashoah commemorations, through the publication of *Martyrdom and Resistance* and through teaching about the Holocaust at a university level. He felt that he survived for the
purpose of fulfilling the mission of remembrance.

As an institution that is deeply rooted in the culture and traditions
of European Jewry, Yeshiva University was the ideal venue for the

chair. Throughout its history, YU has maintained strong ties with its European heritage. In the years before and after World War II it attracted continental students and scholars and harbored refugees and survivors of Nazi persecution. The faculty and student body, the majority of whom are of East European descent, include large numbers of survivors and children and grandchildren of survivors for whom the horrors of the Holocaust remain a part of the fabric of their daily lives.[1]

In speaking about the significance of the chair, Dr. Belkin said: "For the first time there will be a higher educational program in Holocaust Studies sufficiently comprehensive to enable students to major in the field at both the undergraduate and graduate levels. We plan to offer young men and women of commitment the skills to become teachers, scholars and specialists in Holocaust Studies who can create and implement programs in the field at other universities, in high schools, other educational institutions and cultural centers."[2]

On this occasion, Eli received the university's prestigious Heritage Award "as a pioneer of major endeavors to perpetuate the memory and lessons of the Holocaust . . . and in recognition of the outstanding leadership in advancing the cultural and spiritual heritage of Judaism through sustained achievement in behalf of the educational causes promoting the enlightenment of our young people." Announcements about the establishment of the chair appeared in general-readership as well as Jewish newspapers throughout the country, including the *New York Times* and the *New York Post*.[3]

In subsequent years several Heritage Award Dinners were held in support of the chair. Among those honored were Sam and Stella Skura in 1981 and Isak and Sally Levenstein in 1986.

The Zborowski chair has been the central resource in the development and coordination of Holocaust Studies at Yeshiva University. Under the guidance of the first chairholder, Professor Lucy Dawidowicz, more than a dozen courses in a wide range of Holocaust Studies—historical, philosophical, theological, literary, pedagogical— were taught each year in the undergraduate and graduate schools. As a scholar and author, Dawidowicz inspired students to enter careers in Holocaust Studies and to become teachers in universities, Jewish day and afternoon schools, and public schools—all of which urgently needed qualified instructors on the period of the Holocaust.

The establishment of the chair was a proud moment for survivors. It provided them with the opportunity to employ their experiences, abilities, and services to help shape a fitting memorial so that the grim lessons of the past would never be forgotten. Eli invited many fellow survivors to serve on a Holocaust Advisory Committee that was established in conjunction with the chair. Among the survivors who participated were Joseph Wilf, Joseph Distenfeld, Eugen Gluck, Arie Halpern, Sam Halpern, Mr. and Mrs. Isak Levenstein, Jack Pomerance, Sam Skura, Marvin Zborowski, and Solomon Zynstein.

Dr. Norman Lamm, who succeeded Dr. Belkin as Yeshiva University's third president, vigorously pursued the pioneering scholarly programs of his predecessor. Lamm, who has written and lectured widely on the subject of the Holocaust, supplemented the broad range of courses in Holocaust Studies with the development of a Center for Ongoing Research on the Holocaust.

In 1983, Dr. Jeffrey Gurock, a leading historian of American Jewry, was appointed Yeshiva University's program coordinator for Holocaust Studies, a position he held until 2003. In addition to Dr. Lucy Dawidowicz, chairholders have been Dr. Erich Goldhagen, Dr. Lucjan Dobroszycki, and Dr. Joshua Zimmerman, the current holder of the Eli and Diana Chair of Interdisciplinary Holocaust Studies.

Conferences, Lectures, and Teaching Guides

One of the first projects of the Interdisciplinary Holocaust Studies program was committed to the study of modern Jewry and to laying a foundation for learning from it. In 1976, in conjunction with the Stone-Saperstein Center for Jewish Education, a conference on Teaching the Holocaust was convened. The conference, aimed at attracting educational professionals, tackled the problem of how to teach and what to teach about the Holocaust. An outcome of the conference was the establishment of the Institutes on Teaching the Holocaust. These three-week institutes, held during the summers of 1978 and 1980, provided elementary and secondary teachers with the opportunity to study intensively the history of the Holocaust and various strategies for teaching it.

An educationally significant outcome of the conferences was the publication in 1981 of *Issues in Teaching the Holocaust: A Guide*, edited by Robert S. Hirt and Thomas Kessner This outstanding volume was truly a pioneering effort and is as relevant today as it was at the time of its publication thirty years ago. Part I of the collection of papers focuses on teaching the Holocaust, and Part II spotlights several important aspects of Holocaust history. In the lead essay, Dr. Norman Lamm, president of Yeshiva University and member of the President's Commission on the Holocaust, presents a framework for studying the Holocaust:

There can be no understanding of Jewish character, of Jewish destiny, of the Jew's place in the world, and of the current unfolding of the Jewish drama, without study of the grisly and still incredible events of the World War II period. Moreover, there is also simple and practical urgency to informing the next generation about what happened to the last one.

A Holocaust that happened once can happen again. Once breached, the walls of human restraint remain weakened. . . . We must determine how best to go about transmitting to new generations of Jews what happened to our people that almost made it impossible for Jews ever to survive on this planet. . . . No effort must be spared in keeping the memory of the Holocaust alive for both Jew and non-Jew.

The volume's other contributors are listed below with brief synopses of their essays:

"Jewish and Psychological Factors in the Teaching of the Holocaust" by Dr. Menachem M. Brayer, the Stone-Saperstein Professor of Education at Yeshiva University, presents an argument for the psychological benefits to be derived from a full study of the Holocaust with all of its terrifying questions and lessons.

"Theological and Philosophical Responses to the Holocaust" by Dr. Walter S. Wurzberger, associate professor of philosophy at Yeshiva University, and editor of *Tradition: A Journal of Orthodox Jewish Thought*, discusses a broad philosophical base for interpreting the Holocaust for Jews. It also speaks to the issue of Jewish ethical attitudes toward gentiles after the Holocaust.

"Some Counsels and Cautions in Teaching the Holocaust" by Professor Lucy S. Dawidowicz, author of the acclaimed *War Against the*

Jews, 1933–1945 and other important studies in Jewish history, offers some thoughts on what teachers ought to consider in preparing a lesson on the Holocaust theme.

"Obsession and Realpolitik in the 'Final Solution' " by Professor Erich Goldhagen., Harvard scholar, offers an overview of the role played by anti-Semitism in the Nazi worldview, concluding that Nazi anti-Semitism was *sui generis,* a unique blend of rational calculation and unreasoned fanaticism.

"Christian Response to the Holocaust" by Professor Alice L. Eckhardt of Lehigh University's Department of Religious Studies investigates the issue of Christian response and uncovers a deeper relationship between Christian beliefs and Jewish suffering, giving serious thought to this thorny issue.

"The Response of American Jewry to Nazism and the Holocaust" by Dr. Jeffrey S. Gurock, associate professor of Jewish history at Yeshiva University, surveys the literature on the sensitive question of the American Jewish response to the Holocaust. Offering no easy answers, it makes clear that the unsympathetic atmosphere then prevailing helped limit the kind of aid American Jews could elicit from their host society.

Prof. Lucjan Dobroszycki held the Eli and Diana Zborowski Interdisciplinary Chair in Holocaust Studies from 1984 to 1995. During his tenure, he emphasized the importance of gathering scholars to conduct impressive new research in the field. To this end, he organized a series of conferences that attracted researchers from around the world who produced important monographs in the field of Holocaust Studies. Dr. Robert M. Shapiro, one of Dobroszycki's students who edited two volumes of these conference proceedings, commented that "Dobroszycki was dedicated to a clear-eyed elucidation of the catastrophe that befell the Jews during the Second World War . . . and was committed to principled analysis of events on the basis of contemporaneous primary sources."

Several major conferences that resulted in published works took place under the sponsorship of the Zborowski chair. In 1991, it supported a conference on the Holocaust in the Soviet Union—one of the first academic efforts to use Soviet documents. The proceedings were published as *The Holocaust in the Soviet Union: Studies and Sources on the Destruction of the Jews in the Nazi-Occupied Territories of the USSR, 1941–1945,* edited by Lucjan Dobroszycki and Jeffrey S. Gurock (New York: M.E. Sharpe, 1993).

Similarly, in 1993, a conference titled "Individualization of the Holocaust" led to the publication of *Holocaust Chronicles: Individualization of the Holocaust through Diaries and Other Contemporaneous Personal Accounts,* edited by Robert M. Shapiro (Hoboken, N.J.: KTAV and Yeshiva University Press, 1999). Finally, a 1995 conference examining journalism's role in reporting on the Shoah resulted in the publication of *Why Didn't the Press Shout? American and International Journalism during the Holocaust,* edited by Robert M. Shapiro (Hoboken, N.J.: KTAV and Yeshiva University Press, 2003). This book makes clear that "for a variety of reasons, the press did not effectively cover the Holocaust, one of the central events of the twentieth century. . . . it was one of the greatest ethical, professional and political failures of the news media during World War II."

In 2000 Dr. Joshua Zimmerman, who succeeded Dobroszycki, convened a conference on "Polish-Jewish Relations during the Holocaust and After: New Perspectives." These deliberations were published as *Contested Memories: Poles and Jews during the Holocaust and its Aftermath,* edited by Joshua Zimmerman (New Brunswick, N.J.: Rutgers University Press, 2003).

Subsequently, Zimmerman organized the first international conference on the Holocaust in Italy. These proceedings were published as *Jews in Italy under Fascist and Nazi Rule, 1922–1945,* (New York: Cambridge University Press, 2005)

Zimmerman anticipates that as the Eli and Diana Interdisciplinary Chair in Holocaust Studies approaches its thirty-sixth anniversary it will continue to promote study of the Holocaust through conferences and scholarly publications and to offer Yeshiva University undergraduate and graduate students core courses in the Holocaust and East European Jewish history. Going forward with special seminars such as "From Catastrophe to Sparks of Renewal: Polish Jewry, 1939–2009," it will expose students to the history and culture of East European Jewry since 1945. Zimmerman is convinced that "interest in the Holocaust is far from waning as the grandchildren of survivors fill my classrooms eager to learn. They are passionately committed to Holocaust remembrance."[4]

Martyrdom & Resistance:
The First Newspaper Devoted to the Holocaust

From its inception in 1970, the American Federation of Jewish Fighters, Camp Inmates and Nazi Victims began fulfilling its purpose with a wide range of programs and services. It soon became clear to Eli that this would not suffice unless the Federation's work could be brought to a broader and more influential audience. Although it was not exclusively an educational project, the inauguration in 1974 of *Martyrdom & Resistance (M&R),* a bi-monthly newsletter under the auspices of the Federation, had a major educational impact on the teaching of the Holocaust.

It started as a four-page house organ, with three pages in English and one in Yiddish, *mama-loshen,* the mother tongue of most of its readers. *M&R* was the periodical of record that highlighted the role of survivors, in terms of their personal stories and their achievements in advancing the cause of remembrance.

In an article in the collection *A Legacy Recorded,* Eli describes the genesis of *M&R* and acknowledges with thanks all those who played a pivotal role in the impressive development of the periodical:

I held conversations with Rabbi Luban about the compelling need to have a formal avenue of communications whereby we could express our feelings, give direction to Holocaust studies, inform the public on critical issues, and highlight events the survivors sought to share with others and among themselves. It was Rabbi Luban who introduced me to Dr. Harvey Rosenfeld, then editor of the National Council of Young Israel's *Viewpoint. . . .* This is how Dr. Rosenfeld was brought to the attention of the Federation and that's how *Martyrdom & Resistance* was born, with Harvey Rosenfeld as its editor.

. . . We pay special tribute to our first editorial board: Marysia Felberbaum, Icek Shmulevitz and Roman Weingarten.

Marysia was an articulate force in seeing that the voice of survivors had the proper forum in our paper. . . . Icek, a skilled writer who was so sensitive to the experiences and needs of the survivors, guided our Yiddish pages.[5]

In 1994, in an article titled *"M&R*: A Periodical of Achievement," Harvey Rosenfeld wrote: "It was not long, however, that the publication became more than a platform for survivors. . . . From the beginning readership of less than 5,000 survivors, the paper increased its circulation until it now stands at 50,000. This includes researchers and scholars in Judaica; public and college libraries; rabbis and other religious leaders; Jewish organizations; and government officials. Readers are found throughout the United States, Canada, Mexico, South America, Europe, Israel, South Africa and Australia."[6]

Perhaps the most meaningful praise for *M&R* came from a colleague in another Jewish periodical. In an article for the *Yonkers Jewish Chronicle,* editor Carolyn Weiner wrote: "Among the dozens of newspapers and magazines that cross my desk each month, there is one newspaper that never fails to move me tremendously. It is called *Martyrdom and Resistance* and it is the newsletter for the American Federation of Jewish Fighters,  Camp Inmates and Nazi Victims. It moves me, I believe, because unlike the televised *Diary of Anne Frank* or *Playing for Time* . . . I feel the spirits of the martyred who, in a sense, live on through this extraordinary, informative newsletter."[7]

Teaching the Lessons of the Holocaust

Over the years, *Martyrdom & Resistance* has published articles that provide both insights and practical material on teaching the Holocaust. Dr. Eva Pallay, an educational consultant with expertise in Holocaust curricula, paid tribute to the significant role of *M&R* as an educational tool in *A Legacy Recorded.*

As a professional educator, I can attest to the improvement of my skills through careful reading of the periodical (*M&R*). It is a veritable eye of the Holocaust, with a fascinating blend of material; dreams of the martyred, who did not live to realize them, details of demons and sadists from the Third Reich, reviews of the latest cinema, and poignant recollections from the liberators and the liberated.

One must single out for praise the *Index of Martyrdom and Resistance,* painstakingly compiled by Dr. Harvey Rosenfeld. In tandem with the microfiche, this resource opens a wealth of information for educators. There are more than 350 articles on every type of community programming, Holocaust studies in schools and discussion of curricula in Israel, Canada, Sweden and West Germany, to name a few countries.

In November, 1979, I was privileged to be the Executive Director of an educational program in conjunction with the International Year of the Child. The program was chaired by Eli Zborowski, editor-in-chief of *M&R*, and cosponsored by many prestigious dignitaries, organizations and schools. A memorial was erected at Eisenhower Park in East Meadow, NY and a program was arranged for 2,000 school children. *M&R* fully recorded the program for all to adopt and teach.

Martyrdom & Resistance, whose readers include several thousand teachers, scholars and other concerned with the pedagogical aspects of the Holocaust, has developed into a treasured resource in the ongoing process of learning. . . . To conclude, it will teach young and old—*zachor, gedenk,* remember![8]

Modifications and Impact Today

Inaugurated in the fall of 1974, *Martyrdom and Resistance* was the first periodical devoted to the Holocaust. From 1974 to 1985 it was published by the American Federation of Jewish Fighters, Camp Inmates and Nazi Victims. Since 1985, the American Society for Yad Vashem has continued its publication.

In 2006, Yefim Krasnyanskiy became the editor. Under his stewardship, several modifications were introduced to the sixteen-page format. In addition to changes in content and layout, the paper now includes four color pages. Undoubtedly, the most significant change is the availability of *M&R* on the Internet since the fall of 2006. According to Krasnyanskiy, "This has vastly expanded our readership to include many more young people. One of these young people is a Jewish white-collar criminal serving time in an upstate New York correctional facility. He discovered *M&R* in prison and wrote and asked to be placed on our mailing list."

Today's publication includes news from vastly expanded sources and addresses issues that affect not only survivors, but members of the second and third generations. It also features articles about how the Holocaust has changed the social and political climate in the world. Krasnyanskiy says, "We are looking at the Holocaust not only as the most tragic event in Jewish history, but as a global calamity."

In reflecting on its thirty-six year history Eli says: "In the beginning, I sent *M&R* to anyone I thought would be interested. The primary mailing list was the members of the American Federation. It expanded over the years and there are now about 50,000 people who receive it. On an ongoing basis it generates considerable interest. We consistently receive letters of appreciation and donations ranging from one dollar stuffed into an envelope by an aging survivor in a long-term care facility to checks from the general population that are sometimes in six figures."

Chapter 10 Notes

1. *Yeshiva University Holocaust Studies: An Overview,1975–1985* (New York: Yeshiva University Archives, 1986)
2. *Yeshiva University News,* June 6, 1975
3. Ibid.
4. Prof. Joshua Zimmerman in *HOPE,* American Society for Yad Vashem 2008 Commemorative Journal
5. Harvey Rosenfeld and Eli Zborowski (eds.),*A Legacy Recorded: An Anthology of Martyrdom and Resistance* (New York: Martyrdom and Resistance, 1994), p. 30.
6. Ibid., p.12.
7. Ibid., p. 13.
8. Ibid., pp. 220–221.

❧ Chapter 11 ❧

ON THE WORLD STAGE

Greeting Pope John Paul II
at Yad Vashem

On the World Stage

In 1942, speaking Polish as a member of the ZOB, the Jewish resistance fighters organization, Eli Zborowski assisted Mordechai Anielewicz, commander of the Warsaw Ghetto uprising, in crossing the Polish-German border. Later on, speaking Spanish, he founded a highly profitable import-export business in Argentina, Panama, and Mexico, and then in Portuguese he expanded that business to Brazil, becoming president of Sheaffer Latin America, the number-one pen-maker south of the United States. In Hebrew, he exchanges ideas with fellow members of the Yad Vashem Directorate, and in English, he engaged the late John Cardinal O'Connor on a guided tour of the Yad Vashem campus. Speaking Russian and German, he saved the life of a German soldier facing execution by lying to a Red Army officer. And in 2000, he returned to his native Polish to greet Pope John Paul II at Yad Vashem.[1] Eli has accompanied President Mikhail Gorbachev, Secretary of State George Shultz, Vice-President Al Gore, and President George W. Bush on tours of Yad Vashem. Eli Zborowski is a cosmopolitan who speaks many languages and strides confidently on the world stage.

Polish-Jewish Relations

Immediately following the Six-Day War in 1967, the Soviet Union broke off its diplomatic relations with Israel. Soon afterward all the Communist satellite countries, including Poland, also severed their relations with Israel. As the vice-president of the World Federation of Polish Jews, Eli campaigned to send a delegation to Poland to improve relationships. In 1977, after two years of demonstrations in front of Polish consulates in major cities throughout the world, the Polish government finally allowed the delegation to come to Poland, with the proviso that no Israelis would be among the delegates. The head of the delegation was originally to have been Rabbi Alexander Schindler, the president of the American Federation of Polish Jews. Schindler had been born in Germany, but his father was from Poland and in consequence he identified very strongly with Polish Jewry. At the last moment, Schindler was unable to make the trip. He called on Eli to chair the delegation in his stead.

In respect to negotiating, Eli said "I learned from my father how to think strategically and how to achieve one's goal through reasoned dialogue. Sometimes it is better to back off and take your time to respond rather than to confront immediately. I was, therefore, careful not to attack the Poles on anything specific, but rather to speak of our relationship in its totality."

This approach fostered an open and receptive dialogue. Still, Eli was very outspoken about the ingrained anti-Semitism of many Poles and the need for a better relationship—one in which the young generation would no longer view Jews as outsiders and Christ-killers. Prime Minister Mieczysław Rakowski admitted that it would undoubtedly take another few generations to overcome this prejudice.

The delegation of six people was also received by President Wojciech Jaruzelski. Given Poland's dependence on the Soviet Union, Jaruzelski explained to the delegation, he had to proceed cautiously. Still, he spoke about Israel in a friendly manner.

Eli returned from Poland via Israel to brief the Foreign Ministry on the talks with Polish officials. Dr. Yosef Govrin, former Israeli ambassador to Romania and head of the East European Department of the ministry from 1976 to 1985, described Eli's pivotal role in *Israel's Relations with the East European States: From Disruption (1967) to Resumption (1989–91)*:

> For the first time, a delegation of the World Federation of Polish Jews, which was located in the US, left for Poland to conduct negotiations with the authorities on obtaining historical documents and Jewish ritual and cultural objects, on the creations of memorials at Holocaust sites, and on the fate of Jewish (public) property that remained in Poland. Eli Zborowski, who was part of the delegation, visited Israel on his way back to the US to give his impressions of the visit to the Foreign Ministry in Jerusalem. His main points were the

following: The members of the delegation met with the minister of religions and minorities, with the secretary of the Polish government and with Polish Foreign Ministry staff members. The talks took place in a congenial atmosphere, and there was an exchange of letters dedicated to the topics mentioned above that mainly expressed the Polish government's readiness to begin serious negotiations with the organization—something the Polish authorities had refused to do for many years. Similarly, there was explicit discussion of transferring a number of historical documents to Israel.

On the final evening of the delegation's stay in Poland, Eli Zborowski was invited for a discussion with the minister of religions and minorities, Jerzy Kuberski, who knew that his guest was going to Israel on his way back to the US. The minister asked that he transmit 'to whomever he considered appropriate among the proper authorities in Israel' the main points of his message that the time had come to renew relations with Israel. Poland would not wait until the USSR would do so, and it was preferable to have resumed relations before 19 April 1978 (Holocaust Remembrance Day). Moreover, the minister said that the groundwork for this could be arranged by the invitation of Polish journalists to visit Israel, or through the Israeli representatives conducting negotiations towards the setting up of the Jewish Commemorative Museum at the site of the Auschwitz extermination camp, or by Israel agreeing to allow the Polish press agency (PAP) to post a representative in Jerusalem. The minister went on to say that he himself would look positively at an invitation to go to Israel as part of a delegation from Poland of the Righteous Among the Nations that would visit on the occasion of 19 April (Yad Vashem has such a program).

Zborowski added that, in light of my proposal on the eve of the delegation's departure for Poland, he had drawn Minister Kuberski's attention to the injustice the Poles had done to Israel and its Holocaust survivors by severing relations with Israel, a break that was accompanied by open anti-Semitic agitation, as well as to the damage that the severance had caused to the system of proper relations.[2]

During his negotiations with the Polish government on behalf of the World Federation of Polish Jews, Eli befriended Minister of Religion, Jerzy Kuberski. When Minister Kuberski visited Israel at Eli's invitation, he brought this 18th century menorah as a gift to the Jewish people from the Polish people. The menorah is displayed in the Synagogue at Yad Vashem, built through the generosity of Marilyn and Barry Rubenstein.

These talks paved the way for the Poles to express their desire to repair their image among world Jewry so that they could gain greater financial credit and attract Jewish tourism from the United States to Poland. They also indicated readiness to open negotiations with the World Organization of Polish Jewry.

During the negotiations, Eli developed a warm friendship with several ministers in the government. Among them was Mieczysław Rakowski, who subsequently became prime minister of Poland's last communist government. The day Eli was scheduled to leave Poland Rakowski appeared at the hotel with a package for him. It was a painting of Kazimierz, the Jewish town established by King Kazimierz the Great, who opened Poland to Jews in the fourteenth century. The town became a haven for Jews at a time when they were not allowed to live in the cities.

In his diary[3] Rakowski wrote on November 3, 1988:

Elzebieta and I met with Eli Zborowski and his wife, Diana. . .Through the years, Eli and I became very close. . . Eli is an exceptional person. Although his mother and her children left Poland in 1946, Eli's Polish is beautiful and he is interested in all Polish affairs. . .Eli is an example of a Polish patriot.

Eli with Klemens Podlejski, Mayor of Żarki in September, 2003, on the Avenue of the Righteous at Yad Vashem in Jerusalem.

Over the years, Eli nurtured close ties with several Poles. In addition to government officials and people from his hometown of Żarki, he became a close friend and confidant of Jan Karski, the Catholic Polish underground envoy who conveyed eyewitness accounts of the horrors of the Warsaw Ghetto and the death camps of Belzec and Treblinka to President Roosevelt and British Foreign Minister Anthony Eden. Karki urged them to take action, but failed to move them to save those who were still alive.

Eli and Jan Karski two years before Karski's death in 2000

In 1985, Eli met Professor Karski at a conference for liberators that marked the fortieth anniversary of the end of World War II. The conference took place in the halls of the U.S. State Department in Washington, D.C. Among the participants were generals of the Allied forces. Karski, who was one of the speakers, addressed the audience about his unfortunate encounter with President Roosevelt in which the president ignored his eyewitness descriptions of the atrocities perpetrated against Jews, asking only about the plight of the Polish farmers. As the conference proceeded, the similarity of their perspectives on key issues created a strong bond between Eli and Karski.

Jan Karski wrote to Eli on December 3, 1998:

Dear Sir,

I am older and am becoming weaker. The time has come to thank you, dear Sir, for your goodness and generosity extended to me over many years.

You are a noble man, sensitive to injustice and discrimination. You are always eager to show friendship towards those in whom you believe.

To the end of my life I will try to live up to your standards. I will always remember you tenderly and lovingly.

Now goodnight, dear sir.

Devotedly,

Jan Karski

In 1997, Eli attended a conference on the topic of Polish Jewry during the Holocaust sponsored by the Eli and Diana Zborowski Chair in Interdisciplinary Holocaust Studies at Yeshiva University. There he met Prof. Feliks Tych, a prominent Polish Jewish scholar. From the first they discovered they had a commonality of interests and shared a kindred spirit. When Eli went to Poland, he visited with Tych at the Jewish Historical Institute in Warsaw. On one occasion, at Eli's invitation, Tych accompanied Eli on a trip to Żarki. Tych was eager to see Żarki, but even more interested in spending a few hours with a man whose outlook he found so compelling. He said of his visit:

He was so very different from all the other Polish Jews. Most survivors from Poland are bitter. Eli was never bitter and he was very open to having good relationships with Poles. What I found fascinating was the way in which he interfaced with the people in his native town. He talked about the things he wanted to do for them and I was so pleased about the way they reacted. These were, of course, all gentiles as there is not even a single Jew left in Żarki. He talked to them with such respect and deference! It was really a lesson for me on how to carry on this kind of dialogue. Eli was fantastic! He did not in any way present the persona of the rich, bountiful American. He was very tactful and appeared to be one of them, a person who shared their concerns for this town, not just its past, but its future as well.

He showed me the house where his family had lived which provided me a journey into his past. This trip became a very important element in our friendship. He is one of the most important people I have met during my lifetime and has become a significant part of my biography. He is really a very noble person who carries within him a moral authority. There is between us a real meeting of the minds—a kind of brother-hood.

Eli told Tych of his interest in post-Holocaust research, a field in which Tych was working. Their subsequent collaboration will be discussed in the final chapter.

President   Warsaw, October 4, 2005
of the Republic of Poland

Mr. Eli Zborowski
Chairman of the American Society for Yad Vashem
Vice-President of the World Federation of Polish Jews

Dear Mr. Chairman,

Please accept my best regards on your 80th birthday. This wonderful
event is a perfect occasion to congratulate you on your rich life and life-
long work for Polish-Jewish understanding,

I strongly believe that man should be measured by his effort to help others. You have made great contributions to improve relations between our
nations by giving your best. I thank you very much for it on behalf of
Polish compatriots. I wish you continued strength, many years in good
health, satisfaction and pride in everything you have achieved.

With all due respect,

Aleksander Kwaśniewski

Work on Behalf of World Jewry

Acts of kindness and communal responsibility were part of the fabric of life growing up in the Zborowski household in Żarki. Every weekday at lunch the family was joined by a student from the local yeshiva, and Sabbath meals often included one or more of the local beggars who were warmly welcomed to the family table. On a regular basis, Eli was sent by his father with envelopes of money to be distributed to needy neighbors. Later in life, these traditions impelled Eli to become involved in Jewish organizational life locally, nationally, and globally.

The Conference for Jewish Material Claims Against Germany was founded in 1951 to secure a measure of economic justice for Jewish victims of Nazi persecution. It is an organization that advocates for Holocaust survivors worldwide, For years the board of the Claims Conference was made up of two representatives from each of its member organizations. In 2002, a decision was made to enlarge the board by designating a certain number of individuals as *ad personam* appointments. Eli Zborowski was appointed to the board in this capacity. He is actively involved in the organization, serving on the allocations, executive, membership, and memorial committees, and taking time from his busy schedule to attend meetings in the United States, Europe, and Israel. Saul Kagan, former executive vice-president of the Claims Conference, and currently its secretary and a special consultant, says: "Eli is very good to work with. He is well organized, articulate, energetic and determined. In advance of meetings, he shares with others the ideas he wants to present, and he readily engages in discussion of issues."

Eli's fine-tuned negotiating style has not gone unnoticed at the Claims Conference. Julius Berman, the president of the organization, observed; "At the beginning of a meeting, Eli will avoid confrontation. Once, in debate about an educational issue, a member of the board offered an unfounded premise. While Eli totally disagreed with the person, he prefaced his own remarks with 'I think you have said things that are valuable.' He did not let his differing view be known immediately. It took at least three or four minutes before anybody realized that he was disagreeing with the premise. He simply brought everyone along to his way of thinking, and before long he had discredited the other person in a definitive but gentle way." Julius Berman's conclusion: "I think this is brilliant!"

Visit of Pope John Paul II to Yad Vashem

While vacationing in Florida in the winter of 2000, Eli received a telephone call from Avner Shalev, the Yad Vashem chairman in Jerusalem, alerting him that Pope John Paul II was scheduled to make a historic trip to Israel and had expressed a wish to visit Yad Vashem. There would be a ceremony at Yad Vashem at which the pope was to deliver a special message to the Jewish people. Six survivors who had been saved by Christians were being invited to meet the pope. In his capacity as the distinguished founder and chairman of the American Society for Yad Vashem, and as a survivor who had been hidden by two Polish families, Eli was invited to be one of the six.

Eli's memories of the role of the Catholic Church in fostering anti-Semitism left him hesitant about accepting this invitation. While he felt that the Polish people, on the whole, were not anti-Semitic, he had very strong feelings about the church's influence in turning Poles from small villages against the Jews, especially those whose sole access to information and opinions was what they heard in church. Eli ultimately overcame his reluctance and decided to accept the invitation. He was the only American in the group of six. This generated a media frenzy in the United States even before he left for Israel.[4] The first article to appear was in *Newsday,* which sent a reporter to Eli's home as he was packing for the trip. It described Eli's wartime experience, and his communal activities, and then continued:

> The pope's planned visit to Yad Vashem has acquired special significance in recent weeks. Last Sunday, the pope apologized and asked forgiveness for the sins committed by Catholics against humankind over the last 2,000 years. That apology did not specifically mention the Holocaust, spurring calls by some Jewish leaders for a stronger statement from John Paul. Many Jewish leaders expect the pope to elaborate on his apology when he visits Yad Vashem. "The pope's statement last week was a very important step toward recognizing the

church's role in persecuting Jews," said Zborowski. "But the pope can say something more direct to the Jewish people about the Holocaust and church's silence during this period."[5]

The ceremony at Yad Vashem took place on March 23, 2000 in the awe-inspiring Hall of Remembrance, which houses the ashes of concentration camp and extermination camp victims and a large *ner tamid*, an eternal light. Eli recalls the historic moment when the pope walked over to meet the six eyewitnesses to the Holocaust:

I was the first of the six survivors to greet His Holiness. He walked over with his hand stretched out. I greeted him in Polish, saying, "We are very pleased to see His Holiness in the land of Israel, the independent Jewish state." We then spoke for a moment about my hometown, Żarki, which was close to a monastery with which the pope was familiar, and a few words about my Polish rescuers. While we talked, the pope squeezed my hand and did not let go of it.

Pope John Paul later met separately with survivors and their families from Wadowice, his hometown. He asked after Jews whom he had remembered, like the baker where his family bought rolls each morning. He remembered people by name, and exhibited tremendous humanity in his interest and desire to connect with those who came to pay their respects to him. I could see tears rolling down his cheeks when a letter was read from a mother to the Christian woman who was hiding her child. The mother pleaded with the woman to wrap her child in a shawl when she took him out into the cold.

When Eli returned home, he was again interviewed by several media outlets from all over the world. He told *Catholic New York* that at Yad Vashem the pope told the Jewish people that the church is "deeply saddened by the hatred, acts of persecution and displays of anti-Semitism directed against the Jews by Christians at any time and in any place." While there were many who were disappointed that Pope John Paul did not address the silence of Pius XII during the Holocaust, Eli was grateful to the pope for recognizing the Jewish state by making the visit and by meeting officially with Israel's president, prime minister, and chief rabbis. Eli considers this encounter one of the most memorable experiences of his life, because it enabled him to be a witness to a historic moment that signaled a change in the attitude of Christians toward world Jewry.

Eli with Prime Minister Yitzhak Rabin of Israel

Secretary General Kofi Anan and Eli at the United Nations

Eli with Russian Prime Minister Mikhail Gorbachev at Yad Vashem

Eli with Prime Minister Ariel Sharon of Israel

Advocating World Justice and Understanding

When Eli arrived in the United States, the first apartment he rented was in a low-income, racially mixed neighborhood in the Bronx. While his friends questioned this decision, Eli harbored no racial prejudice. He was comfortable with, and respectful of, his neighbors, many of whom were new immigrants like himself. They, too, had to struggle with the English language and with trying to eke out a living and make a better life. His experiences both before, during, and after the war have made him a true citizen of the world. He has been a vocal advocate for justice and understanding in a variety of public forums.

In 1991, a series of riots in the Crown Heights neighborhood of Brooklyn unleashed a barrage of anti-Semitism among African-Americans who lived in the area. Eli responded with an opinion piece in the *New York Amsterdam News,* a newspaper read mostly by African-Americans:

THE NEW YORK
AMSTERDAM NEWS
Saturday, October 12, 1991

Blacks, Jews and Adolph Hitler
By Eli Zborowski

Blacks in Crown Heights are chanting "Heil Hitler! How little people learn from history. At the 1936 Olympics in Berlin, Jesse Owens, the Black track star, stepped up to compete in the broad jump. The stadium was hushed for the man who was expected to break a world record that day. Adolph Hitler decided to leave rather than watch a Black man disprove his theories of racial superiority.

As was the American custom, Owens took a practice run straight through the broad jump pit. The German referee called it a fault! Only three tries were permitted, and Owens had lost one. He ran down the track and made a winning jump. The German referee ruled that Owens had stepped over the takeoff mark.

Carefully, so that everyone could see, Owens drew his own line six inches ahead of the official takeoff. Then he walked back to the starting point and with a six-inch disadvantage won the gold medal. Much later, Jesse Owens remembered the event in an interview with TV Guide: "There were no more angry people than Black Olympic competitors in Berlin in 1936. We had insults thrown at us by our host nation; Hitler didn't accord Negroes and Jews the same courtesies he did others who came to Berlin. That made us more determined to prove that in the eyes of God we were every bit as good as any man."

This was not the first time that Hitler linked Blacks and Jews. After World War I, France occupied the Rhineland with Black troops. In his insane hatred of non-Aryan people, Hitler wrote in *Mein Kampf:* "It was and it is the Jews who bring the Negroes into the Rhineland, always with the same secret thought and clear aim of ruining the hated white race by the necessarily resulting Bastardization."

It is foolish to think that those who hate Jews will be friends of Blacks. We must as Ben Franklin said, "hang together or we shall surely hang separately."

An article in *The New York Times* in March 2001 addressed the issue of Polish-Jewish relations, but failed to discuss some of the nuances that Eli experienced during and after the war. His response to the article exemplifies his sense of fairness, and his willingness to credit acts of courage in the midst of overwhelming hatred and murder.

Eli's letter to the editor, which appeared on March 22, 2001, was titled, "Poles Who Killed, Poles Who Saved." Although Poles had murdered his father, he said, "the remaining members of my family—my mother, my two siblings and I—were given refuge by Polish neighbors who kept us hidden for 18 months at the risk of their own lives. Given this, how can one possibly generalize about the Polish people? While the rescuers were few in number, compared with the murderers, their heroism has been given substantial recognition.. . . In addition, thousands of ceremonies honoring Christian rescuers in the Garden of the Righteous Among the Nations at Yad Vashem Jerusalem have been widely publicized in the world media."

In 2001, murals painted by the famous Polish Jewish artist Bruno Schulz were found hidden behind the wall of a food pantry in Ukraine. With the approval of local authorities in Drohobycz, where the murals were found, the artworks arrived at the Holocaust Martyrs' and Heroes' Remembrance Authority in Jerusalem. This set off a flurry of outrage in Ukraine and in the worldwide art community. Eli's response, the lead letter in the *New York Times* on June 20, 2001, defended Yad Vashem's actions.

The Battle Over the Murals of Pain

To the Editor:
June 20, 2001

Re "Artwork by Holocaust Victim Is Focus of Dispute" (front page, June 20): Leaving Bruno Schulz's artwork shrouded in a pantry in Ukraine is tantamount to posthumously victimizing this Polish Jewish artist who perished in the Holocaust. Given the horrendous conditions under which his murals existed, all the protests about their being removed to Yad Vashem, the Holocaust Martyrs' and Heroes' Remembrance Authority in Jerusalem, ring hollow.

On the contrary, the Polish and Ukrainian authorities should be pleased that evidence of the tragedy that befell Bruno Schulz as a Jew should be returned to the Jewish people in their homeland. After the war, the Polish Jews who survived primarily relocated to Israel. Housing these creative treasures at Yad Vashem brings them back home to this population and to the millions of tourists who visit the world's largest repository of Holocaust artifacts.

ELI ZBOROWSKI
Chairman|
American Society for Yad Vashem

As part of a program marking Holocaust Remembrance Day in 2009, the United Nations planned to present the documentary film *Forgiving Dr. Mengele.* The film follows Eva Kor, a twin who survived the Holocaust, as she decides to forgive Dr. Josef Mengele for the torturous experiments he and his staff inflicted on her and her sister. In response to advance notices that the film would be part of the program, Eli wrote a letter of protest to the secretary general of the United Nations.

AMERICAN & INTERNATIONAL SOCIETIES
FOR YAD VASHEM, INC.

500 Fifth Avenue, 42nd floor, New York, NY 10110

212 220 4303–800 310 7495 – Fax 212 220 4308

www.yadvashemusa.org

January 12, 2009

Hon. Ban Ki-moon, Secretary General

The United Nations

Dear Mr. Secretary,

It is with profound distress that I write this letter concerning the United Nations' choice of showing the documentary film, "Forgiving Dr. Mengele," as part of the United Nations' Holocaust Remembrance Day. The film follows Eva Kor, a twin who survived the Holocaust, as she decides to forgive Dr. Josef Mengele for the torture he inflicted on her and her sister. The showing of the film, particularly by the United Nations, imparts the wrong message regarding one of history's most tragic times.

As you know, the atrocities performed by the Nazis and Dr. Mengele as the "Angel of Death" included systematically and "scientifically" torturing, maiming, and exterminating millions of innocent and helpless people, many of whom were children. This is beyond the world's forgiveness. Instead of forgiving, the world must hold those who committed these crimes eternally accountable to remind future generations of the perils in repeating this history.

Ms. Kor's forgiveness of Dr. Mengele is a personal choice. Forgiveness is the sole, personal choice of each victim of the Holocaust . Moreover, no person holds the moral right of assuming forgiveness on behalf of those who were murdered. By screening the film, the United Nations advocates a decision that many victims and those devoted to remembering the brutalities of the Holocaust feel is inappropriate. Sponsorship of the film sends the dangerous message that the world should collectively forgive those who perpetrated crimes during the Holocaust. It is particularly troubling for the United Nations—a body founded in the wake of World War II and devoted to combating brutality throughout the world—to be communicating this, and anathema to its founding principles. We therefore respectfully request that the United Nations not sponsor this film.

>Respectfully,
>Eli Zborowski
>Chairman

Within ten days, Eli had a reply from Kiyo Akasaka, United Nations undersecretary general for communications and public information. He said that the United Nations had received protests from numerous survivors and partner organizations, all of whom felt that the film was an inappropriate choice. In consequence, the United Nations had decided not to include the film in the Remembrance Day program.

Chapter 11 Notes

1. "Eli Zborowski, Of Things Past," *Lifestyles Magazine* profile, 2001
2. Yosef Govrin, *Israel's Relations with the East European States: From Disruption (1967) to Resumption (1989–91)*, (London: Vallentine Mitchell, 2011), pp 188–189.
3. Mieczław F. Rakowski, Political Diaries 1987-1990 (Editorial ISKRA, 2005), p. 298
4. The visit of Pope John Paul II to Yad Vashem was featured on 1,000 television news programs and generated more than 2,000 newspaper articles.
5. Mohammad Bazzi, "Forest Hills Holocaust Survivor to Meet Pope in Israel," *Newsday,* March 20, 2000.

❧ Chapter 12 ❧
FORGING A PARTNERSHIP WITH YAD VASHEM

Yitzhak Arad, Eli, and Avner Shalev

Forging a Partnership
with Yad Vashem

In the Beginning

Yad Vashem was founded in 1953 with funding provided by the Israeli government and a substantial grant from the Conference on Jewish Material Claims Against Germany. As a member of the Yad Vashem Directorate since 1969, Eli regularly attended quarterly meetings. He soon realized that it was consistently difficult for Yad Vashem to cover its expenses. A consummate problem-solver, he suggested that Jews all over the Diaspora should partner with Yad Vashem by contributing to its expenses in order to make it as vibrant and effective an institution as possible. However, there was a cultural disparity. The Directorate was not prepared to accept the understanding that fundraising is a respectful and compassionate way of supporting the mission of an institution such as Yad Vashem. They viewed asking for money as tantamount to being a *shnorrer,* a beggar. It took almost a decade, until about 1980, for them to appreciate that raising money in the Diaspora was a necessity in order for Yad Vashem to move forward.

Dr. Yitzhak Arad, chairman of the Yad Vashem Directorate talks about coming around to Eli's point of view: "I realized that despite the important work being done, extensive development was needed to turn the institution into a world center commemorating the Holocaust and its victims. . . . To attract visitors, the site had to be developed and enlarged. It was impossible to do so with the financial resources we received from the Israeli government. It was obvious that we needed a strategic partner, and the most natural partner would be the community of Holocaust survivors organized into a suitable framework."[1]

Once he had the support of the Directorate, Eli arranged a meeting
with Arad in New York, and invited Elie Wiesel to join them. As there
was already talk about the establishment of a Holocaust Museum in
Washington, Eli felt that it was particularly important for Yad Vashem
to establish a foothold in the United States and throughout the world.
Having decided to move ahead, they were faced with the need to de-
fine the nature of the relationship. Eli was opposed to being perceived
merely as "Friends." From the beginning, he viewed himself and other
survivors as partnering with Yad Vashem:

> In naming the organization, we were looking for the ap-
> propriate descriptive. Elie Wiesel was very helpful in this and
> suggested that it be known as a "Society." With this sugges-
> tion, two separate organizations were officially registered in
> the State of New York in December 1981—the International
> Society for Yad Vashem and the American Society for Yad
> Vashem.
>
> The people who had expressed an interest came from var-
> ious parts of the world. There were people from Brazil, where
> I was doing business. I also had contacts in Germany among
> survivors who went there after the war and did not relocate
> elsewhere. I told Yad Vashem that if these individuals were to
> be loyal donors, they would need some recognition for their
> philanthropic endeavors. This thought was very alien to the
> Directorate. While I spoke forcefully about the need to give
> recognition to donors, they were not ready to acknowledge in-
> dividual contributors by name. Nevertheless, I began raising
> funds, promising the donors that I would do something, but I
> didn't know what that something would be.

Launching the American Society for Yad Vashem

Alan Deutschman, who has extensively studied the key elements
of leadership, says that "leaders need to have an extraordinary belief
in their own ability to overcome obstacles as well as the potential for
their people to change."[2]

In preparing to launch the first meeting, Eli invited survivors he
had known and worked with in establishing the American Federation
of Jewish Fighters, Camp Inmates and Nazi Victims. They had been

inspired by his leadership in that venture and were willing to follow him in this one. These were people who were committed to Holocaust remembrance but were as yet unaccustomed to supporting an Israeli institution. To provide the necessary link with Yad Vashem, Eli invited Dr. Arad to be present at this meeting.

The meeting took place in the spring of 1981 in the home of Stella and Sam Skura of Hillcrest, New York. Also present in addition to the Skuras and Diana and Eli Zborowski were Rabbi Israel Mowshowitz, the spiritual leader of the Hillcrest Jewish Center, Paula and Henry Major, Paula and William Mandel, Etta and Henry Wrobel, and Celina and Marvin Zborowski. In his remarks, Dr. Arad underscored the centrality of Yad Vashem as the world's first and foremost institution dedicated to perpetuating the lessons and legacy of the Holocaust. Eli spoke about the funds needed to promote research and to disseminate information about the Holocaust, highlighting its lessons for generations to come. He secured $16,000 in pledges.

Following this success, a series of fundraising parlor meetings were held in various locations, each attracting another group of survivors. Those who served as hosts were Mr. and Mrs. Israel Krakowski of New York City, Mr. and Mrs. Isak Levenstein and Mr. and Mrs. Sam Halpern of Hillside, New Jersey, Mr. and Mrs. Mark Palmer of Chicago, and Mr. and Mrs. Solomon Gross of Rosedale, New York. Roslyn The interest and enthusiasm generated by these events was infectious. Arad observed that "not only was Eli willing to take the mission on himself, he knew how to gather around him a group of wonderful people . . . like Sam Skura, Arie and Sam Halpern, Harry and Joe Wilf and others."

The success and growth of the American Society for Yad Vashem was paralleled by the expansion of the International Society for Yad Vashem. Groups were established in Brazil, Canada, Chile, England, Mexico, the Netherlands, and Switzerland.

The first officers of the American Society were Eli Zborowski, chairman; Sigmund Strochlitz and Miles Lerman, vice-chairmen; Sam Skura, treasurer; and Sam Bloch, secretary. From time to time, Dr. Arad traveled from Israel to attend meetings. Here is Eli's account of one of them:

With Yitzhak Arad present, I outlined a plan to hold a series of parlor meetings for purpose of raising funds. Both Miles Lerman and Sigmund Strochlitz, who were vice-chairmen of our organization and were members of the recently established Council of the Washington Holocaust Memorial Museum, were opposed to this plan. They considered it inappropriate for the American Society to be engaged in fundraising. Sam Bloch agreed with them, and my only support came from Sam Skura. Since we could not come to an agreement, I suggested that we drop the subject.

Shortly thereafter, I called a general meeting and presented a new slate of officers selected by a nominating committee. Those who had been opposed to fundraising were no longer officers.

Decisions for the American Society are made by the board. In the event of an issue arising between board meetings, it is dealt with by the executive board. The major duty of the board is to approve the annual budget of the organization. In the absence of an executive director, the chairman serves in this capacity and is authorized to implement the budget throughout the year. It is the responsibility of the board of trustees to oversee two special funds: the Educational Fund and, since 2004, the 21st Century Fund, chaired by Leonard Wilf, who also serves as chairman of the board of trustees.

The board, originally made up mostly of survivors, began to include members of the second generation more than twenty years ago. Today it embraces members of the third generation as well as people who have no direct connection to the Holocaust but view support for the cause of remembrance as a historical imperative.

The establishment of the societies brought Yad Vashem both a concerned and involved constituency from abroad as well as financial backing for much-needed projects. This enabled Dr. Arad to embark on a plan of renovation of the Yad Vashem memorial site.

The construction of the Valley of Communities, described in detail in the following pages, was the first project for which the American Society for Yad Vashem undertook to raise money. During the nine years needed to build the Valley, the Society embarked on and successfully completed several other projects at Yad Vashem. The first of these was the Jewish Soldiers, Ghetto Fighters and Partisans Monument. Dedicated in 1983, just two years after the Society was established, it is the sole tribute to the 1.5 million Jews who fought Nazi Germany during World War II. Spearheaded by Frank Blaichman and Eli Zborowski, the project was chaired by Jack Pomeranc and Sam Skura, former partisans and active members of the American Society. On that memorable day, the monument was dedicated as Isadore Karten spoke on behalf of the partisans and Defense Minister Yitzhak Rabin delivered the major address.

In this first decade a number of other ventures were undertaken. The Children's Memorial is a tribute to the 1.5 million Jewish children who were brutally murdered during the Holocaust. Dr. Arad asked the talented, world-renowned architect Moshe Safdie to submit a model for the Children's Memorial. In Safdie's powerful and imaginative rendition, candles are reflected infinitely in the dark, creating an impression of millions of stars shining in the heavens as a voice recites the names of the children. This project was brought to fruition by the generosity of Edita and Abraham Spiegel and their friends from Los Angeles in memory of the Spiegels' son Uziel, who was murdered in Auschwitz at the age of two and a-half.

Other projects included the Yad Vashem Candelabra, a gift of Stella and Sam Skura and Celina and Marvin Zborowski; the Auschwitz Chimney, sponsored by David Feuerstein of Chile; and the Cattle Car Exhibit, a memorial to the thousands of deportees who perished on the way to the death camps. At Arad's request, the Polish government donated a cattle car to Yad Vashem in 1990. Moshe Safdie also designed and implemented this exhibit, a gift of Bernice and Izzy Merin of the United States and Benjamin Merin of Belgium.

The Valley of Communities and the Beit Hakehilot

Origins of the Valley

"Cargo. They were cargo . . . I rarely saw them as individuals . . . It was always a huge mass . . . naked, packed together, running, being driven with whips."[3]

This was the cold, heartless, impersonal assessment of Franz Stangl, commandant of Treblinka, as he looked down at the Jews being herded through the passageway that led to the gas chambers. Treblinka, one of the three death camps, along with Belzec and Sobibor, known as Operation Reinhard, was fifty miles northeast of Warsaw. Originally a punitive labor camp for Poles, it was converted in July 1942 to kill Warsaw Jews and later Jews from other areas in Poland and Western Europe.[4] Among them were the Jews of Żarki—Eli's childhood friends, good neighbors, and his beloved grandparents, uncles, and aunts.

As Eli approached the Treblinka site on a visit to Poland in 1977, images of the selection process cluttered his mind He could see before him the arrival in crowded cattle cars of those who were too weak to walk and were summarily shot and those who were able-bodied, segregated by sex, stripped of their clothing, their valuables, and their hair. Within hours they were all gassed to death.

Yet, at the time of Eli's visit, there was nothing left of the death camp save the ashes and bones of the people who perished there. The guide who accompanied the group was careful to point out where the ashes were buried. In 1966, the Polish government had erected engraved stone walls at the entrance of the Treblinka death camp as a memorial to the 840,000 Jews who were put to death there by the Germans. They also erected a cemetery-like memorial with tombstones for each of the towns from which Jews were brought to this death camp. Entering the snow-laden grounds on a gray, blustery December day, Eli recalls:

Despite the frigid weather, I slowly began to review the towns, most of which I recognized. I was really very impressed with this memorial built exclusively by the Poles. It was moving to see that they chose to have these towns remembered. I soon spotted towns from my immediate neighborhood, but I could not find Żarki. I became overwhelmed with desperation. Could they have forgotten Żarki? How is that possible?

The other people in our group, for whom this did not have the personal connection it did for me, were preparing to leave for our next destination, Majdanek. Although I did not have any means of transportation to rejoin the group in Warsaw, I decided not to leave and to continue my frantic search for Żarki. It was dreadfully cold and my nose would not stop running. Before long I ran out of tissues and had no more dry handkerchiefs. In the end, I could not find my town and began to walk away from this memorial of towns. When I looked back at the cemetery with pain and disappointment, I suddenly spotted the stone marked "Żarki." Because the inscription faced outward rather than toward the inside, and was situated at the very edge of the memorial, I had been unable to see it.

I ran back to the stone, fell to my knees, and began to sob. It was as if all my relatives and townspeople who had perished had gathered around me in a warm embrace. I was so overcome with emotion, I can no longer recall how I got back to Warsaw. I did not go to Majdanek—a site I have not seen to this very day.

Building a Monument to the Destroyed Communities

Eli returned from Poland via Israel. There, in addition to giving his report to Yosef Govrin, the ambassador for the countries behind the Iron Curtain, as mentioned in an earlier chapter, he met with the chairman of Yad Vashem, Yitzhak Arad, and shared with him this profound experience in Treblinka. At that time, Eli was a member of the Yad Vashem Directorate. He and Arad were in very close contact and continually engaged in discussions about how best to fulfill the Yad Vashem mission. Out of this interchange emerged the idea of erecting a memorial in tribute to the more than 5,000 Jewish communities that were destroyed during the Shoah.

Arad announced a competition to select architects for such a memorial. Lipa Yahalom and Dan Tzur, the architects chosen, proposed designing the memorial as a quarried remnant of a deep ravine, dug out of the existing rock with massive stone columns on which the names of the communities would be engraved. At Arad's suggestion, the Valley was constructed in the shape of a map of Europe. Arad's passion for the project impelled him to direct its implementation with tenacity and infinite attention to detail. To this very day, more than two decades later, the Valley of Communities stands as a matchless tour de force among Holocaust memorials.

The budget for this project was presented at $4.6 million. Eli felt that $6 million would be a more realistic figure and would also symbolize the six million Jews who perished. The first parlor meeting for the Valley was held in the home of Ellis and Israel Krakowski in Manhattan, with Gideon Hausner, then chairman of the Yad Vashem Council, as the guest speaker. Eli was barely able to raise $6,000 from twelve to fifteen of the almost sixty people who attended. He says: "I then revised my thinking and decided to ask for $60,000 from each potential donor. I easily got twenty donors. Interest in this project escalated rapidly among hundreds of donors. Individuals and organizations around the world were forthcoming with significant contributions, and we were ultimately able to cover the $14 million cost of the Valley."

The cornerstone for the Valley of Communities was laid at Yad Vashem in 1983 and the completed project was dedicated in 1992. It is a massive two and a half acre monument blasted out of natural bedrock. The names of over 5,000 communities are engraved on the thirty-foot-high stone walls of the Valley. The overall structure depicts the map of Europe and North Africa as it was at the time of World War II. Each name recalls a Jewish community that existed for hundreds of years and was destroyed during the Shoah.

Yitzhak Navon, President of Israel, Dr. Yitzhak Arad and Eli at the site on which the Valley of Communities would be erected in 1983

Eli and Diana in the Valley of Communities with grandchildren Ori and Tamar in 1992. Diana points to her hometown, Drohobycz.

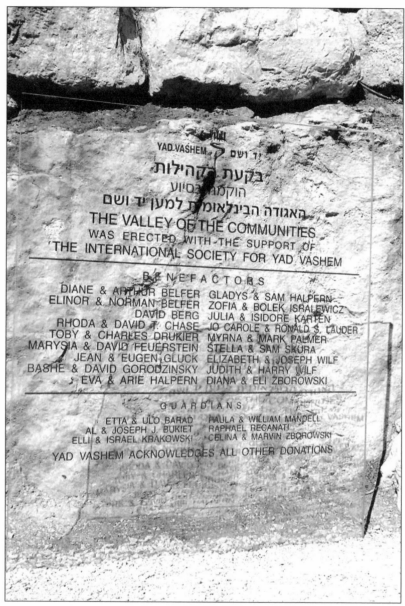

Valley of Communities Benefactors and Guardians

Preserving the Vibrant Life That Was Destroyed

In the center of the Valley of Communities stands the Beit Hake-hilot, the House of the Communities. Through changing exhibitions, lectures, and concerts, the Beit Hakehilot brings to life a world that no longer exists. It was created to elucidate the meaning and purpose of the Valley. As an educational and research center dedicated to dis-seminating computerized information about the vibrant religious, edu-cational, and cultural life of the communities that were destroyed, it enables visitors to appreciate the lives and livelihoods of those who perished.

The Beit Hakehilot was established through the generosity of Di-ana and Eli Zborowski in memory of their parents who perished dur-ing the Shoah.

Eli and Diana gather with family and friends at the Beit Hakehilot in 1993

Yad Vashem
The Holocaust
Martyrs' and Heroes'
Remembrance Authority

Ministry
of Education and
Culture Central Office
of Information

PROGRAMME

Inauguration of the
Valley of the Destroyed Communities

Under the patronage of his Excellency
the President of the State of Israel

Mr. Chaim Herzog

With the participation of the
Prime Minister of the State of Israel,

Mr. Yitzhak Rabin

Har Hazikaron, Jerusalem
Thursday, Tishri 5753
October 15, 1992
at 17:30

Entrance of the President of the State of Israel

National Anthem

Opening Remarks
Chairman of the Yad Vashem Directorate
Dr. Yitzhak Arad

Opening Address
The President of the State of Israel
Mr. Chaim Herzog

Greeting
Chairman of the International Society for Yad Vashem: Mr. Eli Zborowski
Chairman of the World Zionist Organization: Mr. Simcha Dinitz
President of the World Jewish Congress: Mr. Edgar Bronfman
Chairman of the International Council for Yad Vashem: Dr. Yosef Burg

Lighting of the Torches

Sound and Light Presentation on Jewish Communities Lost in World War II

Participants:
Chava Alberstein

The IDF Orchestra Aviv Choir
Conductor: Lt. Col. Izhak Graziani

The Ankor Choir
Conductor: Dafna Ben-Yohanan

Cutting of the Ribbon his Excellency the Prime Minister of the State of Israel
Mr. Yitzhak Rabin

Special prayer for the Destroyed Communities

Rabbi Yisrael Lau - Chief Rabbi of Tel Aviv-Yaffo

Master of ceremonies: Mr. Amikam Gurevich

Production of the programme:
Yad Vashem and Central Office of Information

Shein Audio-Visual Projection Ltd.

N.B.   Following the ceremony, The Valley of the Destroyed
Communities will be illuminated and remain open to visitors until 21:00

Impact of the Valley

Visitors come to the Valley to remember what was, to search for the communities in which they or their family members were nurtured. Walking through the courtyards, one feels dwarfed by the sheer size of the monument and awed by the enormity of what was lost. The following article by Esther Farber indicates the powerful impact of the Valley on visitors. In many ways it mirrors Eli's visit to Treblinka that inspired the building of the Valley.

We stood quietly on a hilltop at Yad Vashem, looking down into this national museum's newest, though yet unfinished, memorial to the six million victims of the Holocaust.

Small wildflowers, new life, pushed up among the terraced hillsides of Jerusalem stone, while far below us, rose up the walls of The Valley of the Destroyed Communities. Columns of massive stone blocks, jagged and roofless, lifted skyward. The pillars and walls symbolize the countries that contained the 5,000 Jewish communities that were totally annihilated in the Holocaust.

We maneuvered down a winding path among construction materials and unset slabs of stone and marble, until we reached the bottom and entered the memorial. A totally new perspective. Now we were looking up at the massive walls open to the sky. We were no longer in our beloved Jerusalem, but standing inside of Hungary, Poland, Austria, Germany, Czechoslovakia, and Russia. On the rough-hewn stones and polished marble were carved the names of the communities.

As we walked through, I became lost in the maze, in the story, and in my memories. I searched the pillars, scanning the etched names, hoping to find my birthplace, Bratislava, Czechoslovakia.

My father was born in Satmar and raised in Topolcany. My mother was born in Lemberg and grew up in Vienna. Both my sister and I were born in Bratislava. Had my father's family survived, I would have had ten aunts and uncles instead of only the two who escaped when we did.

I had seven cousins on my father's side, ranging in age from three to thirteen, all of whom were put to death in the camps.

I passed Berlin, Leipzig, Munich, Warsaw, Lodz, and Lublin, impatient and intent on finding one of my family's home towns. Knowing that our time was over, I almost gave up and started to head back to the entrance. There would be other visits, other years. Then, one of my friends came through a passageway and said, "I just saw Czechoslovakia, there to the left. I'll go with you."

We hurried back into the labyrinth and came to Hungary. Now there was a flash of recognition as I saw "Topolcany," my father's home. We took a picture to bring home to my dad. In the adjacent space was Vienna. Another photo. Finally we came to Bratislava, and as I posed beneath the column, my feelings crowded in at once. With barely time to explore what I was feeling, we walked away to rejoin our group.

Thinking back, the experience of standing inside The Valley of the Destroyed Communities was an awesome one, a mixture of sadness and love. I felt the presence of my lost family, who had only known me until December 1939, when I was a toddler, and who are now only shadows to me. Of the six million Jews, the five thousand communities, those few had held me and played with me. They were my powerful connections. I felt thankful that my parents had managed to escape to America, and grateful for the many years of life I have enjoyed. How lucky we were!

And then I thought of my three wonderful grown up sons, who got the chance at life and made so much of it, and I could no longer hold back the tears. How blessed I feel to have been spared, to have given life to three bright and accomplished members of a new generation, all of them committed to the vitality of Judaism. They and I stand in place of those who perished. [5]

Memorializing Victims through Pages of Testimony

For more than five decades Yad Vashem has led the historic mission to recover the names of the six million Jews murdered in the Holocaust. Under Eli's stewardship, the American Federation of Jewish Fighters, Camp Inmates and Nazi Victims joined with Yad Vashem in 1970 to assist in recording the names of Holocaust victims on Pages of Testimony.

In 1999 the American Society for Yad Vashem launched a nationwide Pages of Testimony campaign. This was a worldwide project to record information on all Jewish victims of the Holocaust and to archive them in Yad Vashem's Hall of Names. At the inauguration of the project, Eli said, "The victims deserve to be remembered not as cold anonymous numbers, but as individual human beings. Pages of Testimony will restore the unique identity and personal dignity that the murderers tried so hard to obliterate. The victims' last wish was, *zachor*—Remember! To understand this imperative, we need to understand that in the Jewish view, death is not seen as an end, but rather as another passage. The soul, which survives the body, demands that its identity be preserved."

This endeavor has deep roots in Jewish tradition. The biblical commentaries compare the people of Israel to stars that God counts when they come out and again numbers and names when they cease to shine. The Shoah victims went to their deaths without burial shrouds, without memorial prayers, and without gravestones. For the innocent victims, Pages of Testimony placed in Yad Vashem's Hall of Names serve as symbolic graves for the martyred Jewish people.

Through a massive media campaign and with the help of hundreds of volunteers trained for this specific task, the American Society has been responsible for collecting 10,000 Pages of Testimony. A central database of the names of more than four million Shoah victims can be accessed at www.yadvashem.org.

Changing the Yad Vashem Landscape

In 1993 Avner Shalev succeeded Yitzhak Arad as chairman of the Yad Vashem Directorate. Concerned with preparing Yad Vashem for the challenges of the next century, Shalev initiated the Yad Vashem

2001 master plan, a project encompassing an unprecedented expansion and renovation of the Yad Vashem complex to include a Holocaust History Museum, a Museum of Holocaust Art, an Exhibition Pavilion, a Visual Center, and a Synagogue.

In Shalev's words:

Together with the survivor generation we are responding to the challenges of the coming generations. The memory of the survivors and their legacy are the stones with which we build the bridge between the past and the future. As the generation of survivors dwindles, we have to find new ways to impart their story and their legacy. . . . The young generation shows great interest in the Holocaust and is seeking new ways to connect to the tragic history and the void that has been created in its wake. In order to address this quest we have devised the master plan Yad Vashem 2001. It will promote the development of new educational concepts, founded upon the expansion of our archives and library collections and scientific research, and will employ modern technology in the service of memory through the computerization of our databases and the production of innovative educational programs.[6]

In 1996, Shalev presented his vision for the transformation of the Yad Vashem complex to the board of the American Society. He spoke enthusiastically about the need to appeal to future generations with state-of-the-art technology and multimedia resources. Eli and the board wholeheartedly commended Avner's farsighted vision and agreed to become partners in Yad Vashem 2001. Joseph Wilf, a vice-chairman of the American Society, was appointed chairman of the Yad Vashem 2001 campaign. The contribution of the American Society to Yad Vashem 2001 was one-third of the total cost of $100 million.

The master plan was completed in 2005. Under Eli's dynamic leadership, members of the American Society for Yad Vashem assumed responsibility for a host of projects:

Eli, Joseph Wilf, Avner Shalev, and Ira Druckier at Yad Vashem in 1999

Eli, Leonard Wilf and Moshe Safdie at Yad Vashem in 2001

The Partisans' Panorama: Julia and Isidore Karten, Harry Karten, Marcia Toledano, and Berne Bookhamer

The Survivors' Wall, honoring Holocaust survivors: Gale and Ira Drukier

The Entrance Plaza, serving as a bridge between the everyday world and the sanctity of Yad Vashem: the Wilf Family in memory of Harry Wilf

The Visitors' Center: David and Fela Shapell

Bridge to a Vanished World: Mr. and Mrs. Jan Czuker

The Holocaust History Museum, the centerpiece of Yad Vashem 2001: the Harry and Judith Wilf Family and the Joseph and Elizabeth Wilf Family

Gallery in the Holocaust History Museum, "From Equals to Outcasts: Nazi Germany and the Jews": the Norman Braman Family Foundation

The Synagogue: Marilyn and Barry Rubenstein and Family

The Museum of Holocaust Art: Dr. Miriam and Sheldon G. Adelson

The Learning Center: Stella and Sam Skura

The Exhibition Pavilion: Tina and Steven Schwarz and Rochelle and Henryk Schwarz

Renewal of the Avenue of the Righteous Among the Nations: Gladys and Sam Halpern Family and Eva and Arie Halpern Family

The Visual Center: The Daniella and Daniel Steinmetz Foundation and Steven Spielberg's Righteous Persons Foundation

The International School for Holocaust Studies Building: Marilyn and Jack Pechter and Family

The Family Plaza, commemorating the Jewish family in the Holocaust: Ruta and Dr. Felix Zandman

The Library Building: Patrons of the Library, Marilyn and Jack A. Belz, and Philip Belz and Family

The Warsaw Ghetto Plaza Refurbishment: David and Ruth Mitzner, Ira and Mindy Mitzner and Family, and the Phyllis and William Mack Family

Differences in background and style between Dr. Arad, the outgoing chairman of the Yad Vashem Directorate, and the new incumbent,

Avner Shalev, required a period of adjustment. Yizhak Arad is a survivor who fought as a partisan in the underground. His immigration to Palestine led to service in the Haganah, the Palmach, and the Israel Defense Forces. He ultimately became a highly acclaimed Holocaust historian. There was a sense of shared history that generated acceptance, trust, and comfort between him and Eli. Avner Shalev, born and raised in Israel, came to the chairmanship with an entirely different perspective. Following a distinguished military career, he held key government posts in the fields of education and culture. To his role as chairman of the Directorate, he brought a new creative vision and a set of finely honed administrative skills. Because both Eli and Avner are strong-willed and persistent, their long-standing relationship, marked by mutual respect, has simultaneously been fraught with tension. Early on, however, Eli recognized Avner's ability and the importance of his mission, and he made every effort to be collegial. Grateful for this response, Avner acknowledged Eli's efforts to help make Yad Vashem 2001 a reality in the American Society's twentieth Anniversary Journal:

> I would like to pay tribute to my dear friend and colleague, Eli Zborowski, who in a pioneering initiative founded the American Society for Yad Vashem. He has been a partner ever since in fulfilling the sacred mission of commemoration and remembrance. In contending with the enormous challenges, Eli shouldered the mighty responsibility and brought an unrelenting devotion and enormous loyalty to this task. His words, *na'aseh v'nishmah,* "we will do and we will obey" (uttered by the Jewish people in the Book of Exodus upon receiving the Ten Commandments), still echo in my ears, and they have accompanied me throughout these many years of cooperation and deep friendship.[7]

The redeveloped Yad Vashem complex was designed by architect Moshe Safdie. Avner Shalev is the chief curator of the Museum complex.

With the new Holocaust History Museum as its centerpiece, the complex attracts more than two million visitors each year. The museum is a prism-shaped triangle, piercing the mountain with both ends cantilevering out into the open air. At the entrance, the interior is several feet high, and features scenes of prewar Jewish life. It narrows as chronologically successive exhibits depict the constricting options facing the Jews. As the museum nears its end, the floor begins to rise, the triangle opens up again, and the museum exits dramatically from the mountain's northern slope to a breathtaking view of Jerusalem.

The museum's exhibitions were designed by Dorit Harel to engage audiences through the personal narratives of eyewitnesses to the Shoah. To help visitors relate to the tragedy inflicted upon its victims, exhibits feature authentic artifacts, testimonies, diaries, and letters. This imbues the memory of the Shoah with depth and meaning, ensuring that the memory of those who perished and the voices of survivors will resonate for all generations. Visitors emerge from the museum experience with greater empathy for the fate of the Jewish people and a stronger will to work toward a more tolerant and humane world.

* * *

The partnership between the American Society and Yad Vashem continues to grow and flourish. Since its inception, the American Society has remitted more than $100 million to Yad Vashem. Eli views with pride the promise and potential of future generations in perpetuating the legacy.

Chapter 12 Notes

1. "A Message from Yitzhak Arad," *Yad Vashem, the Global Guardian of Holocaust Remembrance,* 25th Anniversary Journal of the American Society for Yad Vashem, 2006.

2. Alan Deutschman, *Walk the Walk: The #1 Rule for Real Leaders* (New York: Portfolio, 2009), p.164.

3. Franz Stangl in an interview with Gitta Sereny in *How Was It Humanly Possible? A Study of Perpetrators and Bystanders During the Holocaust,* ed. Irena Steinfeldt (Jerusalem: Yad Vashem International School of Holocaust Studies, 2002), pp.141–142.

4. Yehuda Bauer, *A History of the Holocaust*, rev. ed. (Danbury, Conn.: Franklin Watts, 2001), p.153.

5. Esther Farber was an American journalist and activist. This story, titled "Visiting the Valley: Sadness and Love," appeared in *Martyrdom & Resistance* 18, no. 9 (May–June 1992).

6. Avner Shalev in *A Time to Build—Eit Livnot: 20th Anniversary Journal of the American & International Societies for Yad Vashem,* 2001.

7. Ibid.

❧ Chapter 13 ❧
MILESTONES AND PASSAGES

Receiving Honorary Doctorate from YU

Left: Rabbi Dr. Norman Lamm
Right: Dr. Herbert Dobrinsky

Milestones and Passages

Educational Dreams

Moshe Zborowski was only eleven years old when World War I broke out. This catastrophic event brought with it the end of his formal education. While he went on to become a successful businessman, he frequently voiced his regret that he never had a full education. As a result, he was ferociously determined that his own children would be educated. When his three children were in elementary school, Moshe postponed his dream of going to Palestine so that the children would have at least completed high school before the family emigrated. This dream ended with the outbreak of World War II in 1939. For Moshe's son Eli, the turn of events was both turbulent and ironic:

> I was only thirteen years old. Even though Jewish children were not permitted by the Germans to attend school, my father made valiant attempts for our education to continue through private tutors. However, as the war escalated this too became impossible. Ironically. I found myself in the same position that my father did in his teen years. I, too, deeply regretted that the circumstances of the war brought an end to my education.
>
> I came to the United States without knowing English, and, with no time to go to school because I had to make a living for my family. Trying to get a formal education was totally unthinkable. I learned English through listening, from reading the paper, and from watching television.

It was not until half a century later that Eli would receive recognition from an academic institution, something that had eluded him earlier in life: the award of an honorary doctorate from Yeshiva University. At the university's annual commencement exercises in the spring, in addition to conferring degrees on its graduates, honors are bestowed on those who have made singular contributions in the fields of education, communal service, or government service or who have provided support to enhance the university's educational programs.

In March 2001, Eli received a letter from Rabbi Dr. Norman Lamm, president of Yeshiva University, informing him that he would receive a degree of Doctor of Humane Letters, honoris causa, at the spring commencement ceremonies. This letter provided a stunning interlude in a busy, hectic day at the office. While it filled him with joy and pride, it also elicited pensiveness and reflection. In his acceptance Eli wrote:

> It is at times like this that one cannot help but recall the traumatic journey that one has traveled in the more than five decades since the Shoah. At the tender age of sixteen, I went, in an instant, from being a carefree youngster to being orphaned, homeless and the person to whom my mother and siblings looked for safety and protection.
>
> In the intervening years, my wife and I have struggled to build a life and family in our adopted country. Personal burdens of having witnessed death and destruction have evolved into a communal commitment and responsibility. I thank the Almighty for having given me the strength to participate in this awesome task.
>
> Rabbi Lamm, I am profoundly grateful to you and to the esteemed institution over which you preside for bestowing this distinction on me.

The day of commencement, May 24, 2001, started with a breakfast in a private dining room at Madison Square Garden for dignitaries, the honorary doctorate recipients, and their guests. Eli shared this honor with several beacons of the Jewish community: Rabbi Ephraim Buchwald, founder of the National Jewish Outreach Program; Rabbanit Chana Henkin, founder and dean of Nishmat, the Jerusalem Center for Advanced Jewish Education for Women; and Ambassador Richard C. Holbrooke, chief negotiator of the Dayton Peace Accord, who was the commencement speaker. There was an air of exhilaration as the honorees greeted family and friends and picked up their academic caps and gowns. Amidst all the excitement, Eli had one additional surprise: His daughter Lilly, her husband Avner, their youngest daughter, Maya, as well as Eli's sister Tzila had flown in from Israel to be present for this momentous occasion. With his family gathered around him, Eli said, "To be joined for this important milestone by my brother and my sister with whom I grew up in Żarki, by my wife, my children and my grandchildren, is at least some compensation for the events that so disrupted our goals and dreams."

Eli had come to accept that his role in any graduation ceremony would forever be as a spectator but never an active participant. Now, on May 24, 2001, he stood proudly on the stage of the theater at Madison Square Garden, wearing a cap and gown as the citation was read before several thousand people, and his loyal and respected friends Julius and Dorothy Berman placed the academic hood around his shoulders.

Rabbi Dr. Norman Lamm with Eli as he is hooded by Dorothy and Julius Berman at the Yeshiva University Convocation in Madison Square Garden, 2001

Marking Fifty Years of Yad Vashem

In 1953, Israel's minister of education, the historian Professor Ben-Zion Dinur, presented the Knesset with the Yad Vashem–State Remembrance Authority bill. It established a Memorial Authority known as Yad Vashem in Jerusalem to commemorate the six million members of the Jewish people who died a martyr's death at the hands of the Nazis and their collaborators.

Dinur wrote: "The Yad Vashem Law, 5713-1953, is unique in that it has no precedent in any other country, since the topic with which the statute concerns itself is also unique and unparallel in human history. Yad Vashem also conveys the meaning of a place[1] . . . a place and a name, a name and a place. . . . The name also says that Israel, our land, and Jerusalem, our city, is the place for them and for their remembrance."[2]

Years later, on the fiftieth anniversay of Yad Vashem, a Declaration of Remembrance was issued at the residence of the president of the Israel, stating: "We now know the awesome voice that bursts forth from there, from the abyss, from the millions that were never laid to rest and from the words of the witnesses that have seared our souls. The sin and the crime give no rest and will continue to disturb humanity for all time to come."[3]

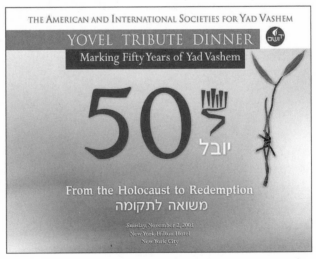

The American & International Societies commemorative journal marking the 50th anniversary of Yad Vashem in 2003

Delegations from all over the world traveled to Israel to attend the events marking this milestone. Before numerous dignitaries, including the president and prime minister of the State of Israel, foreign diplomats, and Avner Shalev, Chairman of the Yad Vashem Directorate, Eli Zborowski, who headed the delegation as chairman of the American & International Societies for Yad Vashem, delivered the following address:

I am deeply honored to have been invited to speak at this milestone event as a survivor of the Shoah and on behalf of the worldwide Societies for Yad Vashem.

As I stand here in front of the Warsaw Ghetto Monument, I am reminded of an unforgettable day early in 1942 in my hometown of Żarki, Poland, when Mordechai Anielewicz came through our town. He was on his way to the Zaglembia District to take command of the Jewish Fighters Organization. As an idealistic teenager of sixteen, I was captivated by this 23-year-old tall, handsome, charismatic resistance fighter. My conversation with him left me feeling empowered. His energy and optimism were contagious. He instilled hope in me and in my small group of friends. He inspired us to believe that the fast-growing underground movement could, in fact, resist the Nazi war machine that sought to annihilate us.

As we all know and as the annals of history have recorded, Mordechai Anielewicz became the commander of the Warsaw Ghetto Uprising. He personally led the uprising against the Germans that began on April 19th, 1943, on the eve of Passover.

Shortly before his death, Anielewicz wrote: "My life's dream has come true. I have lived to see Jewish resistance in the ghetto in all its greatness and glory."

Mordechai, had you lived you would have seen your dream for a self-reliant Jewish people expand and flourish. Just five years after you so valiantly gave your life, the world witnessed the birth of a Jewish State. The image of a proud and powerful Israeli Army would surely resonate deeply in your mind and heart, for you were in the forefront of protecting the defenseless.

And Mordechai, how we wish you could have shared our pride in the establishment of Yad Vashem, an institution dedicated to the Cause of Remembrance that stands majestically on *Har Hazikaron* in the heart of Jerusalem. Today we celebrate a half century of accomplishments.

Through our International School for Holocaust Studies, the Valley of Communities, the Historical Art Museum, the Partisan Panorama, the Hall of Names and scores of programs and services, each day we rededicate ourselves to fulfilling the last wish of the countless innocent victims. They hoped that the world would remember how they lived and how they died, and their prayers for the survival of the Jewish people and the Jewish spirit.

And finally, Mordechai, our most enduring achievement lies with our cherished young leadership—our children and grandchildren. They have joined us here today for the fiftieth anniversary and it will surely fall to them to mark Yad Vashem's centennial. How proud we are that we have raised successive generations knowledgeable about and committed to the perpetuation of the Jewish tradition and to the cause of remembrance!

The American Society had only been functioning for about a decade when Eli began to think about its future and embarked on a plan to involve the adult children of survivors. The first person from this generation to become a member of the board was Ira Drukier, the son of Toby and Charles Drukier, both Holocaust survivors. Ira is now a vice-chairman of the Societies and a member of the executive committee. He and his wife, Gale, were the benefactors of the Survivors Wall at Yad Vashem. The validity of Eli's decision is evident in the remarks Ira made at the opening ceremonies of Yad Vashem's fiftieth anniversary.

I am humbled to have been given the honor of delivering greetings at tonight's reception for the American and International Societies for Yad Vashem's extraordinary delegation.

Ira Drukier

This honor is two-fold. To be in the presence of some of the most devoted caretakers of the Shoah's history is itself a special privilege. And to participate in this fiftieth commemoration with the Societies' esteemed Chairman, Mr. Eli Zborowski, makes it even more special. Being here with Eli brings back fond memories of my childhood in our Forest Hills community. It was at the Young Israel of Forest Hills that, sitting with my dear father Charles, of blessed memory, on *Shabbat,* we enjoyed the company of Eli and his family—along with other brave Holocaust survivors who were among the *Shul's* congregants.

This leads me to a few words about my loving parents, Toby and Charles, of blessed memory. Among the many precious values that they instilled in me—even after experiencing the killing of their parents, siblings and only daughter, my sister—was the importance of both remembering the events of the Holocaust and living productive Jewish lives in its aftermath.

We, the generation of the children of survivors, attempt to emulate the actions of our survivor parents in many ways. We have taken upon ourselves the responsibility to honor our parents' heroic plight by establishing the eternal principle that our children's generation and their successor generations never forget the Shoah and its historic reverberations.

I assure you that as we assume the mantle of leadership in the important cause of Holocaust Remembrance, we will continue to support and strengthen the noble

mission and activities of Yad Vashem, the world's premier Holocaust Remembrance Authority. We will never stop pursuing evidence of the atrocities against our
people. With equal energy and determination, we will always acknowledge with deep respect and admiration the
heroic resistance of those individuals and groups who
used various means to oppose the Nazi onslaught. Con-
currently, we will continue to teach about that infamous
period, so as to prevent its recurrence through tolerance,
understanding and mutual respect.

This is our generation's pledge to all of you on this
momentous occasion of Yad Vashem's fiftieth anniversary. We are determined to never let you down. Thank
you very much.[4]

The Passing of Loved Ones

These two events—the Yeshiva University Commencement at
which Eli received an honorary doctorate and the fiftieth anniversary
of Yad Vashem—were the last major milestones at which Diana, Eli's
beloved wife of fifty-seven years, stood at his side. In the waning days
of 2004, Diana passed from this life following a six-month battle with
cancer.

We cannot understand the void that Diana's passing created for Eli
unless we comprehend the depth of their relationship:

Diana was a partner in all I did. When I came home in the
evening, I liked to share the business activities of the day with
her. Strange as this may seem, it was exactly what my father
did after a day of work. He came home and shared everything
with my mother, what he said, what the customers said and
did, what he bought, what he sold. It was therefore natural for
me to do this as well. It was also fortunate that I had in Diana,
an intelligent, receptive ear. She genuinely participated in my
thinking and in my business. She was a partner in my business
life as well as in my communal activities.

She was very smart and alert. She had the ability to ana-
lyze a situation quickly and give me a short answer that was

insightful and wise. Sometimes she assessed something differently than I had and I would find myself re-evaluating my original thinking.

If I was sometimes hesitant to do something that seemed to be the proper direction, she would simply say, "What are you waiting for?" in order to get me to the next step with more confidence. She was very straightforward and could not tolerate people who were not honest. She was fully supportive of all our philanthropic activities, which we always discussed in advance. People often referred to me as the head of a variety of activities. Diana's response was "Let him be the head, as long as I'm the neck, because the head can't move without the neck."

Their relationship was steeped in love and admiration for each other. Whenever Eli was involved in an important meeting in the office, he would have his secretary hold his calls. That meant all calls except from Diana. Those were sacrosanct. The conversation with Diana would begin in English, quickly move to Yiddish, and invariably end up in Polish. He frequently referred to her as *Shepseleh*—my little lamb, or even more endearingly as *Shepsie*. It was very clear that whatever language they spoke, it was always the universal language of pure love.

Their daughter Lilly's reflections on her parents' bond offers some additional dimensions: "They had their differences. My father can be exasperating at times and my mother sometimes had her issues. On the one hand, she appreciated and admired what he was doing, but at other times she was jealous of all the time he gave to his organizations. In the end, they were deeply tied to each other. They were together for fifty-seven years during which they built a really good life out of nothing."

The last six months of Diana's life, Eli was at her bedside day and night. When she was in the hospital, he rarely went home to sleep, choosing instead to stay overnight catching whatever rest he could sitting in a chair near her bed. When she opened her eyes and looked around, she felt better because she could see him. Eli painfully recalls her last moments: "When she opened her eyes the last time, the expression on her face indicated that she had seen me. She then closed her eyes and the nurse said that she was not breathing. I didn't fully comprehend what she meant. I thought maybe she needed her pillow a little higher. But she had taken her last breath."

Eli called Julius and Dorothy Berman, the Zborowskis' longtime friends, when he saw that Diana was fading. They arrived at the hospital just as she drew her last breath. In his eulogy for Diana, Julie reflected on the very special role Diana had played in Eli's life. "He treasured Diana's advice and constantly looked for her input. Diana had business acumen which was just basic *saychel*—innate smarts. Sometimes Eli's desires and goals would overwhelm him. In instances such as this, Diana was there to direct him to more realistic goals in the gentlest way possible."

Eli and Diana in 1991

The death of one we have known and loved brings to the living a sense of loss which can run as deep as any emotion we are capable of experiencing.[5] Eli was truly devastated by Diana's death. At the same time, he was very aware of his feelings, which he freely expressed to close friends and colleagues. His letter of appreciation to Rabbi Lamm, who eulogized Diana, reveals his state of mind:

To any extent that I could have imagined the loss of my partner in life, I am finding it much more painful and devastating than I had ever thought. My grief is deep and pervasive. During these past weeks of emotional chaos, our family has fortunately been encircled by the reassuring embrace of tradition and community.

Rabbi Lamm, I apologize for not having written to you sooner, Your concern during Diana's illness, your moving and poignant eulogy and your visit to our home during the *shiva* period has been a great source of comfort and consolation. My family joins me in expressing our gratitude for your support and strength.

I have returned to the office and have once again become immersed in my work. However, evenings and weekends, and especially Shabbat, are painful and difficult. While the loss will remain with me forever, I hope that the profound pain will lessen in time.

Diana and I always shared respect for the outstanding work being done at Yeshiva University. We were particularly grateful for the leadership role the University took in developing the first chair for Holocaust Studies in the entire country. I wish the University continued success as it guides the Jewish community to a bright and illustrious future.

In its great wisdom, the Jewish tradition offers a roadmap for mourning and emotional recovery. As Lilly noted, her father's grieving process followed this trajectory.

My father was in really bad shape at the beginning. He was in deep, deep mourning. Three months after she died, he came to Israel and stayed with us for Pesach (Passover). This is something he had never done before, always preferring to stay in a hotel. We were very pleased to have him. He speaks Hebrew and he is very good company, but he certainly was not himself. After a year, he said he wanted to come to Israel and do something he had wanted to pursue for a long time—attend an ulpan (Hebrew-language school). He rented a car, stayed in a hotel and drove himself everyday to Ulpan Akivah. After that, he kind of bounced back. He began to be more himself.

Diana had been a guiding light in launching the annual spring luncheon of the American Society for Yad Vashem. It was, therefore, only fitting that the 2005 luncheon included a memorial tribute to her. Diana was remembered by her good friend Stella Skura, as well as by her children Lilly and Murry, and her grandchildren Tamar and Ariel. At this event, Dr. Lilly Zborowski Naveh announced that the family had established the Diana Zborowski Shoah Aftermath Research and Education Center. The work of this center will be discussed in the final chapter of the book.

As the foregoing illustrates, one of the realities of living into the eighth decade of life is the loss one must endure when close friends and colleagues die. Sam Skura's passing in February 2008 was a particularly poignant loss for Eli. His eulogy reflects the depths of his sorrow:

> Friendships formed after the Holocaust were different than most conventional friendships. They were far more intense, more lasting and more meaningful. Because the Shoah robbed us of our families, our homes, and everything near and dear, we needed to recreate a world we could trust and we could believe in. We needed to find friends who understood our plight and who would give us the strength to move on with our lives. How fortunate I was to find such a friend!

> For sixty years, starting in Feldafing, the DP Camp, Sam Skura was my best friend, and my most trusted colleague. Not only were we best friends, our wives were best friends. Stella and my late wife Diana were soul-mates who spoke to each other almost daily. Over a period of six decades we shared each other's celebrations: births, bar- and bat-mitzvahs and weddings. The highlight of any given week was an evening out with the Skuras and some of our other close survivor friends. When I say that we all spoke the same language, I don't refer to Yiddish, English or Polish, but to the language

of the heart and to the language of unspoken words that comes from decades of shared experiences.

In 1970, when I founded the first umbrella organization for survivors, Sam Skura was at my side and served as vice-president. In 1981, the Skuras hosted a small parlor meeting in their home in the presence of Dr. Yitzhak Arad, at that time, Chairman of the Yad Vashem Directorate. This meeting inaugurated the American Society for Yad Vashem. In all these endeavors, Sam Skura was always the first person I called. He listened, he was supportive, he offered opinions and he gave advice. When I got off the phone, I felt fortified and energized. Sam was truly a life-giving person.

The years we worked together on behalf of Yad Vashem were rich, rewarding, and fruitful.

Sam and Stella's devotion to Yad Vashem is visible throughout the Yad Vashem landscape. Together with Marvin and Celina Zborowski, they donated the Yad Vashem Candelabra. Sam chaired the fundraising campaign that enabled the erection of the Monument to the Jewish Soldiers, Ghetto Fighters, and Partisans. The Skuras are Benefactors of the Valley of Communities, and they were the first Benefactors of Project 2001. The Learning Center, an integral part of the new museum complex, was established through their generosity.

Sam and Stella passed along the legacy and lessons of the Holocaust to their daughter Cheryl and to their grandchildren, Iris and Ilana. I am proud of Cheryl's distinguished service to our organization. I recall that when Cheryl and her late husband Mochi were honored at our annual dinner, Cheryl opened her remarks to the thousand guests who gathered for the event with a Yiddish phrase: "*Ich bin alemens tochter*." "I am everybody's daughter." And indeed, that is exactly how we survivors felt about each other and about each other's children—like one big family.

Today we mourn the loss of Sam Skura, an irreplaceable member of the survivor family. His passing creates a void for

Yad Vashem as well as for the officers, the board and staff of the American Society for Yad Vashem. Personally, I have lost a dear and valued friend. The Skura family has lost their champion.

* * *

The great theologian Rabbi Abraham Joshua Heschel said, "Death is the end of doing, not the end of being." Diana Zborowski and Sam Skura are among those who will live on through their descendants, through their deeds, and through their common destiny with the Jewish people.

Chapter 13 Notes

1. The name Yad Vashem is taken from Isaiah 56:5, "And I shall give them in my house and within my walls a memorial and a name (*yad vashem*) . . . that shall not be cut off."
2. Ben-Zion Dinur, Israeli Minister of Education and Culture, cited in The American & International Societies for Yad Vashem Journal, *From the Holocaust to Redemption, Marking Fifty Years of Yad Vashem,* 2003, p.20.
3. Ibid, p. 59.
4. Ira Drukier in The American & International Societies for Yad Vashem Journal, *From the Holocaust to Redemption, Marking Fifty Years of Yad Vashem,* 2003.
5. Howard Congdon, *The Pursuit of Death* (Nashville: Abington, 1977), p. 180.

ॐ Chapter 14 ॐ

ENSURING THE LEGACY

2009 Spring Luncheon
Jeremy Halpern, third generation, shares the family legacy with
his daughter, Brianna, fourth generation.

Ensuring the Legacy

Milestones provide an opportunity to reflect on the past and to project plans for the future. As Eli anticipates the thirtieth anniversary of the American Society for Yad Vashem in 2011, he feels that the envisioned goals he set for the organization have been met or exceeded. However, with each passing year, there are fewer and fewer survivors with direct memories of the Shoah. In response to this challenge, the American Society has developed Holocaust-related educational and cultural programs that will inspire younger people to become invested in preserving the memory of this most tragic period in Jewish history.

Reaching Across Generations

We are accustomed to thinking that memory fades slowly over time in a linear fashion. In the case of Holocaust remembrance, however, we see just the opposite. The grandchildren of survivors are often more engaged than their parents. Children of survivors find it difficult to imagine their parents as powerless. The Holocaust was an integral part of their upbringing, sometimes a disturbing one. In adulthood, the pain and the burden can become difficult to bear. In contrast, the third generation has had the advantage of knowing their grandparents in more normal times, of hearing the stories, but with enough emotional distance to encounter the issue without reservation.

Recognizing this difference, Eli invited Caroline Massel, granddaughter of his good friends Regina and Salo Gutfreund, both survivors, to sit on the dais at the 1996 American Society for Yad Vashem Tribute Dinner. At that dinner, Eli said to Caroline, who had just graduated from college, "I want you to come to board meetings. I want you to get involved because Yad Vashem needs young people."

Caroline, who had known Eli from the time she was a child, recalls her first board meetings:

> I just sat there and said nothing. I listened, as they made these jokes in Yiddish, only some of which I understood. After three meetings, I asked myself, "What am I doing here? They know everything about the Holocaust. I can't possibly teach them anything!" I ultimately did speak to Eli about his expectations and my specific role. He told me that it is very important that young people begin to realize that Yad Vashem is for the future. He felt very strongly that we can't wait until all the survivors pass away before we start involving future generations.

With her excellent social skills, a huge network of friends, and a strong sense of social responsibility, Caroline felt that the best way to test interest in the Yad Vashem mission was to sponsor an event. She organized a committee of young people from various constituencies and made it their responsibility to reach out to their friends for attendance. The event took place in May 1997 at the top of the Mutual of America Building in New York City. Eli M. Rosenbaum, director of the Office of Special Investigations of the U.S. Department of Justice, an expert in hunting Nazi war-criminals was the guest speaker. His talk was followed by a light buffet.

From the outset Caroline was confident that if you have a good event, it will attract people. As a grandchild of survivors, she knew that young people do care about Holocaust remembrance. Eli, however er was far less certain and quite nervous about how the evening would turn out. Caroline recollects how Eli's demeanor at first projected uncertainty but as the evening progressed turned to exhilaration:

> Eli stood with me at the front of the room and watched in total disbelief as one elevator after another came up filled with young people. He was so excited that he ran to the nearest pay

phone to share with Diana this incredible happening. We had a total of 218 people. For me, the best part of the event was watching Eli's unbridled joy at the fact that people who were two generations removed from the Holocaust came out in an evening to learn about this pivotal chapter in Jewish history.

The evening's success was overwhelming. It validated and underscored Eli's belief that he had found the right direction in which to move. This event spawned the American Society for Yad Vashem's Young Leadership Associates (YLA), with Caroline Massel and Elie Singer as co-chairs. It was the first-ever group of third-generation members to be organized.

From the outset the leaders of the YLA decided that its activities would include educational as well as fundraising events. The latter would enable them to sponsor conferences for public school teachers on the methodology and curriculum content for teaching the Holocaust. All YLA events, both social and educational, include informational material about Yad Vashem, either through an exhibit or a handout.

The first YLA-sponsored Professional Development Conference took place in January 1999 in New York City. It became an annual event attracting several hundred teachers each year. Themes for the conference have included "How Do We Teach the Holocaust to Our Students?", "Holocaust Education Towards the Next Century," "Altered Intellectual Landscapes: Lessons from the Past," "Using Survivors' Testimonies: Witnesses to the Past and Voices for the Future," "Identity and Renewal During Challenging Times," "Echoes and Reflections: A Multi-media Curriculum on the Holocaust," and "Children of the Holocaust."

Keren Toledano, a member of the YLA, wrote the following synopsis of the Professional Development Conferences:

Keren Toledano

The Conferences were initiated by the Young Leadership Associates in coordination with the Society's Education Department and the International School for Holocaust Studies at Yad Vashem. In addition to informative lectures from Holocaust educators and Shoah survivors, attendees participate in challenging discussion groups that encourage them to contemplate the lessons of the day. Upon completion of the Conference, teachers are given a wealth of resources to take back to their classrooms, including sample curricula and lesson plans and multi-media teaching aids.

One public school English teacher has achieved major successes in her classroom based on the information and techniques she learned at the Conference. She reports; "My students are very interested in the concept of resistance during the Holocaust. They were amazed to learn about the partisans, the Warsaw Ghetto Uprising, and the revolts in the camps. They learned that armed resistance was not the only kind of resistance, that spiritual resistance was a major part of life during the Holocaust, through forbidden prayer, celebration of holidays, and underground schools."

By transmitting the lessons of history to present and future generations, we hope to increase awareness and foster greater sensitivity to reduce hatred, intolerance, and prejudice.[1]

In summing up her overview of the YLA membership, Caroline Massel concludes:

The driving force behind the YLA are fifty or so grandchildren of survivors. They are young professionals who are extremely devoted to this cause; and they feel that it's their responsibility to perpetuate it. Most people we are reaching have some formal Jewish education, not necessarily a day school education, but Hebrew school in one form or another. Of the 800 people who attend our events, about 90% have a direct family connection to the Holocaust. Yet, among the 10% who do not, we have some very devoted, hardworking members. From the beginning, we always tried to structure our committees with people who came from all streams of Judaism because it is these people who really drive our attendance. The Holocaust affected all the Jews, therefore we would like our events to reflect the broadest possible spectrum of Jewish affiliation.

In establishing the Young Leadership Associates, Eli provided a forum for Holocaust remembrance that reaches beyond the grandchildren of survivors. Adina Schainker Burian is a fifth-generation American with no direct family connection to the Shoah. She became involved in the cause of remembrance while in college and as a young adult joined the YLA so that she could continue to give voice to her convictions. The essay that follows explains her thoughts on the subject.

The Third Generation and Beyond
Adina Shainker Burian

Adina Burian

Holocaust remembrance and transmission has traditionally been the bastion of the survivors and their children and grandchildren, often referred to as the first, second and third generations. Like their parents, the second and third generations feel a powerful commitment to Holocaust remem-brance and education because their connection to the Shoah is so deeply personal. Our Young Leadership Associates, predominantly comprised of members of the third generation, reflects this trend.

However, as the direct lineal connection to the Holocaust weakens with the passage of time and generations, we need to consider Holocaust remembrance and continuity in the framework of the next generation, not just the third generation. Millions of today's generation of Jewish Americans have not grown up with a direct personal connection to the experiences of European Jewry. They have American grandparents and surely understand few Yiddish words. They have never known the Jewish people to lack a homeland with its capital in Jerusalem. This generation has grown up with images of the *Kotel* (the West Wall in Jerusalem) and IDF soldiers. The fabric of their American Jewish existence includes Hillel Houses, Kosher Restaurants, AIPAC and Jerry Seinfeld.

We, as an institution, need to identify with, and address ourselves to, this broader generation of American Jewry. Yad Vashem must embrace the next generation and emphasize those themes that resonate most poignantly to the larger Jewish community.

Survivors and their descendents have felt a raw emotional connection to the Holocaust, and have traditionally focused on themes of persecution and victimization. However, as we move forward in cultivating, addressing and educating the next generation, we cannot, and should not, focus only on our persecution and victimization. Rather, the Holocaust has always been intertwined with the heroic stories of perseverance and survival, on an individual basis, and for the Jewish people, as a nation. The survivors built new lives—new families, communities, successful businesses and institutions. On a national level, we experienced the miraculous creation of the State of Israel and the explosion of Jewish education and culture around the globe. Like a phoenix rising from the ashes, our people emerged from the utter destruction of the Holocaust with a remarkable resilience and strength of spirit that should make all Jews, whatever their background, proud to be Jews.

Understanding the Holocaust in our modern reality allows all Jews to appreciate who and what we are today as a people. One hundred years ago, the majority of world Jewry lived in Eastern Europe. The Holocaust was the modern watershed event that separates our Jewish past from our Jewish present and future. In that context, one need not be the direct descendent of a survivor to understand the importance of Holocaust education as a key to gaining a fundamental understanding of ourselves and our Jewish world.

The next generation better relates to themes of tolerance, Jewish unity, and the bridge between the Shoah and the establishment of the State of Israel. While focusing solely on universal themes would dilute the memory of the Holocaust, focusing entirely on the story of Jewish persecution would not stand the test of time. In order to maintain its role as the Global Guardian of Holocaust Remembrance, Yad Vashem must incorporate and link both perspectives.

The first and second generations built the infrastructure that ensures that our past will never be forgotten. It will be the task of the third generation, and indeed the next generation, to ensure that the past is linked inexorably to the spirit, unity and vibrancy of the Jewish future.[2]

Remembering the Past, Enhancing the Future

The American and International Societies for Yad Vashem Annual Tribute Dinner is the premier event on the organization's calendar. It takes place in early November in a major New York City hotel. Planning for the following year starts almost as soon as the event is over. Attracting 1,000 to 1,500 guests, it is a forceful demonstration of the strength of the Societies. For survivors it is an affirmation, more than sixty years after the liberation, that the memory of the Holocaust has not dimmed. For younger generations it is an inspiring evening dedicated to the "State of Remembrance."

Eli Zborowski is the ultimate driving force behind the event. He is the architect, master builder, and supreme impresario of the dinner. He meticulously oversees every last detail, including selection of committees and honorees, guest speakers, negotiations with the hotel and the caterer, the invitation, and the program. His diligence in attracting attendance is legendary. In the month leading up to the dinner, he spends almost all his waking hours on the phone with friends and supporters ensuring that they will be present. Following synagogue services on Shabbat morning, while others are savoring the *kiddush* (collation), he is busy working the crowd of congregants with reminders to send in their reservations.

There is no aspect of the dinner, however, that so indelibly carries Eli's distinct signature as the dinner-table seating. He spends days choreographing it like a fine ballet. He presides over this task with a master seating plan spread over the vast expanse of his desk. Close at hand are several sharpened pencils and a gum eraser that enable him to move guests around with the deliberation of a chess master. In the early years, before computers were used to assist in the seating arrangements, this operation would only be completed the Saturday night before the dinner. Stella Skura recalls: "The Saturday night before the dinner we would come to the office and stay until about four in the morning. Both Diana and I came along because we wouldn't let Sam and Eli go alone. Eli did all the tables by himself because he knew the people and he knew with whom they should be seated. He would seat 1,000 people including the dais. With very little sleep, we would get up the next day, get dressed and go to the dinner."

Under the auspices of the American & International Societies, the dinner attracts a broad audience. In addition to survivors and their families, business, educational, and cultural leaders, and government officials, the event attracts many members of the diplomatic corps. In order to elevate the dignitaries and make them more visible to other guests, they are seated on a raised dais at the front of the ballroom. As many as 150 distinguished guests are seated in two or three tiers. Dais guests are ushered in by name at the beginning of the program as a video camera projects their entrance on a huge screen.

Abba Eban, Eli, Isadore Karten.

Israeli ambassador Abba Eban was the guest speaker at the first Annual Tribute Dinner of The American & International Societietes in 1985. Photo: Rivka Pergament

Over the years, dinner honorees and guest speakers have included Ambassador Abba Eban, Ambassador Ronald Lauder, Sir Robert Maxwell, Nobel Laureate Elie Wiesel, Edgar Bronfman, Matthew Bronfman, Dr. Miriam and Sheldon Adelson, Fred Zeidman, and Avner Shalev. In 2006, on the occasion of the Societies' twenty-fifth anniversary, Eli was recognized with a Lifetime Achievement Award. In presenting this honor, Eli's longtime friend Julius Berman said:

The Torah repeatedly reminds us to remember and not to forget historical incidents. . . . We are a people of remembrance. We encompass thousands of years and hosts of generations, both in the past and in the future, both ancient and not yet born, historical heroes and champions of the future—all of them encompass one Jewish nation, a nation that God has blessed with the ability and talent of remembrance.

If the Jewish people is a Nation of Remembrance, then I can safely say that we are honoring this evening an *ish hazikoron*—a man who symbolizes in his very being the attribute of remembrance. Eli Zborowski's entire adult life has been consumed with honing this ability, the melding of our past, present, and future. He has refused to forget not only what occurred during those dark, dark days of destruction and persecution, but also the days and years and generations that preceded.

David Halpern, dinner chairman; Rabbi Israel Meir Lau, guest speaker, and Eli Zborowski, recipient of the Yad Vashem Lifetime Achievement Award at the American & International Societies for Yad Vashem 25th Anniversary Tribute Dinner, in 2006

Eli Zborowski's specific achievements are known to all: the Founder and now Honorary President of the first umbrella organization for all survivors—the American Federation of Jewish Fighters, Camp Inmates and Nazi Victims; a member of the Directorate of Yad Vashem in Israel; the organizer of the first Yom HaShoah commemoration in the United States; the benefactor of the Diana and Eli Zborowski Interdisciplinary Chair for Holocaust Studies at Yeshiva University, the first academic endeavor of its kind; the Chairman of both the International and American Societies for Yad Vashem; an appointee of President Carter and again by President Reagan to membership on the United States Holocaust Memorial Council, and on and on.

Eli has dedicated his life to assuring that as the years go by, as generations come and go, the power of remembrance that has been developed by the Jewish people shall never be lost, that we will continue our task to ensure the continuity of our people.

Eli, Nobel Laureate Eli Wiesel, honoree and Israeli Knesset Member Dr. Yosef Burg, guest speaker, at the American & International Societies Annual Tribute Dinner. Photo: David Karp

Eugen and Jean Gluck, and guests of honor Sir Robert Maxwell, Diana and Eli Zborowski at the American & International Societies Annual Tribute Dinner, 1991

Each year, in conjunction with the tribute dinner, the American and International Societies for Yad Vashem publish a commemorative journal. The purpose of this publication is to raise money as well as consciousness about the mission of the organization. In lieu of the customary Gold Pages, Silver Pages, and the Shoah. Through vintage photographs culled from the Yad Vashem archives, as well as personal mementoes of survivors and their families, the story of the Holocaust is thematically retold and remembered. In addition to the photographs, sponsors of a page can pay tribute to honorees, memorialize loved ones, or express appreciation for Yad Vashem's mission. The journals illustrate the transcendence of the Holocaust over the generations and have become treasured keepsakes with enduring interest and value.

The 2000 journal, *The Jewish Child from Then to Now*, a memorial tribute to the 1.5 million children who perished in the Holocaust, won the prestigious Clarion Award in a national competition sponsored by Women in Communication to acknowledge excellence in promotion and publication.

Eli's cousin Esther is married to Zelig Shushan, the Hashomer Hatzair emissary whom Eli met enroute to the kinus in Landsberg, as recounted in chapter 6. Esther Shushan now lives on a kibbutz in Israel. When she received a copy of The Jewish Child from Then to Now, she was overcome with emotion. She wrote Eli a long letter in Yiddish which is here excerpted and translated:

I received the Journal at noon and found it so compelling that I continued to page through it until late in the evening. As I looked at the photos of the prewar children, I imagined that I knew all of them. I was reminded of the large playground near our home in Zawiercie, Poland, not far from Żarki, that was full of children playing, running, and shouting. Sadly, it is a world that has now vanished. The Journal was prepared and presented in such good taste. It evoked in me such wonderful memories and unearthed thoughts from the depth of my soul. I thank you so much.

Praise for the Societies' journals have also come from distinguished communal leaders. Dr. Herbert C. Dobrinsky, vice-president for university affairs at Yeshiva University wrote: "Unlike so many of its ilk, your Journal truly is commemorative and inspiring. The cherished photos illustrate the importance of Yad Vashem's mission in a way more powerful than any words could describe it."

* * *

In 2000, the American Society added an annual spring luncheon to its calendar. Its purpose was to increase the involvement of women in the organization and create another fundraising vehicle. While men are invited as guests, all the arrangements for the event are coordinated by a committee of women. Each year two outstanding women are honored, one a survivor and the other from the second or third generation. The luncheon is a festive event that attracts between 200 and 250 people. At the 2007 event, Eli reflected on Professor Nechama Tec's remarks about gender issues:

At our first Spring Luncheon seven years ago, we honored the noted Holocaust scholar Professor Nechama Tec. At that time, Professor Tec talked about gender differences during the Holocaust. She said that men and women traveled different roads to their final destination. While husbands and fathers were the first to suffer public humiliation and instant death, mothers and wives struggled to keep their starving families away from death. Together, men and women, and each in their own way, demonstrated enormous resilience and courage. Ultimately, however, one's "Jewishness" rather than gender was the determining factor in annihilation.

It is not surprising that following the war, survivors sought mates who had shared this horrific life-experience. Who else, other than another survivor, could possibly understand what we had been through? In marriage, we forged partnerships that produced families and created new lives in new lands. While husbands and fathers went out to make a living, wives and mothers became the backbone of family and communal life. It was the women who enabled families to flourish and the tenacity of these partnerships that made possible the establishment of formal organizations for commemorating the Shoah.

Over the years, the luncheon has featured outstanding Holocaust authors and scholars as guest speakers. In addition to Nechama Tec, the list of guest speakers includes Deborah Lipstadt, Melvin Bukiet, and Sir Martin Gilbert.

Marvin & Celina Zborowski, Eli and Sir Martin Gilbert, guest speaker at the American Society for Yad Vashem Annual Spring Luncheon in 2002.

Marilyn Rubenstein, luncheon chairperson; Eli; Prof. Nechama Tec, guest speaker; Saul Kagan, former executive vice-president of the Claims Conference; and Fanya Gottesfeld Heller, luncheon committee; at the American Society for Yad Vashem Annual Spring Luncheon, 2009.

A Source of Support and Inspiration

Diana's death left Eli filled with sorrow, and at loose ends socially. His friends were very caring, and constantly invited him to join them. However, it was very difficult for him to accept invitations because he felt exceedingly uncomfortable in most social situations without a partner. People exhibited enormous goodwill, but Eli found it very hard to accept their overtures.

After a year had passed, friends offered to introduce him to women in whom he might be interested. When Eli indicated that he was not yet ready, some of them tried to persuade him and to negate the validity of his feelings. He felt they were well intentioned, but unaware of the depth of his loss.

Eli recalls a phone conversation about this with his brother Marvin, who was vacationing in Florida: "Marvin confessed that he wasn't so comfortable about discussing this matter with me, but, since I had already raised it, he said that when I came to Florida, he would like me to meet his neighbor, Dr. Elizabeth Mundlak. He told me that she had produced two films on her own experience as a child survivor."

Following a meeting at Marvin's home in Florida, Elizabeth invited Eli to see one of her films. "I accepted the invitation and we watched the film, *I Was Lucky,* the very sad and heartbreaking story of her survival. When it was finished, I embraced her and gave her the first kiss. I told her that since she had suffered so, I hoped that going forward she would no longer experience sadness. This brought us very close."

Spending time with Elizabeth enabled Eli to learn about her background. She had been born in Częstochowa, Poland. During the war, as a baby, she was taken in by a Christian family, and she considered the woman who had cared for her to be her mother. After the war, she was reunited with her biological mother, but viewed her as a stranger. They were the only survivors of a large family. In 1957 they and their postwar family left Poland for Venezuela. Elizabeth became a chemical engineer with a Ph.D. in environmental health, and was a professor at the Central University in Caracas for many years.

Despite the dislocation and confusion in her life, Elizabeth overcame these obstacles. Because of her wartime experience, she has developed a very deep feeling for other child survivors. She is an active member of the World Federation of Jewish Child Survivors.

Eli found her zeal for Holocaust remembrance very consistent with his own passion. This, combined with the fact that Elizabeth is an intelligent, cultured, and attractive woman, heightened his interest in her. Still, he proceeded with some caution:

> I told Elizabeth that I would like her to meet my daughter. In a telephone conversation between the two of them, Lilly invited Elizabeth to join our family for Passover in Israel. On the way back from Israel, I met Rabbi Lau in the airport. I didn't quite know how to introduce Elizabeth. What is she to me? A girlfriend? A *kallah*—a prospective bride? What should I say? When Elizabeth was occupied with something else, I got close to the rabbi and said, "This is a woman I have an eye on." Rabbi Lau then turned his eyes from me to Elizabeth and back to me and said: "So what are you waiting for?"

Elizabeth and Eli were married on July 9, 2006. Rabbi Norman Lamm officiated, and Rabbi Lau called from Israel fifteen minutes before the ceremony to offer his blessings.

Elizabeth has joined the staff of the American Society for Yad Vashem as its cultural director. She has used her interest and energy in a number of areas to increase the visibility of the Society and Yad Vashem. She has promoted traveling exhibitions and has developed explanatory booklets, and she has coordinated the production of a monograph about the Society titled *Our Legacy.* For the twenty-fifth anniversary of the American Societies tribute dinner, Elizabeth curated an exhibition about its activities. In addition, she has organized the library and much of the archival material. In assessing her contribution, Eli says, "Elizabeth has a very healthy, balanced approach to issues, which I find refreshing and helpful. She is making a great contribution to the Society."

President George Bush greets Elizabeth and Eli Zborowski at Yad Vashem in 2008. Looking on is Yehudit Shendar, Senior Art Curator

President Shimon Perez of Israel, Elizabeth and Eli Zborowski and Avner Shalev at Yad Vashem in January 2008

Rabbi Israel Meir Lau, former chief rabbi of the State of Israel and current chairman of the Yad Vashem Council, sums up Eli's contribution to the cause of remembrance: "Eli Zborowski is the most important and central figure of our generation in perpetuating the holy commandment *zachor v'lo tishkach*—to remember and not to forget." To underscore this thought, Rabbi Lau holds up a silver Sheaffer pen that Eli once gave him as a gift and adds, "Eli Zborowski built an empire selling Sheaffer pens like this one. He could have built an empire twice the size. Instead, he devoted his time and energy to holy causes on behalf of the Jewish people."

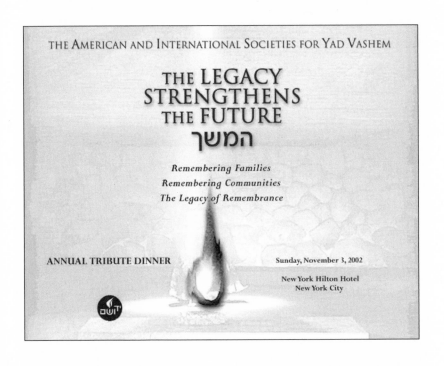

THE AMERICAN AND INTERNATIONAL SOCIETIES FOR YAD VASHEM

THE LEGACY STRENGTHENS THE FUTURE
המשך

Remembering Families
Remembering Communities
The Legacy of Remembrance

ANNUAL TRIBUTE DINNER

Sunday, November 3, 2002

New York Hilton Hotel
New York City

Chapter 14 Notes

1. Keren Toledano is the granddaughter of survivors Isidore and Julia Karten, who were partisans during the Holocaust. This is an excerpt from a longer essay that appeared in the *25th* Anniversary Journal of the American & and International Societies for Yad Vashem, 2006.

2. Adina Schainker Burian, "The Third Generation and Beyond," in *25th Anniversary Journal of the American & International Societies for Yad Vashem*, 2006.

❧ Chapter 15 ❧

THE AFTERMATH OF
THE HOLOCAUST

FELIKS TYCH

Prof. Felix Tych addresses
the International Conference
The Aftermath of the Holocaust: Poland 1944-2010
Sponsored by the Diana Zborowski Center
for the Study of the Aftermath of the Shoah
Yad Vashem, October 2010

The Aftermath of the Holocaust
Prof. Feliks Tych

The aftermath of the Holocaust is as much about how the generations, including the survivors, treat the Shoah, as it is about the impact of this event on them.

After the defeat of Germany, the Jewish survivors thought that they could return to their homes, take up their former roles in society, and resume the normal lives to which they had looked forward. But it was not to be. Unfortunately, anti-Semitism raged on, driving most of the remaining Jews from East European countries. In September 1945, eight months after the liberation of Eli's hometown of Żarki from the Germans, three grenades were thrown into his home, where his mother, his brother Marvin, and his mother's sister and brother were living. Soon thereafter, they left Poland along with many other Polish Jews.

I met Eli Zborowski for the first time at the international conference on "Polish-Jewish Relations During the Holocaust and After: New Perspectives" held at Yeshiva University in New York in April 2000. The conference was sponsored by a grant from the Eli and Diana Zborowski Chair in Interdisciplinary Holocaust Studies.[1] We met again a few years later at the Jewish Historical Institute in Warsaw. At that time I was already thinking about an interdisciplinary research project on the aftermath of the Holocaust in Poland.

I mentioned my ideas in our conversation and described my research design. I had a feeling that Eli was waiting for just such an initiative. This paved the way for our friendship. As Holocaust survivors and witnesses to the first postwar years in Poland, we were both of the opinion that the post-Holocaust condition of the Jews and the state of

Polish-Jewish relations after the liberation of Poland deserved more attention from both Polish and Polish-Jewish historiography. The series of postwar pogroms in Poland, Slovakia, and Hungary show how far the Holocaust's shadow reached, how deep ran the conviction—borne out of the years 1941–1945—that you can kill Jews with impunity. A kind of taboo was still hanging over this topic.

I will never forget our first conversation on this subject. We were unanimous in our opinion that the commonly presented narrative of the Holocaust violated the integrity of the real story. It excluded information about the immediate postwar effects of the Shoah: about the post-Holocaust dramas and personal dilemmas of the survivors, about the conditions they found themselves in and the problems they faced attempting to return to a normal life. Even now, the narrative in most school textbooks still stops with the defeat of the Third Reich. Many Holocaust museums around the world also end their stories with the capitulation of Hitler's Germany and dramatic pictures of the liberated prisoners of the camps, showing piles of corpses and skeleton-like humans. Sometimes the exhibits end with the Nuremberg trials.

Eli wanted a large-scale project that would take in all of the countries affected by the Holocaust, as well as those in which the survivors started a new life. The Holocaust survivors built families. Seeking a new reality and a new source of self-esteem, in time some were extraordinarily successful, especially when contrasted with other immigrants of similar background, circumstances, education, and language barriers. How was this achieved? What distinguished the most successful from the least successful? How did various factors in the new environment affect this success and its distribution among survivors? Most important, how did the Holocaust influence these experiences? How was the moral condition of the survivors affected, and their postwar status in the countries where they were born?

Such a pan-European project would require that researchers in each country affected by the Holocaust start a parallel program which would present the postwar situation of the survivors. This would pave the way to a comparative approach to the topic; however, in many European countries, such research was not as advanced at that time as it was at the beginning of the twenty-first century in Poland. Therefore, his visionary idea of starting with a pan-European project was ahead of its time, but the conditions were ready to start such research in Poland.

Research about the way the returning survivors were received by residents of their native towns and villages was also important because it offered the key to reconstructing the real social and moral environment in which the Holocaust took place. How shall we understand that there were Poles who murdered Jews—including Eli's father—and other Poles who risked their lives every day to save Jews—including himself, his mother, and his siblings? Few historians dealing with the immediate postwar period were ready to speak up on this matter.

Eli Zborowski has been our project's benefactor from the first stages of our research. His patronage gave us confidence that we would be able to complete the project. Eli visited Poland several times during our work on the project. His frequent calls from New York gave me a feeling of his support and true caring about the project.

Our recently published 900-page compendium, *The Aftermath of the Holocaust: Poland, 1944–2010*, is the result of research conducted by a team of twenty-seven social scientists: historians, sociologists, anthropologists, lawyers, ethnologists, demographers, and experts on Jewish literature. The authors are associated with five Polish universities, one Swiss university, three Polish research institutes, two museums, and the Foundation for Preservation of the Jewish Heritage in Poland.

This massive interdisciplinary publication was the fruit of intensive discussions in a series of seminars, which I started and held regularly at the Jewish Historical Institute (JHI) in Warsaw during 2007–2010. These meetings provided an opportunity for exchange of opinions and ideas among researchers of various disciplines, from different generations and different centers, working on the issues of the Holocaust and its consequences. When he visited Poland, Eli always made time to attend our seminar meetings. All the participants in the seminars appreciated his and his wife Elizabeth's moral involvement in the project.

Most of our authors used sources never published before. Our compendium is addressed both to specialists and to a broader audience.

Its authors introduce the reader to the world of Jewish life in Poland, and to Polish-Jewish relations, from 1944/45 until the first decade of the twenty-first century. While the book addresses only the Polish perspective, it deals with problems equally relevant to other countries affected by the Holocaust. That is why an English version of the book will soon be published.

The Polish project was presented on October 3–6, 2010 as "The Aftermath of the Holocaust: Poland, 1944–2010," at the inaugural international conference of the Diana Zborowski Center for the Study of the Aftermath of the Shoah at Yad Vashem—an endeavor that was underwritten by Eli Zborowski and his family, The conference also featured a group of Israeli scholars as well as two distinguished guests from North America—Prof. Jan Tomasz Gross of Princeton University, and Prof. Antony Polonsky of Brandeis University

According to Dr. Bella Gutterman, the director of the International Institute for Holocaust Research at Yad Vashem, "The conference looked at how Polish society deals with the fact that their country was the main arena for the murders. We examined the immediate postwar events—extreme anti-Semitic expressions and pogroms—through the communist era and then from the fall of communism until today. Much of what was presented was new research and findings undertaken in the past two years, and we look forward to broadening our scholarly investigations as a result of the conference."[2]

This inaugural event was a triumph for both our research team and the Zborowskis. Eli's forceful remarks at the conference resonated with everyone present:

A spotlight has been turned on the importance of the post-Holocaust period, and it is already revealing facets previously ignored, overlooked or hidden.

Through these non-judgmental studies we can at last begin to understand not only the full dimensions of the Holocaust's aftermath, but also why this particular path emerged. For the Holocaust to take its proper place in history, it is essential that the ongoing influence of this greatest crime be documented and understood.

If our bold declaration "Never again!" is to be realized, it will be through the efforts of researchers like those represented here. Your work promises to create a model for future study on survivor communities worldwide, primarily in Germany, the United States, and Israel. This is both critical and urgent. *V'im lo achshav, aimotai*—if not now, when?

Prof. Feliks Tych was born in Poland in 1929 to a traditional Jewish family. During the war he was in the Radomsko ghetto and later in Warsaw with Aryan papers. He was saved by a Polish teacher's family. Prof. Tych is a renowned historian who held the position of Director of the Institute of Jewish History in Warsaw between 1996 and 2007. Among his numerous publications are eight books and twenty-six volumes of archival sources. Prof. Tych currently heads the Seminary and Research Project, The Aftermath of the Holocaust 1944-2008, The Polish Case. He is Editor-in-Chief and co-author of The Aftermath of the Holocaust in Poland, 1944-2010 which will be published in 2011.

Chapter 15 Notes

1. The papers presented at the conference, edited by Joshua D. Zimmerman, were published three years later as *Contested Memories: Poles and Jews during the Holocaust and Its Aftermath* (New Brunswick, N.J.: Rutgers University Press, 2003).
2. In "The Fate of Polish Jewry" by Prof. Zeev Mankowitz, *Jerusalem Report,* November 8, 2010.

Glossary

aliyah
Hebrew "ascent." Used to refer to emigration to the Land of Israel

babche
An endearing Yiddish term for grandmother

bar mitzvah
Hebrew: "one (m.) who is commanded." The age of thirteen years and one day when a boy becomes obliged to observe religious commandments; also used to refer to the boy himself

bat mitzvah
Hebrew: "one (f.) who is commanded." The age of twelve years and one day when a girl becomes obliged to observe religious commandments; also used to refer to the girl herself

Beit Hakehilot
Hebrew: "House of the Communities"

Beit Hanoar
Youth House

bocher
Yiddish: young man

Bricha
The organization that arranged illegal *aliyah* for Jews in postwar Europe from the time of liberation until the establishment of the State of Israel in 1948

brit milah
Ritual circumcision ceremony during which an eight-day old boy enters the Covenant of Abraham

Bund
Jewish Socialist political movement founded in Vilnius in 1897

chai
> Hebrew word for "life." The Hebrew letters, when read as numbers, add up to eighteen

chalutz
> Hebrew: pioneer

cheder
> Hebrew religious school for young children

chol hamoed
> The intervening days between the two holidays at the beginning of the festival and the two at the end, during Passover and Sukkot.

daven
> Yiddish: pray

gedenk
> Yiddish: "remember"

gefrishte broit
> Yiddish: "refreshed bread." French toast

gemilat chesed
> Hebrew: acts of loving kindness

hachnoses orchim
> Hebrew: providing for guests

Haggadah
> Hebrew: "recitation." The book used during the Passover seder to tell the story of the Jews' redemption from bondage in Egypt, and to set forth the order of the seder service.

Har Hazikaron
> Hebrew: "Mount of Remembrance," in Jerusalem

Jude
> German word for "Jew"

Judenrat
> German-imposed Jewish council

kaddish
> Hebrew: "sanctification." A prayer sanctifying God, recited during religious services by mourners

kehilla
Hebrew: "community"

kibbutz
Hebrew: "gathering." It is a collective farm or settlement owned by its members in modern day Israel. *Kibbutzim* (pl.) were frequently formed in the Diaspora and members migrated as a group to Israel.

kiddush
Hebrew: "sanctification." The prayer that ushers in the Sabbath and holidays; also, the collation which takes place following religious services

kinus
Hebrew: convention

kotel
Hebrew: the western wall of the Temple Mount in Jerusalem, the most sacred place in Judaism

ma'nishtana
The first two words of the traditional four questions that appear in the Passover *Hagaddah*. The questions, which inquire about "why this night is different from all other nights," are asked by the youngest child present at the Passover *seder*.

madrich
Hebrew: leader

mama loshen
Yiddish: "mother tongue," the Yiddish language

mikvah
Hebrew: ritual bath

minyan
Hebrew: quorum of 10 men required for public prayer

mitzvah
Hebrew: commandment

Mizrachi
Religious Zionist movement

mohel
Hebrew: person who performs a ritual circumcision

opshern
Yiddish: haircut

pater familias
Latin: head of the family

Pirkei Avot
Hebrew: Ethics of the Fathers, a Talmudic tractate containing the ethical teachings and maxims of the early rabbis

rebbe
Yiddish: rabbi

seder
Hebrew: "order." The Passover meal and service.

Shabbes
Yiddish: Sabbath

shaliach; shlichim (pl.)
Hebrew: Emissary from Israel

she'arith hapleta
A biblical term meaning "surviving remnant," now used to refer to survivors of the Holocaust

shiva
Hebrew: the number seven. It is the seven day mourning period observed by a family following burial.

Shoah
Hebrew: "destruction; catastrophe." The Holocaust.

shochet
Hebrew: ritual slaughterer, required if meat is to be kosher

shomer
Hebrew: guard. In this context it refers to a person who attends the body of the deceased from the time of death until burial.

shtibel, shtiblach (pl)
Yiddish: Small house of prayer

simcha
Hebrew: "joy." Celebration

sukkah
Hebrew: "booth." A temporary structure erected for the harvest holiday of Sukkot, celebrated in the fall of the year. It is customary to eat one's meals in the *sukkah*

tahara
Hebrew: "purification." It refers to the preparation for burial of the deceased, which includes ritual washing, purifying and dressing the deceased in white shrouds.

tallit
Hebrew: prayer shawl

tikun olam
Hebrew: "repairing the world." Isaac Luria, the renowned sixteenth century Kabbalist, used the phrase to characterize the true role of humanity in the ongoing evolution and spiritualization of the cosmos.

tisha b'Av
Hebrew: the ninth day of the Hebrew month of Av

tumah
Hebrew: "impurity"

tzizit
Hebrew: "fringes." The fringes on the four corners of a prayer shawl. Similar fringes are attached to an undergarment that slips over the head and is worn by boys and men under their shirts as a reminder to obey the Biblical commandments.

wassertreger
Yiddish: "water carrier"

yartzeit
Yiddish: "anniversary." The memorial anniversary of the date of death

Yiddishkeit
Yiddish: Jewish tradition

Yom Hashoah Ve'Hagevurah

Hebrew: "Day of the Shoah and the Martyrs." The day of Holocaust remembrance designated by the Israeli parliament, which takes place on the 27th day of the Hebrew month of Nissan. It is a day of commemoration for the martyrdom and resistance of victims of the Holocaust

Yom Kippur

The Day of Atonement, marked by a twenty-six hour fast. The fast is broken with a feast shared with family and friends.

z"l

An abbreviation of the Hebrew: *zichrono livracha* or *zichrona livracha*, which mean "his/her memory for a blessing." It is traditional to append *z"l* after the name of someone who has died. Often read as "of blessed memory"

zachor

Hebrew: "remember"

zmirot

Hebrew: songs sung on the Sabbath

ŻOB

Polish: abbreviation of "Żydowska Organizacja Bojowa"–Jewish Combat Organization; a resistance movement known in English as the United Jewish Fighters Organization

Index